Argumentation and the Decision Making Process

Argumentation and the Decision Making Process

RICHARD D. RIEKE & MALCOLM O. SILLARS
University of Utah

John Wiley & Sons, Inc.
New York • London • Sydney • Toronto

Library of Congress Cataloging in Publication Data

Rieke, Richard D
  Argumentation and the decision making process.

  Includes bibliographical references and index.
  1. Debates and debating. I. Sillars, Malcolm Osgood, 1928-   joint author. II. Title.

PN4181.R48   808.53   74-20900
ISBN 0-471-72165-4

Printed in the United States of America

10 9 8 7 6 5 4 3 2 1

In the autumn of 1974 more than thirty scholars from all parts of the United States met in Sedalia, Colorado, as a part of the National Developmental Conference on Forensics. We were included in the group. One of the goals of the conference was to explore the most modern thinking in the field of argumentation and to relate it to the forensic activities that are provided by most high schools and colleges. Often, study in argumentation and debate is virtually synonymous with involvement in forensics. Occasionally preparation for forensic competition yields credit in argumentation and, usually, courses in argumentation use the forensic model as their basis for study.

Having just completed the manuscript for this book, we had a particular interest in the National Developmental Conference on Forensics, since it was dedicated to broadening the scope of study in argumentation and decision making without damaging the important educational role of forensics in any way. We entered this field because of our participation in forensics in high school and college and, for many years, we worked as directors of forensics at the university level. We are convinced that forensic activities constitute one of the most beneficial educational experiences available to our students. However, we think that a study in argumentation and decision making should reflect the best modern scholarship and should provide a content-oriented body of knowledge that can be taught with forensics in such a way that both subjects are mutually complementary.

We oriented our approach to argumentation and decision making around an audience-centered perspective. In this perspective, argumentation is a unified study that examines how people give reasons for their beliefs and actions. Its applications, however, are different, depending on the special situation in which it is used. We use the term "general argumentation" to represent everyday reason-giving. We also discuss, specifically, three specialized applications in the law, scholarship, and competitive school and college debate. Many more specialized applications of argumentation (such as theology, physical science, legislation, business, and formal logic) are mentioned throughout the book.

We include references to modern scholarship where we feel it will help to generate an understanding of the process, without regard for the perspective or methodology employed in that scholarship, and even though it is in conflict with ideas that have long been held. We try to avoid the prescriptive posture of providing students with "the correct way." We openly and directly present our point of view; but, we also present it side by side with conflicting ideas where necessary to let students in interaction with each other and their instructor make a choice among approaches.

Although our viewpoint, at times, differs with traditional thinking, our objective is to strengthen contemporary studies in argumentation and current programs in forensics. Probably the most important characteristic of our approach is that it does not denigrate anyone's concept of argumentation. Instead, it explores a variety of concepts so that each reader can decide what is most valuable from what we have provided.

Many people contributed significantly toward the preparation of this book. We are particularly grateful for the constructive criticism of Professors Jerry M. Anderson, Walter Fisher, Robert Bostrum, and Edward L. McGlone. We thank Charlane Sillars for many manuscript-preparation activities.

Richard D. Rieke
Malcolm O. Sillars

Contents

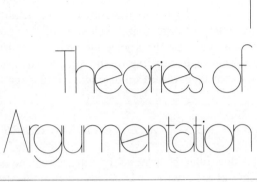

Theories of Argumentation

This book consists of arguments. Taken as a whole, it constitutes a case for a point of view concerning argumentation and decision making. Please keep in mind that the book is an exercise in the subject under investigation, since in it we will advance arguments and ask you to give adherence to those arguments.

The argument that this book advances will be rooted in an audience centered theory of argumentation. This chapter will introduce you to that theory in basic form, and subsequent chapters will develop constituents of it in detail. The theory involves the thoughts of several individuals and, thus, this chapter contains a review of how some influential writers of other years have theorized about argumentation. Necessarily, some new terms will be introduced. In addition, since audience centered argumentation is not the usual theory, new meanings for old terms will be introduced.

CONSTITUENTS OF AN AUDIENCE CENTERED THEORY OF ARGUMENTATION

We have chosen to designate our theory of argumentation as audience centered because that is its most distinguishing characteristic. Other writers, who will be discussed later, have chosen other focal points. We will

1

be concerned with argumentation as a process in which persons make claim statements ranging from such a simple assertion as, "It's a nice day," to complex ones such as, "The State of Israel has no legal basis for existence," and in which other people respond to such claims by offering or denying adherence to them.

Adherence, as the objective of argumentation, will perhaps need some clarification. We hold, with Chaim Perelman, that the objective of argumentation is adherence.[1] Others may legitimately question whether an argument meets specific tests of formal logic, conforms to established standards of probability, changes attitudes, beliefs, or values. All of these may, in one way or another, affect argumentation, as you will see. The ultimate test of argument is whether or not people give their adherence to claims made by the arguer by stating concurrence or behaving accordingly. This understanding of the reason why we advance claims and give reasons for them dictates a distinctive understanding of argumentation.

HUMAN BEINGS ARE REASON-MAKERS AND REASON-USERS

To illustrate the process of advancing claims and granting and withholding of adherence, it is necessary to understand how people make and use reasons. Reason-making is a characteristic of most human beings. Essentially, a reason is what is provided in response to the question, "why?" A satisfactory reason is one to which members of the audience can grant adherence.

Think for a moment of the conversations you have heard during the past few days. If you are able to recall any in some detail, you probably will notice how many reasons were given, sometimes voluntarily and often on demand. However, it may well be that you were not even aware of them, and cannot recall them, because they are so much a part of our language. See if such comments as these are not familiar.

"I'm not going to class today."

"How come?"

"I've got to get started on my reading assignments."

"Yeah, I should do that, too."

Notice a few things about this conversation. First, the colloquial expression, "How come?" is one of a number in our language meaning, "Give me a reason." Such statements are typically given without a "please," or other amenity and tend to constitute a demand: "Give me a reason in connection

---

[1] Chaim Perelman and L. Olbrechts-Tyteca, *The New Rhetoric* (Notre Dame, Indiana: University of Notre Dame Press, 1971), p. 1.

with your previous behavior or comment!" "You and I both know that it is unacceptable in our society to speak or otherwise act without being able to supply one or more reasons for doing so." If the respondent should refuse to give a reason, the questioner could be expected to feel hurt at this rudeness or embarrassed at having opened up an apparently sensitive area. It is unlikely to cross his mind that the first individual really did not have a reason at hand, unless the topic or action were one so trivial that the answer, "no reason," could be used to indicate it is not important enough to state.

A second observation is this: the question, "why?" or "How come?" is typically considered a legitimate one that requires response. One might imagine a society in which the question, not the refusal to answer, is rude. For example, you might reply, "You are impertinent to inquire after reasons for my behavior." "I do not have to justify my actions to you." But in twentieth century North America, and many other parts of the world, one would expect to hear such a comment rarely, if at all.

A third observation about the above is the freedom with which the questioner comments on, or otherwise evaluates or assesses the reason given. It is an acceptable role to play, that of judge: "I'll go along with that," or "I'll buy that," or "That makes sense," or "That's reasonable," or "That's logical," or "Right on," and so forth. It is a typical behavior for those hearing a communication or observing a behavior to announce the extent to which they will adhere to the reasons presented. This seems to be so even when they have not been asked to join into the belief or action, and when it has no apparent bearing on their lives. Obviously, if they freely evaluate reasons under these conditions, they can be expected to do so with even greater gusto when the reason-giver wants them to involve themselves somehow.

Finally, and in line with the other three observations, it seems to be important to the reason-giver to win the adherence of the reason-seeker. To illustrate, let's rewrite the conversation:

"I'm not going to class today."

"How come?"

"I've got to get started on my reading assignments."

"Like hell you do! The library's in the other direction."

"Well, I thought I'd get something to eat first. You wanna come along?"

"Yeah, then we can both get some reading done."

The chances are the announced behavior will be withheld until an acceptable reason for it can be generated, or until communication with the reason-seeker is broken off for some reason. The impact of a refusal to accept a reason may range, roughly, from a shrug to a major modification of behavior, and will probably be a function of many variables such as the psychological status of the reason-giver, the interpersonal relationship among those involved, the importance of the behavior under question, and the ego-involvement in the question. But predictably, a refusal to accept the reason given will typically be followed by some further attempt to secure adherence either by reinforcing the original reason or generating others. To summarize, (1) there are a number of ways to communicate the question, "Why?" both verbally and nonverbally; (2) our culture usually considers the question, "Why?" to be a legitimate demand for response by means of reason-giving; (3) once reasons are given, it is considered appropriate for others to evaluate them and grant or deny their adherence in some manner or other; and (4) securing adherence is typically important to those who advance claims to the extent that they may withdraw the claim and associated behavior if insufficient adherence is achieved.

The making of reasons is so important to our behavior that many times we automatically include them in our original statements. We anticipate the question "Why?" Many people argue that reasons are not made, they are discovered. You may believe that people are merely reporting the "true causes" of their behavior, or that they are offering the "true bases" for believing their assertions. An audience centered theory does not make such a claim.

DETERMINING THE QUALITY OF REASONS

The positive or negative evaluation of reasons ultimately must be a function of the willingness of those making the evaluation to do so. When you advance a claim, "Radial tires are better than others because they are safer on turns and last longer," the person to whom you are speaking may respond, "That's right." What does, "That's right," mean? Does it mean your respondent has such knowledge of automobile tires that he can affirm the truth of your statement? The answer may be stated to give that implication, but regardless of the respondent's knowledge, the answer merely means your claim is one to which he can grant adherence.

In the two hypothetical conversations cited earlier in the chapter, the first respondent accepted the need to get started on reading assignments as a reason for cutting class while the second did not. Perhaps you felt that the second respondent, by hard-nosed inquiry, discovered the "real" reason for cutting class, that is, to get some food. In any event, when the food reason was advanced, the second respondent was satisfied. Possibly a less agreeable respondent may have pushed further and discovered some lack of preparation for today's class, and assumed that to be the reason. In fact, a psychoanalyst may have found another reason to adhere to; the student's professor may have subscribed to another; the parents of the student cutting the class may have identified still another reason.

Important to an audience centered theory of argumentation is the idea that "reasons" come from people. Ponder, for a moment, two meanings that often become confused: philosophical explanations of the factors or forces that create and shape reality, and the human communication of reasons that provide the bases for social and personal action. Suppose you think you know why you took a certain course of action but announce some other reason publicly. If those to whom you communicate the second reason accept it, no problem emerges. For them, it was enough of a "reason" to suit their needs. If, on the other hand, you think you know the reason you engaged in some behavior, and announce that same reason, what happens if those to whom you communicate refuse to accept it? For them, your reason is unsatisfactory, no matter how truthful you thought you were being. Remember all this time that if you went to a psychologist or a psychiatrist, or an astrologer, or a theologian, you might learn that none of the reasons you advanced were acceptable. Notice two examples.

Suppose you forgot today was election day until the polls closed, and when friends asked if you had voted, you say, "No. I refuse to participate in such a corrupt system!" They reply with approval and you are one of the group. No problem: your reason was acceptable. In the second instance, you tell your friends you don't want to play tennis this afternoon because you stayed up all night reading for an exam. They shout their ridicule of you demanding that you confess that you were out fooling around. No amount of argument from you will change their mind. The stronger you protest, the less likely you are to be believed. Such a situation will tend to lead to frustration, if not anger.

Consider a more important illustration. The former aide to the President of the United States appears before a Senate committee and says he knew nothing about the criminal events that he agrees were committed by some people close to the White House. Another high level aide says the former witness was indeed involved in the criminal activities. Suppose, for illustrative purposes only, that all the members of the Senate committee believed the first witness to by lying; what can they do? They could lean over the table and shout, "You're a liar, we're sending you to jail!" But instantly your sense of justice is outraged, even if you agree he's a liar. You might respond, "It doesn't matter what you believe, you can't send a man to jail without justification!" And there is a critical distinction.

The process by which human beings come to believe, think, or feel what they do may be different from the public process that they employ to justify those beliefs and the behaviors to which they lead. This is a necessary distinction because we often may not know ourselves why we behave in a certain way; we often may be unable to communicate satisfactorily to others what we truly believe to be so; we often may find that society is unwilling to put sufficient stock in our belief to act on that basis alone. In each of these instances, we must be able to communicate some basis for justifying our behavior that will serve the others involved. This is a uniquely communicative problem; it is an audience centered approach to argumentation.

To reiterate, people constantly believe that they have knowledge that is sufficiently reliable, true, valuable, etc. that it can serve others as well as themselves. How they came to hold that knowledge is the object of study in many disciplines: psychologists search for a variety of phenomena, such as attitudes, values, psychological consistencies, or ego-involvements, to explain our behavior; psychoanalysts have conceived of such forces as the ego and the id, while geneticists suggest that we are the product of our heritage. Theologians argue that a supreme being plays a part in the knowledge we possess, and humanists hold with the working of the freely acting human intellect as the source of truth. Astrologers tell us that everything is ordered according to the movement of the planets and our relation to them, while social psychologists argue knowledge is the consensus emerging from group experiences. There are many other philosophies as well. But it is the thrust of this theory of argumentation that no matter where the claim came from, once it is advanced publicly it must be supported in such a way as to win the adherence of those addressed. History records ample instances of claims once rejected that later were accepted as truth, and plenty, initially accepted as truth, that ultimately were rejected as frauds. It is with the business of advancing and supporting claims, and their success in winning adherence, that the study of argumentation is concerned.

ARGUMENTATION IS THE PROCESS OF ADVANCING, SUPPORTING, AND CRITICIZING CLAIMS

From what we have said it should be clear that an argument consists of the assertion of a claim along with a reason or reasons stated or implied. Because the reasons offered must ultimately be judged by the audience receiving the claim they may take as many different forms as there are differences among people in the audience. By audience, by the way, we do not mean to restrict argumentation to a public speaking situation. On the contrary, we include in our concept of audience any human being to whom an argument is communicated by whatever medium. By the process of argumentation we mean that on-going transaction of advancing claims, supporting them with reasons, and the advancing of competing claims with appropriate support, the mutual criticism of them, and the granting of adherence to one. Even the granting of adherence can provide for a continuation of the new process, since new audiences or new claims built from the adherence will provide for the continued reason-giving.

In complex situations, argumentation may take on a form called decision making. By this we mean a system in which alternative courses of action are considered by those with the power to decide, and the granting of adherence to one that will become a decision. This action may involve any number of preliminary steps that utilize various forms of analysis, but all of these finally become modes of support in claims considered by decision makers. Two key terms appear in this statement: *analysis* and *support*. Both of them take on special meaning in an audience centered theory.

In this approach to argumentation, analysis is not just a matter of acquiring knowledge; it is a process whereby all the constituents of the argumentation situation are related, one to the other, in such a way that what needs to be argued and what it will take to make those arguments convincing is known so that the arguer may more effectively develop his arguments, and support. Support is any material—evidence, values, credibility, language, etc.—which assists the gaining of adherence to the claim. It is a function of what the audience accepts, and not any universal fragment of "truth." In the following chapters we will see that there are many conventions in the use of evidence and other means of support that have come to be regarded as "correct," and which, therefore, will probably be useful in a variety of argumentative situations. But these are nothing more than modes of support that are commonly respected by audiences. Also, we have said that an inherent part of argumentation is criticism. It may take the simple form of granting unqualified adherence, "I'll buy that," or, it may take the form of elaborate and extensive refutation in which counterarguments are advanced and other claims are suggested.

A great deal of the argumentation in which we engage occurs in the ordinary course of life under no particular format. We call this *general argumentation*. Here, there may be no formal statement of claim, no provision for counterargument, and no explicit decision making. It typically is quite spontaneous. In what we call special argumentation the opposite is true. In specialized fields of argumentation such as law, scholarship, forensics, politics, and business, there are, in addition to the conventions of general argumentation, commonly established formats for *special argumentation*. The modes of support employed will usually be heavily drawn from the epistemology, language, values, etc., of the field in which the argumentation occurs. In other words, the arguments will reflect the specialized character of the audience. This will be illustrated in the final chapters of the book. It is in specialized argumentation that one is more likely to find the use of cases, which are overall plans for winning adherence through a combination of arguments that all lend support to a major claim.

CHARACTERISTICS OF RELATED THEORIES

To understand how the theory discussed here is part of a long tradition of study in argumentation, it is useful to have some notion of how other writers have approached similar subjects. Of course, a brief review of literature must necessarily cover only selected key points, and you may want to turn to the complete texts in order to make a thorough comparison. However, the section that follows will provide some highlights of contemporary perspectives on persuasion and argumentation to allow a comparison and a contrast of them with the audience centered approach to argumentation. Then, rather more detailed discussions of classical and modern thoughts on the theory of argumentation will be presented to provide the necessary background for our study.

SOME CONTEMPORARY APPROACHES TO PERSUASION AND ARGUMENTATION

Traditional theories of rhetoric embraced the processes that are now often divided into theories of persuasion and theories of argumentation. This is largely a product of the emergence of the study of communication through the perspectives and methodologies of the social and behavioral sciences. When the methods of science were applied to communication, a body of literature under the label "persuasion" emerged, while many other scholars continued to invest their energies in the investigation of similar phenomena through humanistic methods and perspectives. Although the audience centered theory of argumentation suggested here bears similarities to both groups of scholarship, it will be seen to be somewhat different from them as well. Notice first the various concepts of persuasion.

Persuasion. Wallace Fotheringham observes that persuasion has been conceived in terms of *attempt* (a conscious effort to use messages to modify the thought and behavior of others), *stimuli* employed (the use of messages, or discourse, or some symbolic process), or *ability* (if one secures a change of belief or action, one has persuaded regardless of attempt or method). Fotheringham, himself, conceives of persuasion as a body of *effects* or the meaning generated by messages, which is instrumental to the action desired by the persuader.[2] Howard Martin and Kenneth Andersen suggest that "all communication is ultimately persuasive in that it seeks to win a response to the communicator's ideas."[3] To Thomas Scheidel, persuasion involves both a conscious attempt to influence behavior and the use of audible and visible symbolic cues.[4] Finally, Thomas Beisecker and Donn Parson conclude that an examination of the various concepts of persuasion indicates that the "persuasive message and the process by which it comes to the attention of receivers . . . [is] central to the concept of persuasion."[5] They go on to say that "persuasion inherently has attitude change as its goal."[6]

Because modern thought on persuasion is strongly inclined to deal with cognitive and affective effects of messages, the audience centered theory of argumentation is quite a distinct line of thought. We are not concerned with measurement and inference about processes that occur "inside" people. Nor are we involved in the assessment of the extent to which an argumentative message (or any other kind of message) will modify such factors as beliefs, attitudes, or values. Although there are some similarities to some of the approaches to persuasion, argumentation as conceived here is concerned with the observation of communication that involves the advancing of claims and reasons and the observable act of granting or withholding adherence.

Argumentation. Now examine some of the contemporary conceptions of argumentation. James McBurney and Glen Mills define argumentation to be "a method of analysis and reasoning designed to provide acceptable bases for belief and action."[7] Austin Freeley perceives persuasion and argumentation to be parts of the same process, differing only in emphasis. He would distinguish argumentation by saying it "gives priority to logical appeals while taking cognizance of ethical and emotional appeals.[8] Persuasion, Freeley suggests, reflects the reverse emphasis. Robert Huber sees

[2] Wallace C. Fotheringham, *Perspectives on Persuasion* (Boston: Allyn and Bacon, Inc., 1966), pp. 5, 7.

[3] Howard H. Martin and Kenneth E. Andersen, *Speech Communication* (Boston: Allyn and Bacon, Inc., 1968), p. 6.

[4] Thomas M. Scheidel, *Persuasive Speaking* (Glenview: Scott, Foresman and Co., 1967), p. 1.

[5] Thomas D. Beisecker and Donn W. Parson, *The Process of Social Influence* (Englewood Cliffs: Prentice-Hall, Inc., 1972), p. 4.

[6] Beisecker and Parson, p. 5.

[7] James H. McBurney and Glen E. Mills, *Argumentation and Debate* (New York: The Macmillan Co., 1964), p. 1.

[8] Austin J. Freeley, *Argumentation and Debate* 2nd ed. (Belmont: Wadsworth Publishing Co., Inc., 1966), p. 7.

the relationships similarly by defining argument "as that process in communication in which logic is used to influence others."[9] Walter Fisher and Edward Sayles look more to the character of the messages than their impact on others: "argument may be used to mean: (1) a series of logically related statements, (2) an instance of reasoning in ordinary speaking and writing, and (3) the process of employing any number of instances of reasoning to influence beliefs."[10] Jerry Anderson and Paul Dovre agree that argument implies the use of rational analysis and logical appeals, but they add to its potential ends by saying it is a method "to resolve conflicts, secure decisions, and affect attitude and behavior."[11]

To the extent that these approaches suggest that argumentation provides more "acceptable," or "logical" bases for human belief and action, the audience centered theory is different. Unless, of course, acceptable is defined in terms of the audience and not in terms of some universal criteria of "correctness" or "truth." If the employment of, or emphasis on, "logic" means that argumentative messages can be evaluated apart from the audience by some universal criteria, the audience centered approach is quite different. When these writers focus on messages that audience members perceive to provide adequate bases for adherence and action as measured by their observable behavior, they are similar to the audience centered approach.

SOME CLASSICAL THEORIES

A great deal of the writing by Greek and Roman authors during the Classical Period is relevant to the study of argumentation. It was during this time that the first major developments of a theory of rhetoric occurred. It would not be practical to attempt a full review of this work here, but some examination of the various perspectives, revealed through the work of Plato and Aristotle, will shed light on present day thoughts about argumentation and persuasion, and will, therefore, help locate the audience centered theory within the distinguished tradition.

Plato's Theory. Both Plato and Aristotle dealt with the question of argumentation in relation to the search for truth and the development of belief.

---

[9] Robert B. Huber, *Influencing Through Argument* (New York: David McKay Co., Inc., 1963), p. 4.

[10] Walter R. Fisher and Edward M. Sayles, "The Nature and Functions of Argument," in Gerald R. Miller and Thomas R. Nilsen, eds., *Perspectives on Argumentation* (Chicago: Scott, Foresman and Co., 1966), pp. 3–4.

[11] Jerry M. Anderson and Paul J. Dovre, *Readings in Argumentation* (Boston: Allyn and Bacon, Inc., 1968), p. 3.

Plato labeled his system "dialectic" and it may be described this way: for every question there exists a truth and it falls to the philosopher to persist in his search until it is found. The process of dialectic is a method of discovering truth, not persuading people to your way of thinking. It proceeds through a question and answer process, seeking to define the nature of the topic under discussion and observe its essential constituents and relation to other phenomena. By breaking down the subject to basics, the dialecticians could observe the self-evident truth, and proceed through definitional relationships to develop a correct understanding of complex ideas. Once this truth was found, it was appropriate to communicate to those unable to perceive truth on their own. This, again, is not an instance of appealing for agreement. It is an instruction for those able to understand; failure to agree is tantamount to misunderstanding, and occurs at the peril of the listener. Notice how Plato says this:

"A man must first know the truth about every single subject on which he speaks or writes. He must be able to define each in terms of a universal class that stands by itself. When he has successively defined his subjects according to their specific classes, he must know how to continue the division until he reaches the point of indivisibility. He must make the same sort of distinction with reference to the nature of the soul. He must then discover the kind of speech that matches each type of nature. When that is accomplished, he must arrange and adorn each speech in such a way as to present complicated and unstable souls with complex speeches, speeches exactly attuned to every changing mood of the complicated soul—while the simple soul must be presented with simple speech. Not until a man acquires this capacity will it be possible to produce speech in a scientific way, in so far as its nature permits such treatment."[12]

In this system of argument one does not envision individuals democratically engaged in difference of opinion, seeking to win the adherence of others. Plato provides for audience adaptation but the general audience is never central; it is more of an afterthought to the real problem: the discovery of truth among philosophers. In fact, once truth had been discovered and announced by the philosopher, it would be the responsibility of others to see the truth:

"And are not those who are verily and indeed wanting in the knowledge of the true being of each thing, and who have in their souls no clear pattern,

---

[12] From Plato: *Phaedrus*, translated by W. C. Helmbold and W. G. Rabinowitz, copyright © 1956 by The Liberal Arts Press, Inc., reprinted by permission of The Bobbs-Merrill Company, Inc.

and are unable as with a painter's eye to look at the absolute truth and to that original to repair, and having perfect vision of the other world to order the laws about beauty, goodness, justice in this, if not already ordered, and to guard and preserve the order of them—are not such persons, I ask, simply blind?"[13]

A little further along in the same dialogue, he says, "A pilot should not humbly beg the sailors to be commanded by him . . . neither are the wise to go to the doors of the rich. . . ."[14] Since Plato observed that often the "blind" or unwise persons were not able to recognize the truth when confronted with it, he faced the problem of securing public action on the basis of truth. Obviously, supplication was out of the question as was the continued operation of society on the basis of error. The solution was this:

"Until philosophers are kings, or the kings and princes of this world have the spirit and power of philosophy, and political greatness and wisdom meet in one, and those commoner natures who pursue either to the exclusion of the other are compelled to stand aside, cities will never have rest from their evils,—no, nor the human race."[15]

Obviously, this brief summary cannot do justice to the philosophy of Plato. All that has been given is just enough to suggest the basic outline of his theory of argumentation. This approach in various forms is advanced today by some writers. In suggesting the existence of an absolute truth apart from human judgment, it is in opposition to an audience centered approach to argumentation. In recommending extensive analysis during which ideas are related to the people to whom they are to be communicated, the two approaches are similar. In proposing the establishment of an intellectual elite who can find truth for others and act in their behalf, it is in opposition to the audience centered theory. Nevertheless this perspective is still active in the thinking of many people who suggest the blindness or ignorance of those who will not grant adherence to their ideas. An audience centered theory would call for improvement in the method of advancing and supporting your claims when people fail to grant adherence. The dialectical approach would tend to place most blame on the members of the audience for failing to grasp the truth of the arguments.

[13] Plato, "The Republic," Benjamin Jewett, trans., in Dagobert D. Runes, ed., *Treasury of Philosophy* (New York: Philosophical Library, 1955), p. 936.
[14] Plato, "The Republic," p. 942.
[15] Plato, "The Republic," p. 935.

Aristotle's Theory. Like Plato, Aristotle's ideas have had considerable influence on Western thought to the present time. The rhetorical theory of Aristotle should not be perceived as opposing the dialectic of Plato. In fact, Aristotle could find much in Plato with which to agree, defining rhetoric as a counterpart of dialectic—different but coordinated. The major problem of Plato—what does one do when, after discovering truth, one finds others unwilling to accept it—is the focus of his rhetoric. That is, Aristotle would expect the use of dialectic to help in the discovery of truth, and the use of rhetoric in the process of securing public acceptance of it. This is a subtle distinction, because, as discussed earlier, the processes become intertwined as "false" reasons and policies are publicly accepted as true, and "true" ones are publicly rejected as false. Who can say which is which? Aristotle's solution lies in the process of communication: "rhetoric is the faculty or process of discovering in each case or question, what are the available means of persuasion."[16] If rhetoric, functioning as a system, brings to bear on the question the available arguments, or means of persuasion, then Aristotle would argue that what emerges will be the correct decision, "because truth and justice are by nature more powerful than their opposites; so that, when decisions are not made as they should be, the speakers with the right on their side have only themselves to thank for the outcome."[17] To illustrate, rhetoric can be compared to a chemical formula: if all the ingredients are entered properly, the correct compound will result. If they are not, the failure is that of those who measured and entered the elements involved. Aristotle would say about it, "we see that its [rhetoric's] function is not to persuade, but to discover the available means of persuasion in a given case."[18] If they are, indeed, discovered, the correct decision will be made.

Particularly important to understanding this rhetorical approach to argument is Aristotle's statement that rhetoric and dialectic are counterparts. If dialectic is described as the mechanism for the discovery of truth, as suggested in the previous section, its methods are those of logic and classification. In logic, says Aristotle, there are two processes—induction, the drawing of claims on the basis of the examination of a number of specific instances, and deduction, the drawing of claims on the basis of examining already accepted generalizations. Important to note here is the fact that these are *formal* processes, that is, they are studies of forms, of relationships. In his writing on logic, Aristotle dealt only in the abstract

---

[16] Lane Cooper, *The Rhetoric of Aristotle*, © 1932, Renewed 1960. By permission of Prentice-Hall, Inc., Englewood Cliffs, New Jersey, p. 7.

[17] Aristotle, p. 5.

[18] Aristotle, p. 6.

so that he could concentrate on the forms of relationships. In this sense, logic is comparable to mathematics. That is to say, in the abstract one can say with absolute confidence of the figures, X-R, X-R, X-R, "All X's have R's." This is an example of absolute truth. Similarly, using a deduction this time, one can assert with equal confidence the following:

If all A is B, and
if all C is A, then certainly, and absolutely
   all C is B

Both of these examples are representative of formal logic. In the Aristotelian system, and that of many who came later, formal logic acts as the model toward which human reasoning should aspire, even though it can never fully approximate it because of the conditional nature of the questions dealt with. If formal logic demonstrates necessary conclusions, then rhetorical logic approaches such demonstration to the extent it approaches pure logic in form. Listen to Aristotle on this question:

". . . men deliberate and raise questions about the things they do, and human actions all belong to this class [of uncertainties or mere probabilities]; no human action, so to speak, is inevitable. And we see that, in Rhetoric, for the most part merely usual and contingent conclusions must be drawn from premises of the same sort; just as, in Logic, necessary conclusions must arise from premises that are determined."[19]

The rhetorical approach to argument set up the example as the rhetorical equivalent of the induction, and the enthymeme (a concept that will be explained in detail later) as the rhetorical equivalent of the syllogism or deduction. Aristotle hypothesized that in the realm of rhetoric, not only were arguments advanced from these logical equivalents, but at the same time, from two additional sources, *ethos* (the character of the speaker), and *pathos* (the bringing of the audience to a state of emotion).

Hopefully, distinctions between the dialectical and rhetorical theories of argument are now clear. Plato reasoned that it is possible for human argument to achieve absolute truth, and his method, accordingly, was dialectic. Furthermore, if one has absolute truth, one does not negotiate, compromise, or even supplicate with others—the truth is stated in the clearest possible way for those who are able to understand. Finally, it is intolerable that one who possesses the truth should stand by while those in error lead the world into greater and greater crisis. A moral obligation

[19] Aristotle, p. 12.

would exist for the promulgation of the truth. Plato's ideal solution was to have Kings become philosophers or turn the Kingdom over to philosophers. Understandably, in Plato's Republic there was no need for a system of free speech—deliberation among all the people would not be appropriate.

On the other hand, Aristotle asserted that, for the most part humans argue about their own actions that are never inevitable and about which one could, therefore, never have absolute truth. He did, however, feel that some judgments are more "probably" true than others, and man should strive to discover those. But dialectic alone would be insufficient for this because of the conditional nature of the questions and the need to enter human judgment into the equation. Therefore, he posited a system that would secure on each question all that could be persuasively said. If all competing arguments were examined together, he said, truth and justice would have a natural tendency to prevail. But this could occur only when *all* competing arguments had full and fair opportunity to be examined. This system, obviously, depends completely on a process of free speech within a society. Even more, it requires the establishment of elaborate decision making systems such as legislatures and courts. The system is also more dependent on a democratic political arrangement than is Plato's.

When Aristotle sets up formal logic as the model to which argumentation should aspire, his approach is in opposition to an audience centered one. To the extent he argues that there are aspects of "truth" or "probability," which can be discovered and evaluated apart from human judgment, he is in disagreement with an audience centered idea. However much of his rhetorical theory serves as the inspiration for an audience centered theory of argumentation. The definition of rhetoric as a faculty, art, or system for the generation of all the available modes of persuasion could easily be modified to serve as a definition of audience centered argumentation. It could be said that the process of argumentation functions to permit the relevant audience to consider all competing claims and their reasons to choose from among them. An audience centered theory would differ from Aristotle's in the sense that he argues that the choice would be correct because truth and justice are by nature more powerful than their opposites. The audience centered theory argues simply that if individuals have the opportunity to examine the full range of claims and support related to any decision, they will perceive their choice to be the proper or correct one, at least at that time.

In summary, Plato was concerned with the discovery of truth, and Aristotle searched for a means of selecting from among competing ideas the one most probably true. In doing so, Aristotle was considerably more concerned with communication than was Plato. The audience centered theory of argumentation parts company with these writers by rejecting a concept of truth that exists in the abstract or absolute sense. It does not turn decision making entirely over to whimsey, however, because it posits the tendency to demand and evaluate reasons and, thereby includes as modes of support all the traditional schemes of analysis. It merely puts full emphasis on the communicative process.

SOME MODERN INFLUENTIAL THEORIES

There is considerable contemporary thought on the subject of argumentation as there was in classical times. Again, there is not space to discuss it all. However, two philosophers have published treatises seeking to revise the thinking on the subject that have had great impact on modern thought. Both writers contend that little original thought on the subject of human argument has occurred since the time of Aristotle. They say that instead most of the attention has gone into the development of specialized systems such as mathematics and the use of computers, into more sophisticated systems of formal logic, highly esoteric decision theories that are based on unacceptable assumptions about human behavior, or into greater refinement of models in specialized fields such as law, economics, and scholarship. These two writers—Stephen E. Toulmin and Chaim Perelman —seek to correct that imbalance by turning their attention totally to commentaries on the ways humans seem actually to engage in argumentation.

Toulmin's Theory.   Toulmin began his search for a new theory of argument from the point of view of a formal logician. His question concerned the extent to which formal logic is relevant to the understanding and assessment of actual arguments, and his goal was the development of an orderly system of assessment that could take into account the variability of arguments as actually used by the average person. He had no interest in writing a handbook on persuasion, nor did he concern himself with the psychological problem of how human beings come to behave as they do or assert the claims they do. His concern was, on the contrary, with the ways in which human beings *justify* their actions through argument. He says, "logic is concerned not with the *manner* of our inferring, or with questions of *technique*: its primary business is a retrospective, justificatory one."[20]

His model for the process of justification was the law. Once again, in law, no matter what the judge believes, he is not free to act unless he can generate arguments in justification of the action he proposes. For this rea-

[20] Stephen Toulmin, *The Uses of Argument* (Cambridge: At The University Press, 1958), p. 6.

son, judges may regularly render decisions that are not in agreement with their own predilections, because it was not possible to justify their desired course of action. Thus, specialists in law must be deeply concerned with the manner of evaluating or assessing arguments to learn how best to make a judgment as to what course of action is justified in a given case. Or perhaps, the specialist studies the decision making process to learn how, in fact, the arguments are assessed, and then reports it systematically. In any event, Toulmin concluded that, "logic . . . is generalised jurisprudence. Arguments can be compared with lawsuits, and the claims we make and argue for in extra-legal contexts with claims made in the courts, while the cases we present in making good each kind of claim can be compared with each other."[21]

What is the test of argument, according to Toulmin? He says it is its ability to "stand up to criticism," that is, one that can meet the standards applied by the field in which it occurs. In advancing a schematic method for setting out an argument for criticism, Toulmin's goal is not truth or acceptance, but rather so that the assessment can be "logically candid."[22]

We've already said that the thrust of traditional theories of argument was to discover universal principles by which arguments could be generated and evaluated. If they were successful in that goal, one could assess any argument whether it emerged from gambling, physics, art, or whatever, by the same principles. Toulmin's theory rejects this premise. He asserts that for every argument there is an element that is universal to all arguments, no matter what their subject matter—*field invariant*; and for each argument there is an element that is indigenous to the particular subject or environment from which the argument emerges—*field dependent*. For example, each claim or declaration that forms an argument contains or implies what Toulmin calls a "modal" term such as possibly, probably, certainly, etc. "The Cardinals *may* win their division." "This compound *certainly* does not contain sulpher." "The balance of payments will *probably* remain stable during the next quarter." For each of these modal terms two questions can be asked. First, what is the "force" of its use; second, what were the "criteria" used to select it?

For Toulmin, the force of modal terms is field invariant while the criteria are field dependent. First, think about the meaning of such terms as "may," "will," "might," "possibly," "perhaps," "probably,": "certainly," "absolutely," "in all likelihood," "as far as I can see," "to the best of my knowledge and belief," "at four to one odds," "was statistically significant at the .05 level of confidence," "90% chance," "1000% sup-

[21] Toulmin, p. 7.
[22] Toulmin, p. 9.

port," "approached but did not achieve significance," and as many or more
in the negative sense such as "cannot," or "should not." What meaning or
force do they have, and does it vary according to the argument or is it
field invariant? Toulmin asserts it is field invariant, and in each case
serves to communicate to others the extent to which one is willing to be
committed or held responsible for the claim. "By saying 'S is probably P'
or 'I shall probably do A', I expressly avoid unreservedly committing
myself. I insure myself thereby against some of the consequences of failure."[23] For instance, if you tell your parents you possibly will get home
for the holidays, you authorize them to make preparations but not to be
hurt if you don't show up. How different would it have been if you said,
"I will certainly get home for the holidays." Think of the consequences if
you failed to arrive! Similarly, if you were to make the announcement,
"The Cardinals may win their division," you are carefully guarding yourself against demands that you put up some money to support your assertion or that you face public ridicule and scorn should they fail. Of
course, a sports writer could use "may" in the public announcement of an
opinion, but privately say, "I wouldn't want to be quoted, but in fact the
Cardinals haven't got a chance." Does that mean the writer is fuzzy-headed
or dishonest? Not necessarily, because he may be willing to be held
responsible to a "cannot" prediction in private, where the consequences of
error would be minimal, but commit to as much as a "may" in public to
cover against the unexpected result of a Cardinal victory, at which time he
could say, "I didn't rule that out." The same can be said of a statement
concerning the sulfur content of a compound or the stability of the balance
of payments. Although the claims emerge from quite different fields, each
contains a modal term that serves to communicate the *force* with which
the assertion is made and, therefore, the extent to which the asserter is willing to be held responsible for it. Furthermore, each of the statements could
be made differently in different contexts by the same person, with the same
honest motives of the sports writer. Thus, for Toulmin, the force of the
modal terms is field invariant, even when the term "probability" is
involved. Although that word is often associated with mathematical calculations of frequencies, Toulmin would point out that it has no "tangible
counterpart, referent, *designatum* . . . does not name a thing of whatever
kind, but is a word of such a type that it is nonsense even to talk about it as
denoting . . . anything."[24] Although mathematical expressions of frequencies are certainly one of the criteria used to select or reject the word

[23] Toulmin, p. 49.
[24] Toulmin, p. 65.

"probably," there are many others. And the force of the term, even when expressed mathematically, remains the same.

On the other hand, the criteria used to determine the modal term to be employed, according to Toulmin, vary from field to field. Thus, the factors considered by the sports writer to make a comment about the Cardinals included the talent and health of the team, the quality of the opposition, the remaining games played at home and away, the coaching, and so forth. But the criteria used to make a declaration about the sulfur content of a compound were quite different and involved a process of chemical qualitative analysis. To assert something about the balance of payments calls for still another set of criteria. To assess these arguments, one would need to examine the particular procedures, facts, etc., that are common to the field under investigation. Here, Toulmin suggests that it is not possible to formulate universal measures of arguments, for within each field there will be routines, emphases, perceptions, etc., unique to the field. They are, in other words, field dependent.

There is a major distinction between Toulmin's philosophy and that of an audience centered theory of argumentation in the fact that Toulmin has no expressed interest in the process of communication or the development of ways to construct claims and reasons to win adherence. However, much of his theory is directly adapted to the audience centered approach. This is particularly true in his concept of the justificatory nature of argumentation, his concept of the character of probability as a modal term (field invariant) that describes the force with which one advances a claim, and with his belief that arguments cannot be assessed apart from the field (or audience) to whom they are addressed.

Perelman's Theory. Also writing from the perspective of a philosopher of logic is Chaim Perelman. He became impatient with what he believed to be too little concern on the part of logicians with the methods of proof used to win the adherence of audiences. In fact, he charged that for three hundred years, the influence of Descartes had moved the field of logic deeper and deeper into highly formalized, mathematical investigations of relatively closed systems aimed at regularizing already established relationships. Descartes' interest was in the absolute, self-evident, and the inferences that could be drawn there from. In the large range of conditional questions that occupy most human arguments, says Perelman, the Cartesian logician had virtually no interest. Therefore, Perelman turned to the development of a theory of argument modeled after the rhetorical theory of Aristotle. He sought a theory that could acknowledge the use of reason "in directing our own actions and influencing those of others."[25]

---

[25] Perelman and Olbrechts-Tyteca, p. 3.

More specifically acknowledging his debt to rhetoric, Perelman says, "the object of the theory of argumentation is the study of the discursive techniques allowing us to induce or *to increase the mind's adherence to the theses presented for its assent.*"[26] Throughout his treatise, he stresses again and again that the starting place for argument as well as the source of its evaluation is the audience, whether the discourse exists as writing, speaking, or whatever. So, for argumentation to exist, a community of minds, a common language, a feeling of importance for gaining the adherence of another human being, and some other human who will listen, must be present. In fact, he says there is a commonality of interests between sociology and argumentation, because each human group is distinguishable in part by its "dominant opinions and unquestioned beliefs, of the premises that it takes for granted without hesitation" all of which form both an integral part of its culture and the starting points and sources of connections of ideas necessary to the creator of arguments.[27] Sociologists may usefully study the arguments that have succeeded and failed in order to learn of the group to which they were addressed, just as a student of argument must observe the results of sociological, social psychological, and anthropological research in order to construct arguments.

Critical to Perelman's categories of arguments is his conception of three kinds of audiences. His first audience consists of a conception of all mankind as an audience. Of course, no one ever addresses all mankind, but in this sense it is a construction that one appeals to. Certain ideas that will be advanced as "fact" are actually based on an appeal to all mankind that no reasonable person would deny it. The audience to which scholars and some other writers speak is a conception of the universal audience, for their work must be so structured that it would likely survive the scrutiny of anyone's examination. This notion is related in some ways to the concept of the "reasonable man" in law and the "rational man" in economics. Both concepts deal not with any one person, but with a conception of "everyman" or "anyman" as a basis of determining what *should* be believed or done. Thus, the highest test for an argument to survive is the scrutiny of the universal audience. The argument would have to be judged as consisting of compelling reasons that "are self-evident, and possess an absolute and timeless validity, independent of local or historical contingencies."[28]

The second type of audience, according to Perelman, is the other person or persons to whom one is specifically speaking. It is to this audience that

[26] Perelman and Olbrechts-Tyteca, p. 4.
[27] Perelman and Olbrechts-Tyteca, p. 20.
[28] Perelman and Olbrechts-Tyteca, p. 32.

the creator of arguments looks for those bases of arguments that will win specific adherence. The third audience is that of the maker of arguments himself as he deliberates or creates reasons in justification of his own behavior. This idea of intrapersonal communication (which some scholars reject as a definitional impossibility) is particularly interesting in the study of argumentation, for it brings to mind a picture of individuals trying out arguments for themselves to test the extent that they will wish to be associated with them in public. We will see in chapter 2 that this process has been suggested to account in part for the behavior of human beings in the making of decisions. Others have at least described it as the basis of relieving the psychological pressures that tend to emerge following decision.

To reiterate, lest it fail to be impressed clearly: for Perelman, the test of arguments is in the audience, and it does not emerge from some objective validity that is inherent either in the argument or in the "nature" or "reality" of things. Perelman attacks those theorists who claim that *"the facts, the truths, or at least the probabilities, subject to the calculus of probabilities, triumph of themselves. The speaker plays no essential role, since his demonstrations are timeless, and there is no cause to distinguish among audiences, since all men are supposed to yield to what is objectively valid."* To this, Perelman says, such a belief is nothing more than a "device to be exorcised."[29] Such demonstration, he says, is possible only in such formal, closed studies as symbolic logic or mathematics.

In discussing the practical business of making arguments, Perelman is concerned with two processes: the starting points of argument, and the methods of associating and dissociating ideas once the argument has started. There must be a beginning community among those involved in argument if any further progress is to be made. You can probably recall many times starting a conversation by saying, "Now you can at least grant that . . . ," or "Surely you agree that this much is so. . . ." Perelman would categorize this process of establishing common ground into two classes: the *real*, including such concepts as facts, truths, and presumptions, which emerge from an appeal to the universal audience; and the *preferable*, comprising values, hierarchies, and loci or lines of argument that are a function of the specific group or individual addressed.

The concept of loci deserves some special discussion, because it is a contribution of Aristotle, which Perelman has brought into the present day in somewhat different form. To introduce his discussion of enthymemes, Aristotle first discussed maxims, and then topoi. A maxim is a statement about those things that concern human action—the choices of human con-

[29] Perelman and Olbrechts-Tyteca, p. 46.

duct—which can reasonably be expected to be accepted by any other person. The maxim may be a simple declarative sentence, such as, "It is better to be free than be a slave." Or, a maxim may have a reason appended as in this: "No one is truly free, for we are all subject to the laws of chance." In either case, the maxim constitutes an argument that likely will establish common ground from which further arguments can be built. Creators of argument can develop an encyclopedia of lines of arguments to which they may turn for ways to begin any one of a number of different arguments. A *Topic* or *Topos* is a heading under which such arguments may be grouped. It is, in a sense, a place or *Locus* to which one can turn for ideas on any subject. When spoken of as a collection, they are referred to as *Topoi* or *Loci*. These topics or loci may be as specialized as to refer to a specific subject as discussed within a specific group—when speaking to members of certain groups such as the Alcholics Anonymous, the Women's Christian Temperance Union, or some organized religions, one can expect acceptance of the claim that, "It can be dangerous to consume alcoholic beverages." Or, topoi or loci may be as generalized or as common as to apply to a wide variety of groups and individuals on many topics, such as, "for every effect that occurs, there must be one or more causes."

Notice that these are not subjects on which to speak, nor are they speeches themselves. They constitute an encyclopedia of sources from which arguments can be built. To recognize them is to recognize the fact that for any one claim, there may be many arguments that could be advanced in its behalf. Whereas it is often suggested that one should search for the "correct" argument or proof of a claim as inherent in the claim, Perelman's line of thought urges the creator of arguments to search among the many proofs of a claim to find those that will most likely win the adherence of the audience. It is, in other words, the uniquely rhetorical or communicative element of argument.

Both Aristotle and Perelman take time to indicate examples of topoi or loci, Aristotle indicating twenty-eight common topics. It is not useful to take time to present those lists here because each arguer must create his own such list in relation to the audiences to be addressed, the topics to be discussed, and the time in which the argument is to be made. One of the errors made by some students of Aristotle was to presume that topoi relevant to Classical Greece are relevant to modern man. It would be equally erroneous to assume that the loci conceived by a writer in Belgium in 1958 would be particularly useful in the United States, or anywhere else, in the 1970's and 1980's.

The final major element in the Perelman theory of argument is his discussion of the processes (or loci) of association and dissociation. Again, they draw their strength from the fact that they tend to secure the adherence of those to whom they are addressed. Once common ground has been found through a satisfactory starting point of argument, a case is developed by the systematic association of new ideas to those already accepted, or by the dissociation of ideas accepted on the one hand with others also accepted, leading ultimately to the acceptance only of those ideas advocated in the case being advanced. The most well recognized schemes of association, discussed in greater detail in later chapters, are what Perelman calls "quasi-logical arguments."[30] These are arguments patterned after the processes of formal logic, such as the syllogistic form drawing contradictions and incompatibility, reasoning from identity and definition, part and whole, comparison, etc. In each case, the argument does not have the characteristics of formal logic of intrinsic validity, but it permits the presentation of ideas in such a relationship that audiences will likely grant adherence, assisted in part by its similarity to formal logic. What many readers might presume to be "reality," is found in the Perelman theory as a mode of argument.

Perelman's work is massive in its detail and use of illustration. But probably most useful to the current reader is his rhetorical perspective toward argument. Although other theorists have sought to straddle two worlds—that of dialectic and rhetoric—Perelman comes closer than any other writer to advancing a communication theory of argument. The fact, as suggested earlier, that he is a logician, not a rhetorician, makes this observation even more significant.

CONCLUSIONS

This chapter has introduced the subject of argument by presenting the basic outlines of the theory to be advanced throughout this book and by reviewing some of the significant theories that have been developed by others. Key to the theory of argument presented here is its audience orientation, and its effort to describe how human beings behave as reason-makers and reason-evaluators. Some predictions of human behavior are hypothesized: (1) When behavior, including communication, is made public, it is done with the understanding that one should be able to give reasons for it; (2) Often, individuals will include reasons for behavior at the time it is made public, voluntarily in the expectation that others have a right to know them; (3) The demand, by others, for reasons is typically considered legitimate; (4) The refusal, by others, to evaluate positively the reasons will tend to create additional reason-making or reason-supporting

[30] Perelman and Olbrechts-Tyteca, p. 191.

behavior; and (5) The positive evaluation of reasons, in the final analysis, must be a function of the willingness of those making the evaluation to do so. Unlike many other commentators on argument, this theory does not presume to say how humans *should* think, argue, and decide; instead, it seeks to describe *how* they typically do so. For this reason, the focus of study is on the reasons publicly announced, and not whatever may or may not exist within an individual nervous system; and on the public announcement or action indicating adherence (or refusal) to arguments, again regardless of what may or may not have happened psychologically. Similarly, the focus is on those arguments that win adherence, and not on those that are "correct" or "true" or ought to have been selected.

Plato's theory of dialectic, with its emphasis on the discovery of absolute truth is in sharp contrast to an audience centered one. Aristotle's rhetoric moved substantially toward a communication perspective but still held to an idea of truth or probability that would "emerge." Toulmin's work on the uses of argument as justificatory and evaluated in terms of the field in which they occur is close to an audience centered concept of argumentation. Perelman's modern rhetoric of argumentation, with its emphasis on the audience as the starting point of argument, provides a strong model for the ideas in this book.

PROJECTS

1. For the next twenty-four hours, remove from all of your communication any statement of reasons. Guard carefully in your statements to leave off "because," "for," and other clauses that follow. Also, when others ask you, "why?" or "how come?" etc., simply say, "I do not have a reason to give." Share your observations with others doing the same thing.

2. Keep a journal for the next day or so of the reason-making behavior of others. Observe the variety and types of reasons given, and particularly notice those occasions when listeners refuse to accept reasons, or speakers refuse to give them one.

3. Select specimens of writing from as many different classes of work as you have time for: prose fiction, legal argument, business memoranda, scholarly books, personal letters, political speeches, etc. Comment on the process of advancing claims and providing reasons. Try to evaluate them in terms of Plato's dialectic, Aristotle's rhetoric, Toulmin's argument, or Perelman's rhetoric.

2
Argumentation and Decision Making

Argumentation has been defined in the preceding chapter as the process of advancing claims and reasons and the granting or denying of adherence to them. The objective of argumentation, we have said, is adherence, and the ultimate test of an argument is whether or not it wins the adherence sought. The process of granting or denying adherence can be labeled decision making. This business in which people evaluate arguments and claims and decide whether or not to adopt them as their own and act accordingly is inherent to argumentation and will be discussed in this chapter.

A function of this chapter will be to identify the role of argumentation in the decisions people make. As already suggested in Chapter 1, there are many accounts of human behavior by many disciplines and points of view. We do not mean to suggest that argumentation is the sole or primary *cause* of decisions made. On the contrary, we do not even deal with the causes of human behavior. Instead, we focus on the act of justifying decisions in a social context. We suggest that people tend to generate reasons for their actions and claims, and it is important to them to come up with reasons that justify those acts in their own minds and in the minds of others who are relevant to the judgment. We further suggest that when adherence is denied to the reasons advanced, individuals will tend to search for new reasons, and may even change their decision because of the inability to justify it. Later we will argue that the very act of creating decisions will be

25

influenced by the presence or absence of strong justificatory arguments. That is to say, regardless of the source of the decision (whim, psyche, stars, social influence, etc.) the availability of strong arguments in justification of it may influence whether or not we announce it as our decision and act accordingly, or whether we keep it to ourselves and search for a better one.

Because the making of arguments and the judging of them are so intertwined, it is distorting to study argumentation without considering the decision making process as well. Unfortunately this has occurred. Often argumentation has been viewed solely from the perspective of advocacy. The perspective has been totally that of one who is advancing arguments with the intention of influencing the decisions of others. From this, we can see that the very generation of arguments involves our own decisions about whether or not they can serve as well or ill. One cannot be an advocate without also being a decision maker. Argumentation is not a unidirectional process. Therefore, in the chapters that follow our observations on analysis, characteristics of argument, evidence, values, etc., should be studied both from the viewpoint of the creater of arguments and the judge.

NONARGUMENTATIVE APPROACHES TO DECISION MAKING

There is a substantial body of scholarly literature usually labeled decision theory, which will not be discussed in this chapter because its relationship to argumentation is limited. In fact, these theories are characterized by a desire to discover some approach to the making of decisions that reduces or eliminates the involvement of human argumentation. The role we see argumentation playing in such systems is described in detail in Chapter 12 and will not be given here. For now, let us simply mention these other perspectives on decision making so that they can be distinguished from the concepts developed in this book.

Some writers on decision making have taken it upon themselves to devise an ideal approach to the business of making choices or judgments. Frankly, they have had serious reservations about the ability of human beings to choose wisely. Typically they have written from a basic premise that for every choice there is a right and wrong decision, or at least one that is more right than others. Next, they have been inclined to believe that human frailty is such that we too often choose the wrong course. Thus, they have sought a decision mechanism that reduces as much as possible the human involvement in the process of choice. The philosophers Charles Sanders Peirce and John Dewey were influential in applying the method of empir-

ical science to social situations such as decision making.[1] They believed
that if decisions could be based on carefully measured observation the
harmful effects of human desire could be minimized. This point of view is
still widely held today.

Economists were among the first to try to develop scientific models to
account for and predict human decision behavior. They began from a
foundation of a concept of a rational man who would always choose
according to certain rules, such as selecting that decision that would be
most advantageous to him.[2] From this premise, the economists devised
mathematical formulas for predicting how consumers would act in the
market place. If various possible purchases can be measured as to value or
utility and a quantification given each, then it was hoped that the correct
choice could be determined mathematically.

Other mathematicians, such as Von Neumann and Morgenstern, dealt
with what they called game theory.[3] Careful calculation of strategies
within a conflict situation has concerned some students of decision making,
and game theory has been used in various forms as a model for such study.
Psychologists have used game theory and several approaches to probability
as the basis for experimenting with decision making. Calculations of
probability, including considerable interest in gambling situations, have
formed the basis of psychological studies.[4]

It is important to recall the assumptions made in a good deal, if not
all the research mentioned above. First, it hypothesizes a correct or at
least "better" choice among alternatives. Second, it holds little confidence
in the unguided human to make that choice with any regularity. Third, the
objective is to come up with decision methods that will improve the batting average in selecting "correct" alternatives. And finally, the typical
approach is to build a decision system that reduces as much as possible
human interaction in decision making.

[1] See Charles S. Peirce, "The Fixation of Belief," in Justus Buckler, ed., *Philosophical Writings of Peirce* (New York: Dover Publications, Inc., 1955), pp. 7–18; and
John Dewey, *How We Think* (Boston: D.C. Heath, 1910).

[2] See Ward Edwards, "The Theory of Decision Making," in Ward Edwards and
Amos Tversky, eds., *Decision Making* (Baltimore: Penguin Books, Inc., 1967), pp.
14–15.

[3] See J. Von Neumann and O. Morgenstern, *Theory of Games and Economic Behavior* (Princeton: Princeton University Press, 1944).

[4] See Irwin D. F. Bross, *Design for Decision* (New York: The Free Press, 1953);
Wayne Lee, *Decision Theory and Human Behavior* (New York: John Wiley and Sons,
Inc., 1971); and D. Davidson, P. Suppes, and S. Siegel, "Decision-Making: An Ex-
perimental Approach," in Edwards and Tversky, pp. 170–207.

AN ARGUMENTATIVE APPROACH TO DECISION MAKING

From the argumentative point of view it is not necessary to take issue with these assumptions with the exception of the last one dealing with the reduction of the human element. Here, we suggest that no matter how much human involvement is reduced or controlled during early stages of decision making, it must inevitably be human beings who decide how to construct and program the nonargumentative systems, and it will be through human interaction that a decision is made concerning what if any action is to be taken on the basis of the nonargumentative recommendations. The function, then, of nonargumentative decision systems is to set up limits on the range of argumentative alternatives by providing compelling forms of evidence to be used in argumentative cases.

To illustrate, consider the situation of a large manufacturing company. Some years ago it was difficult to keep track of the huge inventory needed to operate a major industrial firm. With constant use of raw materials, constant manufacturing of new products and selling them, it was difficult at any point in time to say precisely what was the current inventory. When decisions were made concerning inventory, such as whether or not sufficient items were on hand to endure a strike or cope with a shortage of raw materials, a wide variety of alternatives could be argued cogently. Today, with complex computer based inventory systems, the range of arguments is significantly smaller—one could not argue that there was plenty of inventory if the detailed computer report said there was not. The computer or the man could have made an error in calculation, of course, but it is hard to argue with a computer. But the important point here is this: the computer can report the current inventory and project the availability of products and raw materials under a variety of possible future situations, but only the human decision makers in the company can select which course of action to take. The modern technology can provide impressive evidence to support alternatives, but it is the human who ultimately must annouce which alternative will be chosen and take the risk of acting accordingly. This means an argumentative decision process will likely occur under one of the systems described later in this chapter.

Consider another example. The space program is a monument to technology but all its systems have not eliminated human decision making. The nonargumentative processes can report what will likely occur on a trip into space and what can be accomplished by manned and unmanned vehicles. The systems can estimate the probable costs and probable results. But it is inevitably the human decision makers who must select the course of action to be taken and justify it to those who provide money and public support for the program, and to other specialists involved. Certainly the nonargumentative systems provide substantial evidence for that decision, and they set up distinct limits on the range of alternatives. The Director of N.A.S.A. could not, for example, argue effectively for support of a space effort that could not be justified by elaborate scientific data. But the scientific data alone do not make the decision.

Probability has been mentioned in relation to nonargumentative approaches, and that meaning of the term is the one most commonly recognized. But our discussion of an argumentative approach to decision making suggests another form of probability. Here we turn once again to Stephen Toulmin for guidance. He suggests that no matter how probability is defined in the nonargumentative sense, ultimately probability becomes a function of the force with which an individual chooses to advance, be associated with, or be held responsible for, a given claim. For example, you may be wondering whether or not to spend your life living in a large city. You can turn to a variety of nonargumentative systems for guidance. You can study actuarial tables to learn if those who live in cities die younger or live longer. You can turn to medical statistics to learn the probabilities of urban pollutants that damage your health. You can examine crime statistics to find your probabilities of being robbed or murdered in cities as compared with small towns. You can study business data on the likelihood of finding the kind of job you want in cities or towns. You may say now, "I probably will live in a small town." The word "probably" there describes the force with which you advance that claim, but it is a function of the degree to which you are willing to be held to it. What happens when you meet the person who could be your perfect mate, but this wonderful prospect will not live anywhere but a large city? "Well," you say, "maybe I'll live in the city for a while, but I'll probably move to a small town later." But even that "probability" may change when later you are offered a vice presidency of the company that will require staying in the city. The "probably" describes your commitment to the claim and the extent to which you authorize others to hold you to it. You might be shocked when the president of the firm comes to say, "we wanted to give you that vice presidency, but we have all heard you say you want to move to a small town, and you couldn't do that if you took the job." You might reply, "But I didn't mean it that strongly. "Why didn't you give me a chance to weigh the alternatives?"

A MODEL OF ARGUMENTATION IN DECISION MAKING

The role of argumentation in decision making should be clear by now. It may be helpful to examine the elements and their relationship schematically to improve the understanding. Clearly, problems occur within general argumentation and may lead directly to decision. Or when analysis progresses, as discussed in the next chapter, it may be judged useful to route the problem through one of the specialized fields of argument, such as those described in Chapters 11, 12, and 13. Consideration of the problem within a specialized field of argumentation may involve the employment of one of the nonargumentative systems just described. Regardless of the specialized field used, before decision occurs it will be necessary to turn once again to a system of argumentative decision making that may include conferences, debates, negotiations, or merely some form of interpersonal communication. During this final, argumentative, stage, the results of the specialized analysis will serve as evidence or other forms of support for arguments advanced, as described in Chapters 5, 6, and 7. The decision made will include some language that communicates the argumentative probability or "force" with which the claim is advanced and the extent to which others are authorized to hold the decision makers responsible. It will also be expressed within a framework of values where the claim will be related to the individuals involved.

Schematically, a model developed by Maynard Shelly and Glenn Bryan can be modified to show these relationships. They advance their model from a similar point of view. They believe, for example, that "the language for speaking about judgments in an empirical context is becoming more and more the language for speaking about judgments in a decision theoretic context."[5] But they go on to suggest that the solution of a decision problem is not independent of those for whom it is to be a solution, and no matter how refined the specialized languages of decision become, "[We may] never be able to encompass all of an unspecialized natural language within the language of science."[6] That is, they do not believe highly specialized technology will ever take the place of the human, argumentative elements in decision making. Notice in Figure 1 how these ideas are displayed in our modification of their model.

Problems or urges to decision begin in the unspecialized area of general argumentation with which we are all familiar. When the problem begins to take form, it could move directly to decision, or it could go to one of the specific argumentative decision systems for more careful consideration. However, the desire for more careful consideration may lead to one of the many specialized fields existing in a complex society to provide knowledge, information, or analysis to assist in making good decisions. These include all the academic disciplines and specialties with which any

[5] Maynard W. Shelly, II, and Glenn L. Bryan, *Human Judgments and Optimality* (New York: John Wiley and Sons, Inc., 1964), p. 22.
[6] Shelly and Bryan, p. 23.

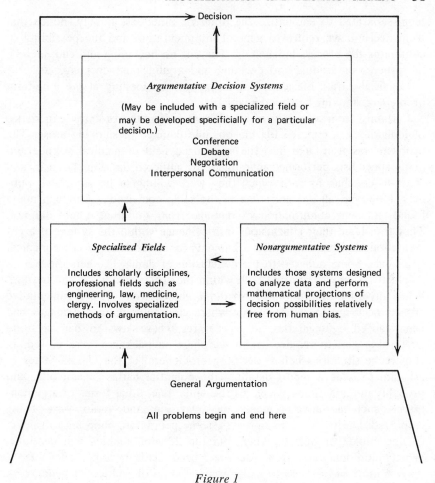

Figure 1

college student is familiar. They include specialists in the many professional areas of endeavor, such as engineers, lawyers, physicians, clergymen, etc. These fields may include the use of nonargumentative systems as discussed earlier, or they may employ them from elsewhere. The decision to seek assistance from a nonargumentative system will be made within the specialized field.

Before reaching decision, however, it will be necessary to employ an argumentative decision system such as conference, debate, negotiation, or some less formalized interpersonal communication. The specialized field may include provision for an argumentative decision system, or members of the field may need to turn to an outside system. On Figure 1, we show them separated to emphasize the different functions. Finally, notice that from decision we return to general argumentation and the possibility of continuing the process indefinitely. There is no beginning and end, merely, the process of arguing and deciding and arguing and deciding, etc.

Let us illustrate the ideas one more time by looking at the long-term problem of smoking and good health.

Certainly from a variety of sources, including the ordinary experience of individuals, a concern for the possible damage of smoking arose. The problem was translated into the specialized field of medical science and many specialists performed investigations, gathered data, analyzed it, and came to conclusions with which they were willing to be associated publicly. However, all did not come to the same conclusion. Although many found sufficient confirmation of damage from smoking, others did not. They translated their conclusions into evidence within the system of argumentation, and presented their arguments for acceptance by other medical specialists. Some adhered to the conclusion of damage, others did not.

The decision was pursued both within the specialized areas and beyond. When investigation continued, so did argumentation. The argumentative aspects occurred in courts of law where civil suits claimed damages had been caused by cigarettes, in legislatures where laws to ban cigarette advertising and to require health warnings on packages were passed, in conference situations before the Surgeon-General of the United States to ask him to issue a report detailing the potential harms of smoking, and probably in many more places. At the same time, other forms of argumentation, such as advertisements on television and radio were being employed. During the entire process, some people are choosing to smoke, or not smoke, or quit smoking, and the decision making will continue. When additional data from the specialized fields becomes available, it may be more or less easy to make arguments on the subject, depending on the character of the research findings. In terms of probabilities, each research report will be expressed in terms of statistical probability, that is, the extent to which the observations made could be explained by chance alone. And each individual that becomes involved in the question will express a decision in terms of a probability that means the degree to which he will be associated with it. For example, some will switch to milder cigarettes, some will switch to pipes and cigars, some will smoke less, some will smoke not at all, and some will make nuisances of themselves by trying to tell their friends about the hazards of smoking. Of course, others will begin smoking, or continue at the present pace, and some will become arrogant about the fact that they still smoke nonfiltered cigarettes just as always. These are expressions of probability within argumentation, just as the statistical comments are within some specialized languages.

ARGUMENTATIVE DECISION SYSTEMS

In Figure 1, the argumentative decision systems indicated three general systems within which argumentation is featured prominently, and where it is employed to facilitate decision making: Conference, Negotiation and Debate. These constitute situations where argumentation is a prominent aspect of decision making. They deal with situations in which two or more individuals share a single decision and those processes in which that is a central focus. The remainder of this chapter will be devoted to a discussion of the application of argumentation to those systems.

In Chapter 1, the variety of situations in which arguments are employed and where argumentation occurs was discussed. Sometimes, these informal argumentative situations lead to decisions, sometimes they do not. On the other hand, it was also pointed out that no clear-cut distinction between argumentation and all other forms of persuasion could be made and the broad scope of persuasive situations includes argumentation in various forms and to various extents. But over many hundreds of years' practice, argumentation has formed into some relatively distinct systems designed to render decisions in the way desired or in the form desired by certain individuals. Although these take on different names and various specific forms from place-to-place, it seems reasonable to group them under one of three headings: Conference, Debate and Negotiation. The general characteristics of each is discussed in the sections that follow.

Conference.   Perhaps you can conceive of situations where one person makes a decision involving no other human beings. It happens in some of our most private thoughts. Indeed, as we have noted, much of decision theory is aimed at explaining such decisions. But a great deal of our decision making behavior necessarily involves others. Even when we have made a decision on our own, it will most often need the cooperation or support of other people. Whenever this situation obtains, some kind of decision making arrangement must be worked out.

Even when two people are interacting in more than a casual or ritualistic way, they will probably fall into some mutually acceptable way of relating to each other. Of course, other disciplines have much to say about the social and psychological elements in such a situation. Our concern here is with the decision oriented arrangements that are made. In a great many of these encounters, it seems reasonable to presume that past associations have set roles and habits of communicating that are employed without conscious effort. Remember, in the main, the human being is a reason-making creature, and that whatever decision behavior occurs will include reasons advanced either explicitly or implicitly and their evaluation by another through choosing to grant or withhold adherence. Virtually no systematic research has gone toward the analysis of such casual encounters, and they are typically not defined as decision making situations, even though they possess most of the characteristics of them. Perhaps as the study of interpersonal communication expands, more scrutiny of this phenomenon will be undertaken.

Frequently, however, two or more people come together with more than a casual interest in reaching a decision in common, or in achieving common approval of a decision that one or more of them has made. Then more attention is paid to the ways to proceed, and social scientists would say that a group begins to emerge. Of three general approaches to decision making that make prominent use of argument, the one occurring most frequently is that in which a task-oriented group forms. This is typically called a conference, committee, a group discussion, or a "meeting." For convenience we shall refer to this as a conference.

There is considerable scholarly literature from specialists in social psychology and group communication relating to task-oriented small groups. From that body of data, we will select only those data that help describe the ways in which argument occurs in a decision situation. Of the many studies concerned with the processes within small groups, only a few have concentrated on communication variables and the place of argument in decision making. Thomas M. Scheidel and Laura Crowell examined the development of ideas as groups move toward a consensus. They sought to study the smallest ideational contribution and thereby discover the ways groups actually proceed. Such elements as assertions, questions, information, inference, restatement, clarification, substantiation, and extension were a part of a pattern of analysis. Their conclusion was that groups move toward consensus in a spiral pattern. That is, an idea is advanced and discussed within a group, and finally comes to be a point of agreement. Then, the group uses that point of agreement as the anchorage from which to try out another idea, and so on, gradually developing a decision. Fisher comments on this study by saying, "The spiral process of anchoring and reach-testing is not linear in that the group constantly retraces its path of idea development." Important to the study of argumentation is the fact that claims, once they achieve general adherence, become support for still other claims.[7]

Ernest G. Bormann theorized that decisions, as well as roles, emerge by a method of residues. This means that within a group there are tasks

[7] See Thomas M. Scheidel and Laura Crowell, "Idea Development in Small Groups," *Quarterly Journal of Speech*, 50 (April 1964), pp. 140–145; see also B. Aubrey Fisher, *Small Group Decision Making* (New York: McGraw-Hill Book Co., 1974), p. 138.

that must be performed and decisions that must be made. In both cases, the evidence suggests that groups do not proceed in a rational-deductive way of setting up problems, facts, criteria, and alternatives and then choosing among them. Rather, individuals within the group make efforts to perform a role, or suggest a decision, and they are either rewarded, punished, or ignored by the others. If the effort is disapproved, or responded to ambiguously, the chances are that the individual will soon abandon the effort and step aside for others to try, or at least it will cease as soon as clear disapproval is expressed. If the effort—either in playing a role or suggesting a decision—is rewarded, the individual will continue the effort and may eventually become strongly fixed in the role, or highly influential in determining the group's decision. Thus, the method of residues means the rejection or denial of adherence by group members, of unsatisfactory efforts one-by-one until a good one comes along, or until the group ends in failure. Bormann mentions two important factors in this procedure: (1) those actions—role efforts or decision suggestions—that group members perceive as beneficial are reinforced; (2) the behavior of each member tends to be channeled into those functions he does best.[8] This latter process, while not related to any of the established logical models for assessing argument and selecting among alternatives, suggests that groups tend to function in such a way as to obtain the best product from the talents and other resources available. Of course, this result is particularly dependent on the effectiveness of the communication achieved within the group. To the extent it is possible to measure the quality of group decisions (and that is highly limited) there are data to suggest that there is a direct relationship between the quality of communication and the quality of the group product.[9]

B. Aubrey Fisher examined more closely the way in which groups come to decisions and the place of argument within that process. His findings are similar to the spiral theory of Scheidel and Crowell in that he observed that decisions come in a series of spurts of decisional activity and not in the steady evolution envisioned by some. A claim may be advanced and supported and then reactions and criticisms would be suggested, but not continued until some final assessment of the claim. Instead, the whole thing would be put aside for a time while the group considered other ideas. Then, later, the same or another member would reiterate the claim with some modification in the argument, a reformulation as Fisher

[8] Ernest G. Bormann, *Discussion and Group Methods* (New York: Harper & Row, 1969), pp. 188–197.

[9] Dale Leathers, "Quality of Group Communication as a Determinant of Group Product," *Speech Monographs, 39* (August 1972), pp. 166–173.

calls it, that ultimately seemed more satisfying to the group, and it was adopted. This describes a process beyond that of discovery, or generating "good" ideas of the sort desired by the decision theorists mentioned earlier in this chapter. Rather, it describes a peculiarly communicative dimension, one of coming up with the argument that others can subscribe to; one on which a consensus can be justified by those involved. This is evidence of the distinction between some idealistic decision theory and the realities of argumentation.[10]

Fisher hypothesizes four phases as typical to groups in the process of decision making, and identifies different functions for argument from phase to phase. Following from the method of residues and the spurts of decision activity, he argues that groups do not consciously select decisions, they permit them to emerge. He says,

". . . members perceive several alternatives for accomplishing their tasks. As discussions· progress, these alternatives are debated, refined, accepted, changed, rejected, etc., until the final task product evolves from their deliberations—largely through a "method of residues" or elimination of available alternatives."[11]

In phase one, called the "orientation" phase, members of a group tend to search tentatively for ideas and ways to proceed. Because members are not yet sure of their relationship to others or the task, there is little effort to assert claims with great strength. Rather, ideas are thrown out to see what, if any reaction they will generate. The second phase, called the "conflict" phase, is characterized by the abandonment of the tentativeness and ambiguity of the first. Instead, members are now ready to advance claims with which they will clearly identify themselves, and they will react critically to other ideas. They will seek to win the adherence of others, and typically coalitions on opposite sides of predominant claims will form. Then, during the third or "emergence" phase, the conflict diminishes along with the clear-cut coalitions. The claims expressed as well as the positions adopted become, once again, ambiguous. "Ambiguity," says Fisher, "then functions in the third phase as a form of modified dissent. That is, the group members proceed to change their attitudes from disfavor to favor of the decision proposals through the mediation of ambiguity."[12] In this phase, the justificatory function of argument is clearly

[10] B. Aubrey Fisher, "The Process of Decision Modification in Small Group Discussion Groups," *The Journal of Communication*, 20 (March 1970), pp. 51–64.

[11] B. Aubrey Fisher, "Decision Emergence: Phases in Group Decision-Making," *Speech Monographs, 37* (March 1970), p. 54.

[12] Fisher, "Decision Emergence . . . ," p. 63.

indicated. By this is meant that the group is at a critical point between indecision and decision. The arguments advanced and the coalitions formed during the second phase have done much to establish a tendency for consensus, but there are those who have identified themselves with other alternatives, and they will find it difficult to abandon them without some justification. And here, justification means a socially acceptable reason for doing so. Although Fisher does not engage in speculation about this phase, it is interesting to do so.

One of the prominent theories of human behavior in decision making situations for many years has been that of cognitive dissonance, identified with Leon Festinger.[13] Briefly described, the theory of cognitive dissonance suggests that human beings seek to maintain a psychological balance, consistency, or harmony. Festinger suggests that when one is faced with a choice situation, the first steps taken will be a collection of information, an evaluation of that information in relation to personal values, and an effort to set up a preference ordering among the alternatives. The relatively unbiased search for information tends to continue, according to Festinger, until the decision maker feels enough is available to warrant a choice without much risk that future discoveries will upset it. The closer together in attractiveness the alternatives are, the more varied the information about them is, the more determined will be the search for information to justify a choice. When a feeling of confidence comes that a decision can be made, the decision maker will gradually begin to change in behavior, looking more for information that will support the decision that seems to be emerging.

During the period of decision emergence, as individuals waiver between doubt and choice, a number of pressures seem to be on them. Festinger speaks of a brief period of regret that commitment must be made. The alternatives may suddenly seem closer together in attractiveness. Jack W. Brehm suggests that because the choice of one alternative rules out the possibility of selecting another, a "psychological reactance" occurs in which the value of the alternative thus denied actually seems to increase.[14] When still more movement toward commitment is made, particularly when public announcement of a decision must be made, Festinger suggests that cognitive dissonance occurs, an upsetting of the psychological balance created by the need to choose among alternatives without clear and compelling support for any one of them. To remove

---

[13] For a full explication of this theory see Leon Festinger, *A Theory of Cognitive Dissonance* (Stanford: Stanford University Press, 1962).

[14] Jack W. Brehm, *A Theory of Psychological Reactance* (New York: Academic Press, 1966), pp. 3–7.

doubt that an erroneous decision might have been made, and to increase confidence and satisfaction in one's choice, there tends to be a search for "consonant" arguments and supporting materials, that is, there gradually comes a search for help in justifying the choice. Of this process Festinger says, "It may very well be that in such a situation [difficult dissonance reduction], without social support and without additional sources of information, dissonance reduction does not prove to be very stable. Outside support may be necessary to help the person continue to believe what he wants to believe."[15]

Roger N. Shepard thinks that the dissonance reduction that Festinger describes may function more prominently during the predecision period than others think to be so. Notice what he says:

"Now consider an individual who is faced with a decision problem of the typical kind in which no alternative is better than every other in all respects. The subjective ranking of the alternative with respect to over-all value will then depend on his current "state of mind," since that is what determines the relevant set of subjective weights. But, at the moment when a decision is required the fact that each alternative has both advantages and disadvantages poses an impediment to the attainment of the most immediate subgoal; namely, escape from the unpleasant state of conflict induced by the decision problem itself. I suggest, therefore that one device that people use to resolve the conflict and to consummate the decision is to "try out" various frames of mind until they find one whose associated subjective weights give one alternative the clearest advantage over its competitors. This principle of human decision making differs from that propounded by Festinger . . . in one important respect: Festinger argues that the change of attitudinal state occurs subsequent to the actual decision and serves to reconcile the individual with a choice already made; I am proposing that the change of state precedes the decision and serves to render the decision possible."[16]

Taken together, Festinger and Shepard urge that during both the pre- and immediately post-decision times, arguments are necessary to help one person or a group justify a decision that seems to be emerging. The psychologists suggest that even when an individual is deciding alone, these arguments must come from outside social sources to work best. It is reasonable to conclude that within small group decision making, during what Fisher calls the "emergence phase three," the function of arguments is to provide this kind of social support: to provide possible "states of mind"

[15] Leon Festinger et al., *Conflict, Decision, and Dissonance* (Stanford: Stanford University Press, 1964), p. 158.

[16] Robert N. Shepard, "On Subjectively Optimum Selection Among Multiattribute Alternatives," in Shelly and Bryan, p. 277.

about a decision to see if they fit well, and to reconcile group members with a decision during what is a difficult state of regret or reactance.

The arguments, therefore, change character from those advanced during the conflict phase. Whereas before, the goal of argument was to provide bases for assessing one alternative in relation to others, in the emergence phase the arguments provide a way of reconciling a previously divided group with a common decision. They tend to stress the commonality of values being served, and they provide a face-saving way for previous opponents to agree. Perhaps, as Thomas Schelling claims, arguments during this phase should provide "key" points on which individuals can hang a common decision. For example, the concept of compromise is a key point: "Let's recognize that we are all giving in a bit from what we would prefer."[17] Fisher suggests that ambiguity is the signal factor during this phase, and arguments probably concentrate on more abstract ideas and values so that more people of different points of view could agree to the same claim.

This form of justificatory argument continues into what Fisher defines as the fourth phase of "reinforcement." Arguments concentrate more and more on finding different bases on which the group can support the decision that has now clearly emerged. Perhaps you have become impatient with group members who continue to argue for a claim that everyone in the group has already accepted. Perhaps you have thought or said, "If we all agree, why do we keep arguing for the decision?" The answer comes from the studies that the group may have all accepted a single decision, but they still need time to reinforce it so that all can become comfortable with it. Argument is serving a vital function in this instance. It may make the difference between a decision that earns unanimous and vigorous support during implementation and one that the group has agreed to but without enthusiasm and with many doubts.

Barry E. Collins and Harold Guetzkow argue that unless a group gives full attention to the establishment of an interpersonal network where the kind of interaction that is described above can occur, the group cannot achieve the full benefits of group decision making. Groups must concentrate not only on the task oriented communications, but they must recognize the interpersonal needs within a group. The need for making use of the resources available among all members, and the individual need for socially acceptable bases for action must be recognized in the arguments generated if the "assembly effect," which indicates a product superior to what the individuals working alone could have achieved, is to result. The

---

[17] Thomas Schelling, *The Strategy of Conflict* (Cambridge: Harvard University Press, 1960).

members must concentrate, says Collins and Guetzkow, not only on generating their own arguments, but they must remember that they have a role to play as assessor of arguments. That is, they must listen to others' arguments and reward through positive evaluation those that seem to assist movement toward the fulfillment of group goals.[18] If, on the other hand, groups can develop this kind of effectiveness of operation, then theorists suggest that they can accomplish not only broad adherence to the choice made, but also produce decisions of higher quality than those made by individuals acting alone, no matter how the quality of decision is measured.[19]

Debate. For many writers on the subject, argumentation and debate are virtually synonymous.[20] For others, the two are synonymous in any situation in which at least two sides of a single claim are presented and defended.[21] Some writers stress the fact that in a debate, care is taken to see that advocates exist for all possible points of view, even to the extent of appointing individuals or groups to represent a position that does not spontaneously generate support.[22] Others feel a critical characteristic of debate is that the decision is made by a party outside the conflict to whom arguments are addressed and whose decision is to be binding on the participants.[23] Two other elements of debate are considered of prime importance: (1) debate typically serves as a system to render a desired process for decision making, such as representation of all interested parties; (2) debate is usually viewed as a way of achieving decisions of better quality than would result from other methods.[24]

[18] Barry E. Collins and Harold Guetzkow, *A Social Psychology of Group Processes for Decision-Making* (New York: John Wiley and Sons, Inc., 1964), pp. 69–87.

[19] For a summation of studies in this area, see Collins and Guetzkow, Chapter 2, and A. Paul Hare, *Handbook of Small Group Research* (New York: The Free Press of Glencoe, 1962), Chapter 12.

[20] Baker and Foster, two founders of modern studies of argumentation, do not even define debate, apparently in the belief that their definition of argumentation served this purpose. See George Pierce Baker, *The Principles of Argumentation* (Boston: Ginn & Co., 1898); and William Trufant Foster, *Argumentation and Debating* (Boston: Houghton Mifflin Co., 1908).

[21] Erwin P. Bettinghaus, "Structure and Argument," in Gerald R. Miller and Thomas R. Nilsen, eds., *Perspectives on Argumentation* (Chicago: Scott, Foresman and Co., 1966), p. 145. See also Austin J. Freeley, *Argumentation and Debate*, 2nd ed., (Belmont, California: Wadsworth Publishing Co., Inc., 1966), p. 2.

[22] James H. McBurney and Glen E. Mills, *Argumentation and Debate* (New York: The Macmillan Company, 1964), p. 4.

[23] Douglas Ehninger and Wayne Brockriede, *Decision by Debate* (New York: Dodd, Mead & Co., 1963), p. 10; Arthur N. Kruger, *Modern Debate* (New York: McGraw-Hill Book Co., Inc., 1960), p. 416.

[24] Ehninger and Brockriede, pp. 3–11. Thomas R. Nilsen, "Ethics and Argument," in Miller and Nilsen, p. 195.

Obviously, from the preceding discussion of conference, many of the characteristics of debate are found in the conference situation. If Fisher's findings are generalizable, the second, conflict phase in group decision making is essentially a debate according to many commonly held definitions.

For our purposes, the concept of debate will be used to designate a highly structured decision making system in which (1) a common commitment to the search for high quality decisions exists; (2) the advocates are consciously selected to insure a broad representation of available arguments and interests in relation to the decisions to be made; (3) a strong commitment to abide by the decision made exists; and (4) decision, as opposed to indecision, is highly valued. Obviously debate is virtually pure argumentation and little further need be said about the role argumentation plays in this decision system.

From these requirements it can be inferred that debate as conceived here is considerably less common than decision through conference. Why, then, do people resort to debate? Often, debate is characterized as a process that comes into play when informal communication or conference fail to generate a decision. For example, suppose your neighbor comes to complain that rainwater drains off your yard and into his basement. You and he talk it over, and you agree to do some work on your gutters. A satisfactory decision seems to have been reached. However, after the modifications, rain continues to drain into his basement, and he comes back to ask for further changes. You suggest a rather formal conference including members of both families and some experts. The conclusion of the conference is that the only way to stop rain from entering the basement is to spend about $1000 to build a retaining wall. This is agreed on by all concerned. Then, however, the question of who should pay the $1000 comes up. Your neighbor says you should pay, and you believe he should pay; no consensus is achieved. Well, you could flip a coin, or, to keep peace in the neighborhood, you could say, "I really don't think it's my responsibility, but what's a $1000 when compared to the cost of losing good friends. I'll build the wall." Or, you could say, "The water is going into your basement, not mine. If you want the wall, build it. I refuse to help in any way."

Any one of these devices could lead to decision. The last statement could lead to negotiation, as will be seen in the next section. But the chances are fairly good that few people will opt for a flip of the coin— the question is too important to leave to chance. Besides, you feel your position is correct, and you want it to be vindicated. Unless you have reached a state in life where that amount of money is meaningless to you,

you will probably resist paying if you do not think you should. Moreover, one might be expected to say, "It's not the money, it's the principle."

So what is to be done? The decision is too important to be left to chance. Both parties feel that they are correct and should be vindicated. Therefore a decision must be reached to prevent further damage to the basement; but neither side will give in. You have already guessed that lawyers will probably be called in, and that the decision will be put to the courts in the form of a civil suit. That is debate.

Consider another situation. Your metropolitan area has grown by 75 percent in the last five years and the state legislature must decide how much money to spend in construction of highways and mass transportation facilities to accomodate the growth. But the legislature was apportioned many years ago and is still controlled by representatives from rural districts. They do not feel justified in using state funds to do the jobs requested. Taken abstractly, it is difficult to say which policy for expenditure of state funds is "true" or "correct" or even "best." The needs of other elements in the state are also critical. The conclusion is typically a reflection of the thorough examination of the combined self-interests of those involved. The correction in this case is not to change the process, but to change the representation. Through reapportionment, each citizen is represented by the same amount of legislative power as every other. Then, no matter what the decision, all can say they had their interest properly considered.

It has become popular lately to say that the debates that go on in legislatures, city and county commissions, and in the Senate and House of Representatives of the United States are meaningless. The "real" decisions, it is said, are made in committee and party conferences and through the work of lobby groups. Here again a distinction between the factors that lead to decisions and the arguments with which they are justified must be made. Of course, the conference work is crucial to legislative decision making but so is legislative debate. It is here that representatives state arguments that go on the record and for which their constituents will evaluate them. It is conceivable that a legislator may want to vote for a bill because of his own value system, but refuse to do so because he could not generate arguments to which his constituents would subscribe. Bills calling for pay increases often are of this kind, as are proposals to raise taxes, and many others. The process of advancing arguments on the floor of a legislature is an important aspect of the decision making process in representative situations, even when every person present has already made a decision.

The procedures of argumentation in a debate setting require that, to achieve the desired decision, the best of the available arguments must be presented for consideration. To achieve this, advocates are consciously selected; in law, professional adversaries are assigned to defend the various aspects of a case; in legislation, the advocates are selected to achieve an equal representation of the parties involved in the policy making. In any case, the roles tend to be formally assigned, rather than allowed to emerge as in the conference. Furthermore, the clear advocacy of positions is much more encouraged, if not required in debate. Because those involved are typically professionals, there is less overt attention to arguments designed to maintain interpersonal relationships than is true in conference. Often, as will be seen in later chapters, specific requirements on the form of arguments to be presented exist. Finally, the decision in debate tends to be relatively binding within a context of appeals, or electing new representatives and voting again.

In what situations does debate occur? Legal and legislative debate have already been mentioned. But there are many other contexts for debate as well. When, for example, the administrative head of a unit in any organization assigns his subordinates to prepare presentations on various alternatives pursuant to a policy decision, a form of debate occurs. It must be apparent that this is a common practice in business decision making when individuals are invited to make their presentations to the appropriate board. This seems to be common in the decision making in the White House—the President will make the decision alone, but before that, aides are assigned to prepare and defend personally memoranda on various alternatives.[25] In the appeal process from personal arguments, deadlocked conferences, negotiation situations, and so forth, it is common to call in a respected outsider to act as a mediator. Each side will present its case, and the mediator's decision will either be accepted as binding, or it will become highly influential in reaching a decision by the former means. When a contract is to be let, it is common to permit those interested in doing the work to present their case along with their estimate of the costs. Commonly, the lowest cost is the best argument that can be presented, but it is not the only one. If a higher cost can be justified on the grounds of such factors as superior workmanship, quality of materials, or reliability of the firm, a higher bid might be accepted. This is a form of debate.

Some writers would make a distinction between a situation where an outside party decides the outcome of the debate and one in which the debaters themselves are the decision makers.[26] In this view, a court of law is debate but a legislature is not. Such a distinction would be one way to distinguish between debate and conference. However, we suggest that

[25] Theodore Sorenson, *Decision Making in the White House.*
[26] Ehninger and Brockriede, p. 10.

the formal structure of the situation, the assignment of advocates, the commitment to a certain quality of decision, as well as the commitment to decision over indecision make enough of a distinction. In addition, conference usually involves a small group, less than 20, and thereby can function without the structuring of debate.

Negotiation.   Little will be said about the literature of negotiation because most of it deals with its game rather than its argumentative aspects. Some would even suggest that argument has little to do with the outcome of a negotiation. We disagree, and this section will briefly outline where argumentation plays a part in negotiation.

In negotiation, the parties are committed to reaching a decision, but will prefer no decision to one that grants them less then what they consider to be minimally acceptable. If a buyer and seller negotiate, they would like to come to agreement, but the seller will probably not take a loss, and the buyer probably has an upper limit that will be paid. Negotiation can occur, however, if the ranges of acceptable settlement of the parties overlap.

What form does argument take in negotiation? First, we have regularly said that human beings are reason-makers, and even when the outcome of negotiation is largely to be determined on the basis of power, coercion, or trickery, they will typically engage in argumentation to justify what they are doing. Second, the prime goal of negotiators is to discover their opponent's maximum (or minimum) settlement without revealing their own. Thus, the credibility of arguments becomes critical. For example, in labor-management negotiations, business will often prepare elaborate cases to argue that higher salaries will be destructive of the business. If labor believes this, they would prefer to settle for less money than lose their jobs altogether. Labor leaders in turn advance arguments designed to show that they could not accept a lower settlement and still maintain their position with the union. If management accepts that argument, they may conclude that negotiations will break down before their offer is accepted.

Argument serves three other important roles in negotiation. First, arguments are advanced to modify the opponent's concept of acceptable settlement. For example, when attorneys are negotiating before facing a trial, each will make arguments to show the strength of his own case and the weakness of the opponent's. When one accepts the argument that he will lose the case if it goes to trial, his willingness to settle will change.

Second, argument is used with outside parties to demonstrate the undesirability of the opponent's position and thereby bring pressure toward settlement on him. For example, an argument to the prosecutor that one's opponent is engaging in conspiracy to restrain trade may bring legal pressure for a lower price. Similarly, labor and management regularly take space in newspapers to argue to the public that the other side is unreasonable and ought to be censured. If the public subscribes to the arguments on one side, they will bring pressure toward settlement.

Finally, negotiation may be used as an argument itself. By engaging in negotiation one may seek to communicate to constituents the reasonableness of a position. Judges often insist that attorneys get together and search for settlement. Refusal to do so may be interpreted negatively by the judge. If one can claim to have worked as hard as possible for settlement, it may become an argument for a favorable decision from the judge. This can apply to most other situations such as subordinates presenting policy proposals to a superior or one nation meeting with another to end a war. There may be little interest in settlement by negotiation, but it is used as an argument for decision by debate.

CONCLUSION

Two approaches to the study of decision making have been discussed: those dealing with individuals making decisions of the highest possible quality, and those in which argumentation is heavily involved and which seek human adherence to suggested alternatives. A model was described in which all decisions, no matter how "objective," must ultimately turn to systems of persuasion, including argumentation, to become effective.

Within the individual decision theories, attention was given to the efforts to remove human judgment from the decision process, and replace it with the method of science. Economic, mathematical, and psychological efforts along this line were briefly described. Considerable attention was given to the varying meanings of "probability." In a classical sense it means a ratio of all alternatives possible and the good ones available. To mathematicians, it means an objective, quantitative expression of the expected frequencies with which phenomena occur. Psychologists speak of personal or subjective probability that adds to the objective concept a human dimension derived from an ideal conception of human judgment, or generalized from experimental observations of real subjects.

Three decision systems that rely on argumentation were discussed: conference, debate, and negotiation. Conferences were suggested as the most common form of argumentative decision making. They proceed through a process in which arguments are advanced, evaluated, put aside, reinforced, rejected, and ultimately emerge rather than being selected. Argument serves different functions at different stages or phases of the conference. Debate is a system in which persons search for the best possible decision by the Aristotelian prescription of bringing to bear on the question all possible means of persuasion. Participants are carefully selected and assigned roles, a willingness to abide by the decision is expressed, and a commitment to decision or indecision is made. Negotiation is a conflict system in which those with overlapping zones of acceptable settlement seek to achieve the most favorable outcome. Argument serves important but limited functions. It is primarily the device by which negotiating parties communicate their limitations on settlement and bring pressure on their opponent to settle at a less favorable level.

PROJECTS

1. In a group of no more than five to seven people, hold a conference on a subject important to all, such as, "What should be the minimum requirements to achieve credit for this class?" Tape record your conference, and then as a group listen to yourselves and evaluate the argumentation. Did you go through the four phases? Did the nature of argument change from time to time? How was a decision finally made?

2. Interview at least five people who have studied in such different fields as psychology, physics, mathematics, philosophy, and literature, asking each one to define, "probability," and illustrate its use. Summarize their points of view in a paper in which you also give your own conception.

3. Engage in a negotiation with someone on the question of the rain going into the basement and building a retaining wall. Do so in the presence of others in the class, and be sure to tape-record your deliberations. Then analyze the extent to which argument played a role in the final outcome in relation to other strategies.

4. Observe a debate either among students on the debate team, in a legislature, or in a court. Again, analyze the form of arguments employed in relation to the decision to be made.

3
Analysis in Argumentation

Argumentation occurs because of the human necessity for giving reasons and gaining the adherence of others to these reasons. Only through argumentation can consensus, majority vote, or shared agreement be said to exist, for only then does each person know on what basis a decision is made. Unfortunately, however, a problem looking for solution does not rise up in the finished form of legislation, scholar's premise or debate proposition. Problems are problems because people recognize them as such and communicate them to others. For years people could throw paper and cans along the roadside with little attention being paid to it; suddenly, it seemed, litter was a problem. Small pressure groups like the Sierra Club or the Audubon Society could lobby with little effect for conservation and then suddenly, these were powerful organizations that lobbied for millions of people. How does such a phenomenon come about? It comes about because increasing numbers of people become convinced that there is a problem. They advance a claim and arguments to support it; others choose to offer reasons against, and the process we have discussed earlier is begun. But the "problem" was always there and after the argument ends, some part of the general problem will remain. We may, as a nation, agree completely with the most radical conservationists and grant them their every wish, but then we will have the problem of adapting to less power, less roads, less private ownership. Problems always exist and, therefore, potential argumentation never ends, but people do stop arguing.

It is people, then, who determine when an argument begins, when it ends and what course it will take. The individual arguer may join in an argument at any point but that point will always be its real beginning for him. For instance, suppose you have just heard about the problem of preserving the California Condor. You become quite interested in it and you speak to others about the necessity of preserving this endangered species of bird. You must explain the problem as best you can on the basis of what *you* know, as limited as that might be. If you knew more, your arguments might be different. You might even decide to "let the buzzards die." But you cannot argue more than you know so you make do with what you have. You could go on this way, learning more from the corrections of others (perhaps embarassingly) until you had developed arguments that were difficult for others to answer and to which people gave their adherence.

This process could be speeded up, however, if you analyzed the situation systematically before you began to make arguments. Analysis is not just a matter of acquiring knowledge; it is a process whereby all the constituents of the argumentation situation are related, one to the other, in such a way that what needs to be argued and what it will take to make those arguments convincing is known so that the arguer may more effectively develop his arguments, evidence, values, credibility and language. It is not, therefore, as in the hypothetical example used above, that you gain more knowledge about the condor but that you gain more knowledge also about your receivers and their ideas so that you select the claim and support that will bring their adherence to your decision making purpose.

ARGUMENTATIVE TERMS

In order to talk about systematic analysis in argumentation, there are some terms that need to be understood. For the moment we need to understand the terms, argument, issue and claim.

ARGUMENT

We have already discussed argument. Ideally, an argument is a statement with the support for it. For instance, cigarettes are a threat to the nation's health. The Surgeon General's report shows that they cause lung cancer and heart disease. In actuality, any statement is an argument because it is capable of support and may actually be supported in the receiver's mind. Thus, the statement above, without support, "cigarettes are a threat to the nation's health," is an argument.

ISSUE

An issue is the result of the clash of two arguments. If one person argues that it should be illegal to use marijuana because it is a dangerous drug and another argues that it is not a dangerous drug, we have an issue: Is marijuana a dangerous drug? In actual argumentation an issue may be stated any number of ways. For the purposes of analysis, however, it is best to use the question form to help keep clear the distinction between argument and issue.

CLAIM

A claim (frequently called a proposition) is a single statement that a person is prepared to support. It may be the same as a single argument. "Cigarettes are a threat to the nation's health" is a claim. A claim, however, may also be larger than a single argument. It may require several arguments to prove a claim. For our purposes we shall note that there are three kinds of claims: fact, value and policy.[1] Later in this chapter we will see how they interrelate and are used to support one another. For now let us see what they are.

A *factual claim* is a statement that seems to affirm a "factual" truth— one, which a receiver will adhere to because he believes it can be confirmed by objective data.

There are 1600 diplomats representing 132 missions at the United Nations in New York.

---

[1] There has been among students of argumentation, some controversy over how many types of claims (propositions) there are and what their natures are. Gary Cronkhite, "Propositions of Past and Future Fact and Value: A Proposed Classification," *Journal of the American Forensic Association, 3* (January 1966), pp. 11–17; Gerald R. Miller, "Evidence and Argument," in *Perspectives on Argumentation*, eds., Gerald R. Miller and Thomas R. Nilsen, (Chicago: Scott, Foresman, 1966), pp. 30–37; Gerald R. Miller, "Questions of Fact and Value: Another Look," *Southern Speech Journal, 28* (Winter 1962), pp. 116–122; Walter F. Terris, "The Classification of the Argumentation Proposition," *Quarterly Journal of Speech, 49* (October 1963), pp. 266–73. The following discussion draws most significantly from Cronkhite's analysis.

Next year there will be increased benefits for social security recipients.

There is a sharp increase in one parent families.

There will be more suburban theater groups started in the next few years.

Coal is needed in vast quantities to make steel.

These are all factual claims. Each makes a claim that the receiver might verify to his satisfaction by reference to some kind of data. The second and fourth are worthy of special note as they deal with a claim to future facts and might be defined as separate kinds of claims[2] from those that deal with past and present fact because they cannot be checked until after a decision on adherence takes place. Nonetheless, they are treated the same way and if we know that Congress has changed the Social Security law to provide greater benefits next year, for instance, we may give as much or more adherence to the future claim in the second proposition than we would to a newspaper story about the number of diplomats at the New York U.N. headquarters.

A *value claim* is one that makes a judgment about a person, place, thing or idea.

"It [Viceroy] is what smoking's all about."

"Natural gas burns clean, with no smoke and virtually no emissions."

"Gambling is a matter of public morality."

All of these statements make claims about the value of something, a value judgment that cannot be checked against data. They are all value claims.

A *policy claim* is one in which a policy is proposed. Its key word is the word "should" either stated or implied.

"Capital punishment should be the penalty in skyjack cases."

"The American dollar should be devalued."

Some value claims that deal with the future values are policy claims.[3] Even though the word "should" is not included, it is implied. A Bethlehem Steel ad closes with this argument:

"Surface-mined land can be reclaimed responsibly under present state reclamation laws. However, Federal legislation is now being considered that could unreasonably restrict or even ban surface mining of coal. . . .

---

[2] Cronkhite, p. 15.

[3] Cronkhite calls all propositions of policy "propositions of future value," p. 14–15.

"We favor legislation that will make it possible to meet the nation's energy needs and reasonable environmental goals at the same time. But why cut coal production by unreasonable restrictions on surface mining at a time when all other energy sources—except coal—are in critical supply?"[4]

Although there are several value claims here and the final one is stated as a question, that final one means the Federal legislation now being considered to restrict surface mining of coal *should not* be enacted and is, therefore, a policy claim.

THE PURPOSE OF ANALYSIS IN ARGUMENTATION

Argumentation can be a lengthy and involved process with hundreds of arguments and issues developing around a single claim of fact, value or policy. Consider, for instance:

"There is a God."

"Democracy is a superior form of government."

"Individual freedoms should be guaranteed to all persons."

On such claims one might say that there is potentially an infinite number of related arguments because by one chain of reasoning or another all potential arguments can be related. Certainly, that is the assumption of the theologian as he looks at the claim: "There is a God." One would not be stretching things too far to say any argument (if we let the chain run long enough) can be related to any other claim.

If this (or even the modified view with which we began the last paragraph) is true, then the person engaged in decision making through argumentation must reduce the number of arguments to a workable basis in the time limit imposed by the situation. For this reason he must analyze the situation including the audience, the problem, the potential means of resolution, the available arguments and supports to discover first the working claims, arguments and issues, and second, what it will take to resolve issues for his receivers and bring their adherence to his claim.

There are two somewhat distinctive parts to this analysis. One deals with finding claims when the decision to be made is only a vague realization that some problem requires resolution, what Charles S. Peirce called a "feeling of doubt." The second has to do with finding the crucial issues in a situation after the claim has been identified. We will see as we go

----

[4] *U.S. News and World Report*, 75 (July 16, 1973), p. 75.

along that these two overlap and interact, that a single analysis may move back and forth from one to the other but we will treat them separately because they are rather different approaches.

One caution is necessary here. Just as argumentation differs with each specialized type of audience addressed (legal, theological, scientific, etc.) so analysis is different in each of the specialized studies. Our concern here is with the kind of analysis done for purposes of general argumentation where persons are addressed and claims are argued as a part of the general public concern—not the specialized inquiry.

FINDING CLAIMS FROM A FEELING OF DOUBT

In Chapter 1 and 2, particularly Chapter 2, we have discussed an overall theory for the way in which argumentation functions in decision making. Much of what has already been said is applicable here because finding claims is obviously a first step in decision making. We hope now to supplement what you have learned earlier in Chapter 2 and show how certain factors act and interact in the selection of claims.

It is worth repeating that claims in general argumentation are not usually assigned as they sometimes are in legislative debate, classroom, courtroom and intercollegiate debate. An important part of developing an argumentative case can be the selection of the claim. We will discuss the phrasing of claims as an argumentative strategy in Chapter 10 on language. But note the following example of how the selection of the claim, not just its wording, can affect the argumentation. In a western city there was an ordinance permitting builders who had twenty acres or more of land to build condominiums without a public hearing. A group of citizens argued for a change so that every development would require a public hearing. When asked, they said, "We are not opposed to condominiums, we just believe that the people's views should be heard." Thus, one may oppose condominium building but as a means of opposition, argue a quite different claim.

F.S.C. Northrop, in his book, *The Logic of the Sciences and the Humanities*, gives four examples to illustrate how four different authorities would answer a question of what "procedure is to be followed at the very beginning of inquiry."

Francis Bacon: "One must proceed purely inductively, putting all preconceived ideas, or Idols, aside."

Rene Descartes: "One's procedure is purely rationalistic. One intellectually doubts everything which can possibly be doubted and then, from the indubitable minimum, which remains, one *deduces* the remainder of one's knowledge."

Morris Cohen: "Starting with the problem which initiates inquiry, coupled with skepticism with respect to traditional beliefs, one pursues hypotheses, testing them by the method of trial and error."

John Dewey: "Since inquiry begins with a problematic situation, one must first observe the determinate facts, together with the indeterminate uncertainties of the situation, to suggest hypotheses respecting the possible resolution of its problematic character. These hypotheses in turn to be pursued to their deductive consequences and thereby checked operationally."[5]

These four theories are addressed to more philosophical or scientific kinds of problem solving than we are centering on here in general argumentation. However, many writers in argumentation, including one of the authors of this book, have agreed with Northrop that Dewey's method is the best method of analysis.[6]

If analysis is not simply going to find the same claims everyone else has found, the arguer should maintain a healthy skepticism as all of these theorists advocate. Furthermore, the analyst does not want to waste time digging up useless facts and nonapplicable claims. At first glance, therefore, if all the relevant material is to be examined, John Dewey's method would seem the most reasonable answer. Unfortunately, argumentation does not function in so ideal a world as Dewey's methodology would imply. Argumentation and the decision making associated with it spring up in the midst of a problem area. There is no beginning place for it. Women in the sixties who began to become aware of discrimination because of sex may have thought that they were confronting a new problem, or at least an old problem with new awareness, but it was not a new problem and only their own awareness was "new." Women's Liberation is an old phenomenon in America. Soon, whether they stumbled across them accidentally or read about them, they came up with claims that other women had advanced before. Or, by analogy, they borrowed claims from the Civil Rights Movement in which some of them had worked. Thus, in general argumentation we do not have the luxury of John Dewey's methods. We have a phenomenon, something more like the Morris Cohen view as explained by Northrop. We present claims and we test them, change them, discard them, find new ones.

---

[5] F.S.C. Northrop, *Logic of the Sciences and the Humanities*, (New York, The Macmillan Co., 1947), pp. 2–16.

[6] Charles S. Mudd and Malcolm O. Sillars, *Speech: Content and Communication*, (Scranton: Chandler Publishing Co., 1969), pp. 350–51; Northrop, p. 17.

The potential for chaos in such a system is great, but it does not need to occur because every problem has a storehouse of knowledge and standards by which selection takes place. There is a simple control on the mechanism: the human mind, unable to tolerate chaos, moves inevitably to decrease the number of options and focus on something from which it can reason and test.[7] Although an infinite number of claims might emerge on a single problem, they will not. Only a limited number will and soon one will be the focus, however temporarily. This characteristic of human thought is a wonderful thing and it shortens our work in finding solutions enormously, but it has its dangers. The mind may be attracted to easy claims that seem to solve problems but which have grave consequences. That is why analysis should be careful and thorough. That is why a systematic approach to decision making through argumentation can be beneficial to society.

There are a number of factors that influence the closure process. They are the same factors that influence argument at each stage but they are especially applicable here.[8]

Claims are discovered by examining the problem in the light of the interaction of the problem with facts, truths, presumptions, values and hierarchies. Need we repeat again that in all of these cases we mean as they are perceived by receivers? Important to our understanding is that Perelman and Olbrechts-Tyteca classify all of these as "types of objects of agreement." That is, types of objects on which people can agree.

A *fact* is a fact "only if we can postulate uncontroversial, universal agreement with respect to it," says Perelman. But "no statement can be assured of definitively enjoying this status, because the argument can always be called into question later, and one of the parties to the debate may refuse to qualify his opponent's affirmation as a fact."[9] But, within a reasonable period of time, there are a whole host of statements that every party to an argumentation will accept as a fact and permit reasoning from. When we search for a claim, which will resolve a problem, there are innumerable ones that are ruled out because they do not conform with the "facts" as understood by receivers. If there is corruption in the

---

[7] Jerome S. Bruner, *The Relevance of Education* (New York: W. W. Norton and Co., 1971), p. 4.

[8] This section draws heavily on the insights of Chaim Perelman and L. Olbrechts-Tyteca in what they see as the "starting point of argument." The section of their book which we shall use deals with what the arguer does in developing an argument. Since we are concerned with finding claims, we shall extrapolate their views for our uses here. Chaim Perelman and L. Olbrechts-Tyteca, *The New Rhetoric*, (Notre Dame, Indiana: University of Notre Dame Press, 1969), pp. 65–83.

[9] Perelman and Olbrechts-Tyteca, p. 67.

Federal government at the highest level, it cannot be solved by firing the mayor of Seattle, Washington. The Federal Government is in Washington, D.C. It may not be ten years from now, but it is now. Or so we all believe.

And as long as a statement stands as a fact, "there is no need to increase the intensity of the adherence . . . and it requires no justification."[10]

A *truth* is the same as a "fact" in its power to command adherence without further justification but while a "fact" is an "object of precise, limited agreement," a truth is a "more complex system." Scientific theories are examples of truths.[11] They hold that status only so long as they are agreed to by people but while they do, they stand in the same position as facts. Again, like facts, they limit, not as severely as do facts, but nonetheless they do limit significantly the range of claims available in any given problem solving situation.

A *presumption* is a rule that sets down what is "normal and likely," but unlike facts and truths, audiences "expect their adherence to be reinforced at a given moment by other elements."[12] There are many presumptions by which we organize our argument and control its activity. The most obvious presumption is the legal presumption of innocence in a court of law. We know such a presumption to be strong but it also can be ignored and verdicts have been overturned because juries lost sight of this presumption. Richard Whately explained a century and a half ago that "a 'Presumption' in favor of any supposition, means, not (as has been sometimes erroneously imagined) a preponderance of probability in its favor, but such a *pre-occupation* of the ground, which implies that it must stand good till some sufficient reason is adduced against it."[13]

Whately found a whole series of presumptions. Those in favor of existing institutions, of innocence, and against paradox seem like the ones most applicable today.[14] Most of the others have to do with Christianity (Whately was a Theologian) and are not very applicable to general argumentation. Only James McBath, among current textbook writers, defines presumption in a clearly audience oriented manner. He says, "If a

[10] Perelman and Olbrechts-Tyteca, p. 67.

[11] Perelman and Olbrechts-Tyteca, pp. 68–69.

[12] Perelman and Olbrechts-Tyteca, pp. 70–71.

[13] Richard Whately, *Elements of Rhetoric*, Douglas Ehninger, ed., (Carbondale, Illinois: Southern Illinois University Press, 1963), p. 112.

[14] There is some controversy in the field of argumentation over the usefulness of presumption particularly in the way the presumption in favor of existing institutions has been applied in intercollegiate debate. See: Gary Cronkhite, "The Locus of Presumption," *Central States Speech Journal*, 17 (November 1966), pp. 270–76; Patrick O. Marsh, "Is Debate Merely a Game for Conservative Players?" *Speaker and Gavel*, 1 (January 1964), pp. 46–53; Malcolm O. Sillars, "Audiences, Social Values and the Analysis of Argument," *Speech Teacher*, 22 (November 1973), pp. 291–303.

decision is not disconsonant with prevailing social standards, it stands until modified by the group."[15] There are, of course, many contemporary presumptions in general argumentation. There is a presumption against miracles, a presumption for science and a presumption against the veracity of alcoholics, to name but a few.

Even though presumptions, unlike facts and truths, must be supported, they serve as a basis for the analysis of problems and help narrow the available claims.

Values will be discussed in greater detail in Chapter 6. For now let us simply remark that there are value systems at work in general argumentation that provide a basis for the selection of claims. Values are not universally acceptable. They tend to have their greatest credence in specific audiences. That is, certain values are held virtually as truths in specialized audiences. However, while not universal these values are applicable to a large extent in general argumentation. Such values as progress, honesty, democracy and liberty are rather generally accepted as positive values and claims, which were shown to be in conflict with these, would usually not be acceptable.

Hierarchies also function in argumentation. That is, people tend to place some things over others "such as the superiority of men over animals, gods over men."[16] For our purposes we shall maintain that the most important hierarchies are hierarchies of values because in general argumentation the value system under which the group is functioning is the most important fact in argumentative decision making. But, of course, there are also hierarchies of facts, truths, and presumptions.

Some relatively identifiable value systems function in general argumentation within our society.[17] We also know that audiences differ with time and circumstance. Thus, even with a limited number of available value systems, different hierarchies will emerge in different situations. Let us examine the role in a specific situation of one of our most powerful values, "progress." Not too many years ago any proposed new factory was good. It was a part of the progress of an area producing new taxes, new jobs and a better way of life. Today, the mere hint of a new factory will generate powerful opposition. That opposition will have a limited number of points of view. For environmental reasons ("a better way of life"), the factory should not be built. Factories defile "nature," ruining the future for our children and are, therefore, not really "progressive." And so on. The important point to note here is that traditional values represented by such

[15] James H. McBath, *Argumentation and Debate*, 2nd ed., (New York: Holt, Rinehart and Winston, 1963), p. 8.

[16] Perelman and Olbrechts-Tyteca, p. 80.

[17] See Chapter 6, pp. 233–249.

words as, "progress," "better way of life," "nature," and "children" are operative. True, one might argue against "progress" but most often the most effective arguer will deny the value term "progress" to the factory.

It is not in different values, then, but usually in a different hierarchy of values that real argumentation takes place.

What answers does this society permit to claims of fact and value? It may be accepted as fact that it is cheaper to kill people than to keep them on welfare. But, what does our society say about what cheapness or expensiveness are? And, what will it say about other values that may be violated in the interest of a narrow view of expense? We could come rather close to answering some rather vital value questions unanimously on that issue. But our hierarchy of values thus established, of life over financial cost, would shift dramatically were we to discuss the same proposal but with a reference to unwanted cats at the animal shelter. And we know that there can be a quite different hierarchy of values when we deal with the killing of human beings of another country in wartime, though it is easier if we can dehumanize them in our own minds.[18]

Even though a carefully analytical system such as John Dewey's might yield a more thorough and useful solution to problems, such a system is not available in argumentation. In argumentation, people immediately begin to suggest claims. These claims come about because of the interaction of facts, truths, presumptions and values, and the integration of them in hierarchies. Subsequently, these same factors and the arguments generated by opponents help to test and shape the claims.

THE ANALYSIS OF A POLICY CLAIM

A policy claim is analyzed by subdividing it into the factual and value claims that help to establish it. This is done by searching out the claims contained in the crucial issues. These issues are found by looking to the clash of arguments as in a debate. Although many argumentation situations do not involve debate, each is potentially a debate. Anyone who wishes to advance arguments must be prepared to answer objections by giving reasons. If an arguer is never asked to give reasons, it may be because the argument is congruent with reasons the receiver already holds, or because the question is unimportant to him or he doesn't want to hurt the arguer's feelings, but debate is a latent potential in all argumentation.

Therefore, each arguer as he analyzes a claim should conceive of it

---

[18] The preceding two paragraphs are substantially quoted from Sillars, pp. 301–302.

being directed to an audience where arguments for and against will be judged according to the "facts," "truths," "presumptions," and "values" of that audience. It would be best if, for the moment, that arguer would pursue both sides of the claim with equal vigor. Such a practice is frequently impossible but one thing is clear—the arguer who only looks to his own arguments, who does not consider carefully what the possible opposition arguments are is doing no one a disfavor but himself.

A simple method for dealing with this minidebate one carries on with himself is to make a list of arguments for and against and then match them up. Which arguments make issues and which do not? For instance:

Policy Claim: Capital punishment should be mandatory for persons who kidnap and kill the victim, sell narcotics to juveniles, hijack an airplane or kill a prison guard.

For	Against
1. These are serious crimes which should be deterred.	Capital punishment doesn't deter crime.
2. The penalty must be mandatory because parole is too easy to get.	Eliminates the notion of rehabilitation.
3. An eye for an eye and a tooth for a tooth.	This is worn out.
Not if it is mandatory.	4. Capital punishment discriminates against the poor and the minorities.
Not as much as selling narcotics to juveniles and other terrible crimes.	5. Legalized murder saps the moral fiber of the country.
6. It would be cheaper than keeping such killers.	That's a barbarian attitude putting money over human beings.
Courts should be speeded up; they waste too much time.	No, it wouldn't be cheaper, the court cost would be great because of the longer trials and appeals.
No, they aren't. That's a chance we have to take People who engage in such crimes aren't human beings.	7. Innocent people are put to death.

Of course, we have arranged this quite neatly and we have left out some arguments because of the most obvious values of the society. We have not included these, for instance:

No one should be put to death or even go to jail because society is to blame for what they did.

Killing people every now and then helps to keep the rest in line.

As we said earlier, it is possible to connect any argument to any claim if one works at it hard enough. Thus, by limiting to the most prevalent arguments shown above we have let the facts, presumptions and values work, leaving only those arguments that would be given some credence by a general audience of citizens.

Admitting that this example is somewhat oversimplified, what potential issues do we get.

1. Does capital punishment deter crime?
2. Is it best to make the punishment mandatory? (If we are to have capital punishment in these cases, should it be mandatory?)
3. Is the Biblical injunction "an eye for an eye and a tooth for a tooth" applicable in this case?
4. Does capital punishment, even when mandatory, discriminate against the poor and minorities?
5. Will capital punishment sap the moral fiber of the nation or will it strengthen the moral fiber by eliminating people who commit crimes that do sap the moral fiber?
6. Will it be cheaper to kill them than to keep them in prison?
   6a. Is saving money by killing such persons barbaric
   6b. Would it be cheaper to kill such people, particularly if we also passed legislation to speed up court action and cut down on appeals?
7. Do innocent people die under capital punishment?
   7a. Is putting innocent people to death a chance we have to take?

There are a few interesting points about the issues we have just found.

1. If rephrased as arguments for the policy claim, they would all be factual and value claims. 1, 4, 6, and 6b are factual claims, and 2, 3, 5, 6a, 7, and 7a are value claims.
2. Two of the claims, one of value (2), and one of fact (6b) are easily converted into policy claims. We observed earlier that all policy claims are fundamentally claims of future value and issue 2 illustrates that point. 6b is interesting because it illustrates how some argumentation flows on in a continuous stream until one can end up arguing something completely different from what began as the claim. From speeded up court action, we might find ourselves talking about elimi-

nating the jury system, a mandatory retirement age for judges and a host of other claims.

3. As in the case of 6, there is not just one issue but a variety of issues that can be constructed from a single argument because issues depend on what an opponent will say or a listener will think. In 6, the first issue is a factual one because the anticipated opposition response is on cost alone—a presumably measurable factor. But on 6a there is a strong value orientation because the response is such.

Now that we have reduced the policy claim to a workable series of issues of fact and value we can consider the further analysis of the policy claim by analyzing each of the fact and value claims in those issues.

THE ANALYSIS OF CLAIMS OF FACT AND VALUE

The first stage in the analysis of the claims of fact and value is to place them in some order of importance based on the values of the audience addressed. Naturally, audiences will differ one from another. Generalizations about audiences are always hazardous. One must be careful not to fall into stereotyping of people on the basis of limited knowledge. Good audience analysis is the product of a life long habit of mind that makes one continually aware of the truths, values and presumptions most often held by various groups. In the space permitted us here, we are unable to provide all the details of a careful analysis. So permit us for the moment to assume an audience with values that we believe will be close to your own and present a brief analysis of these issues.

The crucial issue is the first one. For most people crime is serious and these crimes are particularly serious (though the receiver of an argument may need some convincing on why these and not some others). A primary concern with crime is how to deter it. If one could prove that capital punishment does not deter crime, he could come near destroying adherence to the claim on that issue alone. Claims about saving money can easily be turned against an arguer because of the high value we place on human beings over money. A similar problem exists with regard to issue 7a where we must accept the idea of being prepared for an innocent man's death. The "eye for an eye" argument will be effective with but a small group of people, particularly since there is the emphasis on such biblical injunctions as "love thy neighbor" and "judge not lest you be judged."

Thus, it appears most reasonable to argue for this policy claim primarily around the issue of deterence with some attention to the general societal issues of protecting the moral fiber (5) and, of course, justifying the mandatory clause (2). Because we see our audience interested in humanitarian values as well as their own safety, we would tread lightly on all the other potential issues.

In arguing against the claim we would also center on the deterence argument but would build also the idea of barbarianism, in the act and the motivation for it.

It would appear from this analysis that the negative position on this claim has the greatest advantage when presented to the audience we have pictured. It probably does with college students but not necessarily in the general population. But the number of issues that tend to lean to one side or another is not as important as firm adherence. There are seven issues listed here and one side or another could get support on six of them and still not gain adherence because the issue of deterence is so important. This may well be a case where one should argue that one issue only. Such a decision the arguer will have to make on the basis of the values that he sees functioning in the audience. The skill of such discovery will not be learned by reading one chapter or a book. Make it a habit to examine what people say and the way they act to understand better the value systems by which they order their lives.

After one has discovered the relative importance of fact and value claims, he can then examine each of them more carefully.[19]

The analysis of claims of fact and value are essentially the same. First, we must establish criteria by defining the judgment term and then test the subject term of the claim against it. To illustrate, we will use the claim of fact: Capital punishment deters crime. Capital punishment is our subject, and we wish to judge it by whether or not it deters crime. To do this we must ask what does "deter crime" mean? Eliminate crime altogether? Lessen it? How much less? Deter compared to what? Immediately we are asked to resolve a whole battery of questions about definition. Obviously new issues could be formed right here and arguments would be developed in defense of particular definitions. It would be nice to have a neat list of points by which capital punishment could be judged. These might be reasonable enough:

1. There will be a significant drop in actual crimes of the types covered.
2. Capital punishment is shown to be the cause of the decline.
3. There will be a general decline in crime attributable to capital punishment.

[19] The essential ideas in this section have been previously explained in Mudd and Sillars, pp. 52–56.

We might even further define the word "significant" to provide some statistical measure.

Even though such criteria are a starting place, they do not adequately account for decisions that have to be made. Criteria, most particularly, are difficult to apply because they tend to be static whereas most argument is comparative. Mickey Mantle was a great outfielder, but was he as good as Henry Aaron is, or Babe Ruth was? Americans have freedom but do they have as much freedom as Britons or Swedes? The University of Iowa has a fine history department, but how does it compare with Harvard, Chicago or North Carolina? Thus, the criteria will generally need to be used on a comparative measure. Comparative measures, while still linked to the criteria, will provide a more convincing basis on which to ask for people's adherence. Here are two comparable states—Michigan and Indiana—both have rural populations, industrial populations, rich people, poor people and minorities in similar proportions. For several years Michigan had no capital punishment while Indiana did. What do the figures show on the commission of capital crimes? This and other comparisons, *which a receiver would accept*, can be used as a basis for making the criteria usable. How many contemporary outfielders must Mickey Mantle be compared to to decide if he is a great one? Only a few. But even though we would not lose sight of criteria such as batting average, home run records and errors, the comparison would help make such criteria clearer.

In the selection of criteria we consider "facts" (what do people consider to be facts of an outfielder's greatness or standards of crime deterence?), "truths" (baseball is a game of skill, not chance), "presumptions" (certainly, in baseball there is a presumption in favor of an outfielder with a high batting average), and the values that govern people's judgments (ability to perform, humility, handsomeness, what values govern judgments about an outfielder?) One might ask what humility and handsomeness have to do with athletic ability, but sports writers apparently think that at least humility is important and Mohammed Ali was prohibited from fighting and stripped of the world championship because of his refusal to enter the armed forces. There are value judgments at work at all times and sometimes they are not the most obvious ones.

All of these factors (facts, truths, presumptions, values) enter into the selection of criteria and, once criteria are selected, they enter into the decision of which of the criteria are most important. On the deterence claim, for instance, while the third criterion, a general decline in crime, appears as a basis of judgment, it would not be regarded as important as the other two factors if we could not prove that it was caused by capital punishment. That is, it would not be regarded as important if it failed to meet the presumption of cause.

In testing whether the subject meets the criteria, there are more alternatives than just accepting or rejecting the claim. We may actually find new claims that are more pressing than the one we have examined. This need not be a matter of a grand change of position. One might make comparatively simple changes such as dropping the mandatory requirement in the capital punishment policy claim. But this would bring about a significant change in the case. Even simpler, the policy claim favoring capital punishment could depend on the factual deterence claim and it in turn could depend on the accuracy of statistics or the comparability of two states like Michigan and Indiana. It is important, therefore, for us to be aware of the locations where issues may be found:

1. Issues are found in controversy over the formation of appropriate criteria for judging fact and value claims.
   a. What is a *significant* decline in capital crime?
   b. How do you know capital punishment *caused* the decline and not something else?

2. Issues are found in controversy over the relative importance of various criteria.
   a. How *important* is a general decline in crime to this question?

3. Issues are formed over whether or not the evidence, values and credibility produced are applicable to the criteria.
   a. Are Michigan and Indiana *comparable* states?
   b. Is the person making the argument too *biased* on this question to be trusted to provide criteria?
   c. Do the criteria reflect the *proper* values?

4. Issues are formed over the acceptability of the evidence, values and credibility produced.
   a. Are the statistics *accurate*?
   b. Is the source for them *trustworthy* and *competent*?
   c. What *value* can we place on statistics as compared to what "the good book" says?

Policy claims depend for their adherence on the acceptance by the receiver of one or more fact and value claims. The arguer must discover what claims are most crucial to this adherence. That is, he must determine which constitute issues for the receiver. He does this by looking on the analysis as a debate in the mind of the receiver, and observing the major locations where issues will be found, eliminating claims that "facts," "truths" and "presumptions" support. One also eliminates those issues where audience values give a clear verdict. The issues remaining will be limited and can then be clearly identified as those requiring support. How they are approached in terms of strategy of organization will be covered in Chapter 8, Case Building.

CONCLUSIONS

It is people who determine where argumentation begins. It is they who discover problems and determine how these problems shall be resolved. They frequently do this in a hit or miss fashion from limited knowledge and analysis. The adherence of others can be more easily developed if the analysis of problems takes place systematically rather than hit or miss.

In order to understand how to engage in such analysis, some terms need to be understood. Any statement can be considered an *argument* although the ideal argument form is the statement and its support. An *issue* is created when there is a clash of opposing arguments. A *claim* (frequently known as a proposition) is the single statement that a person proposes to support. It may be a single argument or it may involve several arguments. There are three kinds of claims: factual, value and policy. Each depends on the audience for adherence but they are different in that one claims a fact to be in existence, the second claims the value of something, and the third argues for a particular policy.

Because any statement may be linked to any other statement and thus generate an infinite number of claims, the number of arguments must be reduced to some workable basis. This is achieved in two parts: First, the process of finding a claim when only a general problem (a "feeling of doubt") is realized and, second, the process of finding the crucial issues in the argumentation after the claim has been identified.

Claims are found from a "feeling of doubt" by testing possible claims against the facts, truths, presumptions, values and hierarchies that audiences will apply in the situation. By testing claims, changing them, discarding them and looking for new ones, one can narrow to the most usable claim for the situation. But the selection of the claim is not the end, for persons may at any time determine to abandon that claim and return to the procedure for selection of a claim.

Once a claim has been determined, it can be more specifically analyzed. A policy claim is analyzed by looking for the clash of arguments as in a debate. Thus, by looking at both sides of the claim, the arguer can discover the issues of fact or value that are likely to be most crucial. Value and factual claims are analyzed by finding criteria by which to measure the subject term. Criteria are discovered by again testing by facts, truths, presumptions, values and hierarchies. Issues about fact and value claims will be found in four conflicts:

1. Over the formation of appropriate criteria.
2. Over the relative importance of various criteria.
3. Over whether or not the evidence, values and credibility produced are applicable to the criteria.
4. Over the acceptability of the evidence, values and credibility produced.

When the claim is identified, the issues discovered and their specific natures identified, the arguer can then determine what must be argued and how best to argue it.

PROJECTS

1. With a small group of your classmates, discuss a general problem area such as America's energy needs, crime prevention, mideast peace, world hunger, the future of higher education. How many policy claims can you generate? What kinds of claims did you leave out because they conflicted with your facts, truths, values and hierarchies? What did you learn about narrowing to a claim?

2. Examine the "facts," "truths," and "values" of a special group to which you belong (a fraternity, church, club, or even your own age group). To what extent are they different from the general society?

3. Find the issues in the following controversy. On November 7, 1972, the voters of California were voting on a highly controversial proposal for an amendment to the Penal Code on the subject of obscenity. The following statements are taken from the pamphlet distributed to all California voters by the Secretary of State, *Proposed Amendments to Constitution, Propositions and Proposed Laws, Together With Arguments, General Election, Tuesday, November 7, 1972*, pp. 45–48. What issues do you find in the clash of arguments? Which do you consider most important? Why?

OBSCENITY LEGISLATION

Initiative. Amends, deletes, and adds Penal Code statutes relating to obscenity. Defines nudity, obscenities, sadomasochistic abuse, sexual conduct, sexual excitement and other related terms. Deletes "redeeming social importance" test. Limits "contemporary standards" test to local area. Creates misdemeanors for selling, showing, producing or distributing specified prohibited materials to adults or minors. Permits local governmental *agencies to separately regulate these matters. Provides for county jail term and up to $10,000 fine for violations. Makes sixth conviction of specified misdemeanors a felony. Creates defenses and presumptions. Permits injunctions and seizures of materials. Requires speedy hearing and trial. Financial impact: None.*

ARGUMENT IN FAVOR OF PROPOSITION 18

The U.S. Supreme Court has recognized the right and duty of states to provide for their children an environment conducive to their healthy emotional and moral development. That is the purpose of this measure. Its restraints are reasonable. They will be welcomed by those sincerely concerned about the welfare of our society and its children.

Recent experience clearly has demonstrated that California's obscenity laws are inadequate. Hardcore pornography has saturated many communities and threatens to engulf the state. It blatantly is flaunted in public places without regard for the sensibilities of our children. Law enforcement is handcuffed by statutes which give complete license to smut-peddlers.

Eminent students of human behaviour have expressed grave concern about the damaging effects of pornography, especially upon the young. They have identified these interrelated destructive influences of smut upon individuals and society:

1. Early exposure to pornography cripples emotional development and diminishes the consumer's ability to mature sexually.
2. Pornography is addictive and is as destructive of personality as narcotics.
3. Pornography dehumanizes sex. Humans become objects to be used rather than persons to be loved. Animals also become things to be used for the consumer's degenerate sexual gratification.
4. Pornography glorifies sexual violence.
5. Pornography encourages promiscuity among the young, with its consequent spread of venereal disease and unwanted pregnancies.
6. Pornography depersonalizes sex. Robbed of its meaningful, interpersonal relationship, sex becomes a warped and degenerate activity.
7. Dehumanization and depersonalization of sex produce defective personalities which ultimately produce a defensive society.
8. History attests that societies which tolerate widespread public indulgence in deviant sexual practices suffer marked cultural and political decline.

The inability of law enforcement effectively to cope with the problems of pornography is the result of these weaknesses in our statutes:

1. The requirement that, to be considered obscene, material must be *without any* redeeming social importance. The requirement is unnecessary and undesirable. It has allowed even the hardest pornography to escape censorship.
2. Vagueness of present language works a hardship on merchants and prosecution alike.
3. Because there is no means for stopping obscene materials prior to their dissemination, much damage is done *before* the law can act.
4. No mechanism exists for allowing local community control of pornography.

THE PURPOSE OF THIS MEASURE IS:

1. To protect our children from the debilitating effects of obscenity by eliminating hardcore pornography.
2. To give some control over pornographic materials to local communities.
3. To conform California law to pronouncements of the United States Supreme Court.
4. To help law enforcement conserve funds through more efficient use of its resources.

WHEN ENACTED BY THE PEOPLE THIS MEASURE WILL:

1. Eliminate the "social importance test" from our statutes.
2. Within reasonable limits, allow local communities to regulate the moral climate in which they wish to live.
3. Place interested parties on notice as to specific activities which are proscribed.
4. Within reasonable and constitutional limits, allow law enforcement to stop dissemination of harmful matter before the damage is done.

JOHN L. HARMER
State Senator, 21st District
WOODRUFF J. DEEM
District Attorney, Ventura County
HOMER E. YOUNG
Pornography Specialist
Federal Bureau of Investigation, Retired (1955–1972)

REBUTTAL TO ARGUMENT IN FAVOR OF PROPOSITION 18

Vote NO to the censorship initiative. The supporting argument fails to tell you these important facts.

The censorship initiative is not primarily concerned with minors. Over 80% of its provisions directly limit the rights of adults to read or view matter. But it could limit adults to matter which is fit only for children.

The censorship initiative will not ban pornography. Our highest court has explicitly said that our existing obscenity law bans "hardcore pornography."

The censorship initiative will ban matter that is not obscene. It creates hundreds of new crimes, crimes so broad that recent academy award movies Patton, Cabaret and Godfather would be subject to prosecution.

The censorship initiative does not give control over pornographic materials to local communities. Local police, sheriffs and district attorneys are already empowered to enforce our law banning pornography. But it does give cities and counties the right to "further regulate" the right to read and to create more censorship laws.

The censorship initiative is not necessary to protect minors. California passed a special statute in 1969 to prohibit distribution of harmful matter to children.

The censorship initiative will not bring California into conformity with our Constitution. Rather, the initiative, by repealing such constitutionally required provisions as the social importance test, will subject our existing law to invalidation. The social importance test does not impede the prosecution of obscenity. Our highest court has said that hardcore pornography is utterly without redeeming social importance.

Vote "NO" to the obscenity initiative.

FATHER CHARLES DOLLEN
Library Director
University of San Diego
RT. REV. RICHARD MILLARD
Suffragan Bishop to California
Episcopal Bishop of San Jose
CHARLES WARREN
Assemblyman, 56th District

ARGUMENT AGAINST PROPOSITION 18

Vote "NO" on Proposition 18. It would not regulate obscenity. It would create wholly new crimes banning matter which is not obscene. It would create the most drastic censorship law ever proposed to the citizens of California. It would impose censorship on books, newspapers, motion pictures, sculpture, paintings, records and all forms of distribution including libraries.

Proposition 18 would abolish the protection now given recognized works of art and literature. It would deny adults the right to read or view matter which is not obscene. It would deny adults in many cities the right to read or view matter freely available elsewhere. It would create sweeping new crimes subjecting motion picture artists and others to criminal prosecution. It would give power to government officials to seize books, newspapers or motion pictures without a search warrant. It would restrict the matter which newspapers could freely circulate. It would empower cities and counties to create hundreds of even broader censorship laws.

Proposition 18 goes far beyond banning obscene matter. California already bans obscenity to the extent constitutionally permissible. It would create wholly new crimes banning matter which is not obscene. The new crimes are so sweeping and vaguely worded that adults could be prevented from seeing the academy award winning motion pictures French Connection, Patton and Midnight Cowboy, or award nominees Love Story, MASH, Cabaret, Butch Cassidy and the Sundance Kid, Five Easy Pieces and The Last Picture Show. The producers and stars of such movies could be subject to criminal prosecution.

Proposition 18 is a badly drafted measure of over 6,000 words. It is so broad that it would make it a crime to exhibit to an adult a motion picture or magazine containing a single photograph "that shows the nude or nearly nude body," or that utilizes slang words referring to the human body. Playboy magazine would obviously be banned as would many major motion pictures.

Proposition 18 repeals the protection now given recognized works of art and literature, such as Michelangelo's statue of David, by repealing language protecting matter of redeeming social importance. This drastic proposal was rejected by the people of this state in 1966 when they soundly defeated an identical initiative proposal.

Proposition 18 could also spawn hundreds of new censorship laws. It empowers cities and counties to pass censorship laws going beyond those in the initiative and to ban what is not tolerated by their local standards. Matter could not circulate freely in the state. Adults in one city would be denied matter lawfully available in another city. Only the most bland and innocuous of matter would survive this oppressive network of censorship laws.

The drastic proposals contained in Proposition 18 are opposed by newspapermen, motion picture artists, librarians and many others.

Proposition 18 would create a vast bureaucratic jungle of censorship laws strangling our freedoms of speech and press. Our police are needed in the streets preventing crime, not in our libraries censoring books.

Vote "NO" on censorship.

FATHER CHARLES DOLLEN
Library Director, University of San Diego
RT. REV. RICHARD MILLARD
Suffragan Bishop to California
Episcopal Bishop of San Jose
CHARLES WARREN
Assemblyman, 56th District

REBUTTAL TO ARGUMENT AGAINST PROPOSITION 18

Opponents' review of Proposition 18 must have been superficial. Their argument contains many *gross misstatements of fact*, any of which would be obvious to a careful reader.

The charge of "vagueness" is false. The measure is long *because* it is clear and specific. "broad and vaguely worded" documents require few words.

The emotional appeal to the specter of censorship clearly is misplaced. Because the measure is extremely specific, it would in fact *reduce* the incidence of arbitrary censorship.

The concepts advocated here are not new. They have been adopted by other states, including New York and Oregon.

Some facts:

1. California law *is* unduly permissive. Many states *never have* adopted the "redeeming social importance test." Others have abolished it. No majority opinion of the United States Supreme Court requires it.

2. None of the movies listed by opponents would be banned, nor would "Playboy" or Michelangelo's "David." What is banned is the obscene exhibition of human genitals, sexual conduct and excretion.

3. Broad defenses within the measure protect works of art and other matter which is not obscene. Opponents conveniently overlooked these. As it concerns adults, the measure is directed at hardcore pornography, nothing more.

Opponents' argument should be rejected, just as the conclusions of the Presidential Commission on Pornography were rejected by conscientious scholars, Congress and the President himself, because of its utter disregard for the facts.

We urge a YES vote. We must protect ourselves against the commercialization of degenerate sex. This proposition may be our last chance.

JOHN L. HARMER
State Senator, 21st District
WOODRUFF J. DEEM
District Attorney,
Ventura County
HOMER E. YOUNG
Pornography Specialist
Federal Bureau of Investigation, Retired (1955–1972)

4

Characteristics of Argument

It may be useful to review briefly what has been discussed elsewhere. Argumentation is not a single rational system of decision making; it is a composite of systems, sometimes intermixed and sometimes functioning alone, designed to provide justification for a particular decision. There are characteristics of general argumentation that can be identified, but there are also understandings of what is acceptable argumentation, which are appropriate to rational decision making in each specialized system. In Christian theology, the Bible is the basic authority from which one reasons by analogy to present understandings and actions. Scientists reason to find and use natural laws. They seek to discover it by particular means of induction and tests of probability. When a behavioral scientist says that there is believability for his idea at the .05 level, he means that there is a possibility of his conclusion resulting from chance of only five out of a hundred. Why not zero out of a hundred? Because that kind of certainty is never attained. Consequently, knowledge in that field is established on that level of probability, and men draw elaborate conclusions from the combination and relisting of such knowledge.

Some humanists look to the words of great men and reason from that authority. If the idea was espoused by Plato or Shakespeare or John Locke, it is worthy of note and worthy of organizing our lives around. The legal system determines right action through an intricate system of legal statutes, customs and precedents, and judges and juries are expected to reason from them. If a judge simply said to a defendant, "I think you are as guilty as sin and I intend to lock you up and throw away the key," he would be making an argument about a person's moral state and what should be done with him, but it would be a legally unacceptable argument. So, his decision must be based on evidence and reason within certain carefully defined limits. "This is a nation of laws," we frequently like to say, "not men." Each man, whether he begins from the United States Constitution, the *Koran, E=mc²*, Milton's poetry, the *Book of Mormon* or a host of other starting places, has a method of arriving at what he and others will perceive as truth. In this chapter we will attempt to examine some of the forms that arguments take and see how they are tested within belief systems.

Inherent in this discussion is the idea that there is no one proper way to reason. In 1925 at the Scopes "Monkey" Trial in Dayton, Tennessee, William Jennings Bryan could charge that the Darwinian hypothesis was a "guess" because that is what a hypothesis is, a guess. He could contrast that guess with the certainty that the Bible gave of man's eternal salvation. His opponent, Clarence Darrow, could question the "scientific truth" of the Bible about whether Joshua made the sun stand still. Each could argue and gain or reinforce the adherence of others to his position. Similar disagreements today exist over the relative merits of a psychological study and the observations of Aristotle. But we will not concern ourselves with assessing the value of one method of reasoning over another. Our concern is with the forms of argument as they develop in general argumentation where they are used by persons from a variety of systems to gain the adherence of receivers.

Later in this book we will look rather specifically at four of the main special applications of argumentation. In this chapter we are primarily interested in the arguments that go to make up what we have called general argumentation: those kinds of arguments, which would appear to the average person in his personal, social, economic and political life. Of course, general argumentation is not totally distinctive from special cases of argumentation. When one finds himself engaged in an argumentation about legalizing abortion, for instance, he frequently hears arguments that draw from specialized theological, scientific and legal argumentation. Argumentation is the study of what audiences will give adherence to and the designation of quality that we give an argument is in terms of a standard, which is functional for our receivers. Thus, there are special kinds of argumentation (such as theological, scientific, literary, mathematical and legal) that in certain circumstances function as the sole standard and at other times function as applicable in general argumentation. There are also some standards for general argumentation that result from the inter-action of specialized kinds but most particularly there are standards that are rooted in one kind: formal logic.

ARGUMENTATION AND FORMAL LOGIC

General argumentation is related to a variety of specialized kinds of argumentation, both are particularly indebted to formal logic. Argu-mentation and formal logic are not the same, nor does formal logic necessarily strengthen argumentation. There is ample evidence to show that people do not follow the laws of formal logic when they argue. The mere existence of fallacies clearly proves that.[1] But there is also evidence to show that in the human thought process many of the "sources of cogni-tive linkages" and the actual linkage, which takes place in thinking, are quite similar to those that formal logic attempts to describe.[2] A careful analysis of the psychological literature has led one psychologist to the conclusion that the errors of reasoning can be accounted for while still acknowledging that human reasoning is substantially "logical."[3] Another accepts the same but attributes human logicality not to the nature of human thinking but to the education one has undergone.[4]

Whether we believe that human beings accept logical rules by nature or by training is not vital to our interests here. Tradition and contemporary research support the idea that our reasoning processes are sometimes related to the rules of formal logic. Perhaps this is only because of our training and perhaps it is "according to as yet only dimly understood principles of what might be called 'psycho-logic.' "[5] The problem with the

[1] Morris R. Cohen, *A Preface to Logic*, (New York: Henry Holt and Co., 1944), pp. 2–3.

[2] Karl E. Weick, "Processes of Ramification Among Cognitive Links," *Theories of Cognitive Consistency: A Sourcebook*, Robert P. Abelson et al., eds., (Chicago: Rand McNally and Co., 1968), pp. 512–519. Weick does not make this point but the processes he identifies contain most of the processes identified by formal logic.

[3] Mary Henle, "On the Relation Between Logic and Thinking," *Psychology Review*, 69 (July 1962), pp. 366–78. See also, Daniel K. Stewart, "Communication and Logic: Evidence for the Existence of Validity Patterns," *Journal of General Psychology, 64* (April 1961), pp. 297–305.

[4] John Dollard and Neal E. Miller, *Personality and Psychotherapy*, (New York: McGraw-Hill, 1950), p. 120. Studies in mathematical probability show that the ability of children to select according to probability rules improves with age. John Cohen, "Subjective Probability," *Scientific American, 197* (November 1957), p. 128.

[5] Robert P. Abelson, "Psychological Implication," *Theories of Cognitive Con-sistency: A Sourcebook*, p. 112.

application of formal logic to argumentation is that it is too often offered as the paradigm of perfection. The assumption that formal logic will yield "truth" if all the rules are obeyed—like all systems based on the assumption of objective truth has made the study of argumentation too often sterile, and occasionally ridiculous. Formal logic is important to argumentation, not because it yields ultimate truth, but because it is a better approximation than many other systems of how the human mind works and, more important, because it can test an argument by a means which large numbers of people accept. Consequently, in this chapter we shall not look directly at the rules of formal logic, but instead look at a method of examining individual arguments to discover what kinds of claims are being supported and how they are being supported.

Much of the traditional study of argumentation has drawn its interpretation of the characteristics of arguments from traditional logic. It has assumed that the study of the formal rules of induction and deduction in generalization, example, syllogism and enthymeme, would provide a basis for learning to improve the quality of argumentation. As we have noted here and in Chapter 1, although such a study is useful, it is not flexible enough as it is based on an assumption of universal principles of argument when we know that arguments are claims that we present and support in the hope that they will "stand up to criticism" and be adhered to by a particular audience. We know that each contains a field dependent element, a criterion of selection that will determine its acceptability, not on universal principles, but based on the specific standards of a specific audience.

THE FORM OF AN ARGUMENT

If we are to acknowledge the usefulness of formal logic to argumentation but question its forms and rules, where will we turn? The most profitable source for ideas about the forms of argument are not traditional logic, we believe, but in Stephen Toulmin's book, *The Uses of Argument*.[6] Professor Toulmin's point of view on argument has received considerable comment by students of argument and logic.[7] Some of his major

---

[6] Stephen Toulmin, *The Uses of Argument* (Cambridge: Cambridge University Press, 1958).

[7] See: Wayne Brockreide and Douglas Ehninger, "Toulmin On Argument: An Interpretation and Application," *Quarterly Journal of Speech, 46* (February 1960), pp. 44–53; J. C. Cooley, "On Mr. Toulmin's Revolution in Logic," *Journal of Philosophy, 56* (March 26, 1959), pp. 297–319; J. L. Cowan, "The Uses of Argument—An Apology For Logic," *Mind, 73* (January 1964), pp. 27–45; Albert L. Louis, "Stephen

contributions were discussed in Chapter 1. The primary use that we will make of Toulmin in this chapter is to take the graphic form that he gave to argument and adapt it to our purposes here. Our model, like Toulmin's, is an analytical device that could be used before or after the actual written or oral argument is prepared (or after it has been heard). Before the argument it may be used to predict from the audience's position what the audience will do with the claim. After the argument, it can be used similarly to judge the strength or possible vulnerability of the argument so that refutation may be planned.

Let us sketch out briefly the basic form of an argument and a modified form of it, define each of the terms, illustrate each form and then consider some of the applications of these forms in different types of arguments.

The Basic Form of Argument

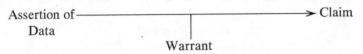

The Modified Form of Argument

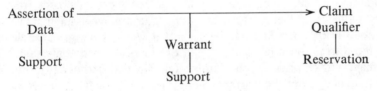

Terms

CLAIM: The conclusion to the argument. The statement that is advanced for the adherence of others. It may be actually stated or it may be implied. It may be a universal statement or it may be qualified as shall be seen.

ASSERTION OF DATA: Any assertion that an arguer makes about persons, conditions or events, which asserts that data are available to support a claim.

Toulmin: A Reappraisal," *Central States Speech Journal*, 23 (Spring 1972), pp. 48–55; Peter T. Manicas, "On Toulmin's Contribution to Logic and Argumentation," *Journal of the American Forensic Association*, 3 (September 1966), pp. 83–94; Jerie M. Pratt, "The Appropriateness of a Toulmin Analysis of Legal Argumentation," *Speaker and Gavel*, 7 (May 1970), pp. 133–137; Jimmie D. Trent, "Toulmin's Model of Argument: An Examination and Extension," *Quarterly Journal of Speech*, 54 (October 1968), pp. 252–259.

WARRANT: A statement of general principle that establishes the validity of the claim on the basis of its relationship to the Assertion of Data.

SUPPORT: Any material that is provided (specific instance, statistics, testimony, values or credibility) by the arguer to make the Assertion of Data or Warrant more believable to the audience.

QUALIFIER: A qualification placed on the universal applicability of some claims (frequently in the form of such words as possibly, probably or most likely.)

RESERVATIONS: The basis on which the claim will not be acceptable.

In 1962, President John F. Kennedy spoke in Berlin and said: "All freemen, wherever they may live, are citizens of Berlin, and therefore, as a free man, I take pride in the words, 'Ich bin ein Berliner.'" This argument will illustrate the basic form.

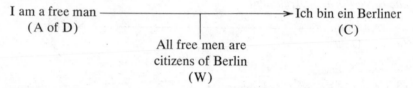

I am a free man ⸻⸻⸻⸻⸻⸻⸻⸻→ Ich bin ein Berliner
  (A of D)   (C)

All free men are
citizens of Berlin
(W)

The argument, according to all reports, gained great adherence from that mass audience of Germans on that day. The argument might have been less stylistically appealing but we suspect it would have gained adherence had the warrant been left out and had President Kennedy only said, "As a freeman, I take pride in the words, 'Ich bin ein Berliner.'" Arguments will frequently omit the warrant and let the audience fill it in. Or suppose he had left out the assertion of data and said, "All free men, wherever they may live, are citizens of Berlin, and therefore, I take pride in the words, 'Ich bin ein Berliner.'" Again that audience would have filled in the missing assertion. Thus, arguers may adapt their argument to provide only as much as is necessary to gain the adherence of their receivers. Indeed, common sense would tell us that filling in all the premises would make an argument boring. Aristotle gave this warning in his discussion of the enthymeme. "You must not begin the chain of reasoning too far back, or its length will render the argument obscure; and you must not put in every single link, or the statement of what is obvious will render it prolix."[8]

But what if the assertion of data and the warrant are questioned by an audience or are likely to be so questioned? In that case an arguer may do

[8] Lane Cooper, The Rhetoric of Aristotle, © 1932, Renewed 1960. By permission of Prentice-Hall, Inc., Englewood Cliffs, New Jersey, pp. 155–156.

either or both of two things. He may provide support for the questionable statement or he may admit to a qualification in his claim. Both of these are illustrated in the modified form diagramed earlier. Here is a complex argument that Walter Lippmann made in 1939, as World War II began, concerning the nature of freedom of speech, which illustrates how qualification functions. Subsequent arguments will illustrate support. The examples of Russia and Germany are dated but the argument is one we might hear today.

"The despot shuts himself off from the truth that no man can dispense with. We know all this well enough when we contemplate the dictatorships. But when we try to picture our own system, by way of contrast, what picture do we have in our minds? It is, is it not, that anyone may stand up on his own soapbox and say anything he pleases? . . .
"If the democratic alternative to the totalitarian one-way broadcasts is a row of separate soapboxes, then I submit that the alternative is unworkable, is unreasonable, and is humanly unattractive. It is not true that liberty has developed among civilized men when anyone is free to set up a soapbox, is free to hire a hall where he may expound his opinions to those who are willing to listen. On the contrary, freedom of speech is established to achieve its essential purpose only when different opinions are expounded in the same hall to the same audience.
"For even though the right to talk may be the beginning of freedom, the necessity of listening is what makes the right important. Even in Russia and Germany a man may still stand in an open field and speak his mind. What matters is not the utterance of opinions. What matters is the confrontation of opinions in debate."[9]

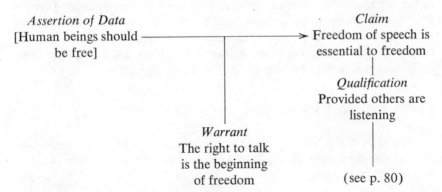

Assertion of Data
[Human beings should be free]

Claim
Freedom of speech is essential to freedom

Qualification
Provided others are listening

Warrant
The right to talk is the beginning of freedom

(see p. 80)

[9] Walter Lippmann, "The Indispensable Opposition," copyright © 1967, by the *Atlantic Monthly Company*, Boston, Mass. Reprinted with permission, (August 1939), pp. 186–190.

Reservation
The necessity of
listening to the
confrontation of
opinions through
debate is what
makes the right
important

|

Support
Even in totalitarian
states a person may
still stand in an open
field and speak

There are several points that may be noted. Some of the steps in even a complex argument may be left out (the assertion of data in Lippman's argument is in brackets to illustrate this). Support may be presented in a specific way (by citing examples or providing testimony) or where the assertion of data or warrant are accepted by all in the audience being asked to give adherence. This is unnecessary. Qualifications can be placed on claims but, although we know that all claims have some reservations to them, we infrequently argue that way. Note the confidence with which John F. Kennedy claimed "Ich bin ein Berliner." With the full understanding that particular principles all have reservations, in general argumentation, we tend to argue that for this case, under these circumstances, with this audience, the claim is valid. This is particularly true in the argumentative decision systems of debate and negotiation. Conference may be more prone to more tentative arguments with greater use of qualification and more subject to reservations. However, an important reality about the way we argue is that although we know argumentative decisions are tentative, we frequently argue as if they were not.

TYPES OF ARGUMENTS

Even though the form we have illustrated here will help to clarify the general characteristics of arguments, it will be useful to look at some rather distinctive types.

ENTHYMEMATIC ARGUMENT

The closest parallel to formal deductive logic is enthymematic argument, and while all deductive argument in the broad sense is enthymematic, we chose to use that term here in a narrower sense to mean only those arguments that are quite clearly deductive. The example given earlier of President Kennedy is such an argument. So is the following quotation from President Richard M. Nixon's "1970 State of the Union Address:"

"Our land, this land of ours together, is a great and good land. It is also an unfinished land and the challenge of perfecting it is the summons of the seventies."[10]

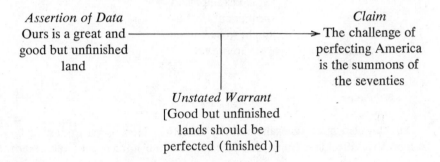

ARGUMENT BY GENERALIZATION

The closest parallel to pure induction is argument by generalization. It proposes to look at a series of instances and from them claim a general principle. Here is an example from Edmund Muskie's Election Eve address in 1970:

"And what are we to think, when men in positions of public trust openly declare that the party of Franklin Roosevelt and Harry Truman, which led us out of depression and to victory over international barbarism—the party of John Kennedy who was slain in the service of the country he inspired— the party of Lyndon Johnson who withstood the fury of countless demonstrations in order to pursue a course he believed in—the party of Robert Kennedy murdered on the eve of his greatest triumph. How dare they tell us that this party is less devoted or less courageous in maintaining American principles and values than are they themselves. This is nonsense, And we all know it is nonsense. And what contempt they must have for the

---

[10] Richard M. Nixon, "1970 State of the Union Address," *Contemporary Political Speaking*, L. Patrick Devlin, ed., (Belmont, California: Wadsworth Publishing Co., 1971), p. 66.

decency and sense of the American people to talk to them that way and to think they can make them believe it."[11]

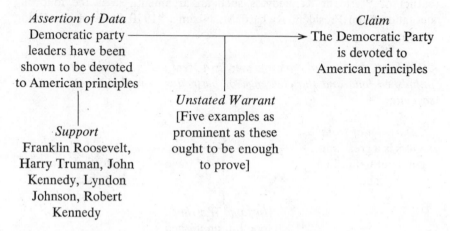

One can also have generalization by statistics: Here is an argument by former Vice President Spiro T. Agnew about the influence of television:

"First, let's define what power. At least 40 million Americans every night, it's estimated, watch television news. . . . According to Harris polls and other studies, for millions of Americans the networks are the sole source of national and world news. In Will Roger's observation, what you knew was what you read in the newspaper. Today for growing millions of Americans, its what they see and hear on their television sets."[12]

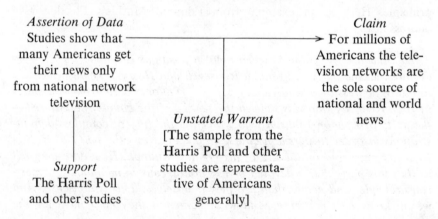

---

[11] From a text supplied by Senator Muskie's office.
[12] Spiro T. Agnew, "Address Criticizing Television News Coverage," Devlin, p. 43.

CAUSAL ARGUMENT

We have already noted on a number of occasions in this book that Americans tend to assume cause and effect relationships. For every event there must be a cause, is a common though not universal assumption. Causal reasoning is, therefore, quite important to us. One can reason from cause to effect or from effect to cause. This example from a 1970 Gubernatorial Campaign Address by Governor George Wallace of Alabama illustrates reasoning from effect to cause:

"Have you picked up the Birmingham News and seen a full page ad that says, "Call your loved ones by telephone;" or "Alabama Power builds Alabama." Why do they have to advertise when they are a monopoly? They advertise because they put thousands of dollars of your money in the pockets of the newspapers of Alabama. And then when they want a rate increase of multimillions of dollars there is no one to oppose them."[13]

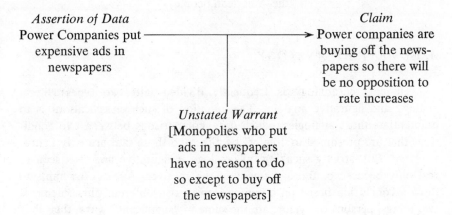

Assertion of Data
Power Companies put expensive ads in newspapers

Claim
Power companies are buying off the newspapers so there will be no opposition to rate increases

Unstated Warrant
[Monopolies who put ads in newspapers have no reason to do so except to buy off the newspapers]

ARGUMENT BY SIGN

A similar argument does not claim a cause for something but is merely an indication (a sign) of its existence. Argument by sign means what its name implies. In this argument the arguer reveals a sign that tells us something abut another person, thing or event, just as a "for sale" sign on a car tells us that that car is for sale. Edmund S. Muskie's election eve address in 1970, which we cited earlier, has sign reasoning in it.

[13] George C. Wallace, "Gubernatorial Campaign Address," Devlin, p. 84.

"How dare they tell us that this party is less devoted or less courageous in maintaining American principles and values than are they themselves. This is nonsense and we all know it is nonsense. And what contempt they must have for the decency and sense of the American people to talk to them that way and to think they can make them believe it."[14]

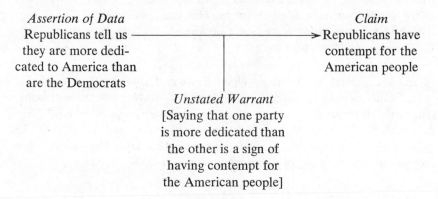

ARGUMENT BY ANALOGY

Argument by analogy is frequently divided into two types: literal analogy and figurative analogy. The intention of such classifications is to differentiate those analogies, which draw comparisons between two conditions that are presumed to "really" be alike and those that are only figuratively so. But, strictly speaking, all analogy is figurative and it is seen as real only because of the agreement of the receiver. Analogy attempts to draw a conclusion based on a comparison of two different phenomena. If two things, persons or events, are the same in "significant" ways, then they are the same in the claim being made. But, two women or governments, or holidays are alike in many ways and unlike in many ways. In no way are they "literally" the same. In analogy what one looks for is the similarities that count in the mind of the receiver. Here is a historical analogy from John F. Kennedy's "Cuban Missile Crisis Speech:"

"The 1930's taught us a clear lesson: Aggressive conduct, if allowed to grow unchecked and unchallenged, ultimately leads to war."[15]

[14] Muskie text.
[15] John F. Kennedy, "Address to the Nation, October 22, 1962," *U.S. Department of State Bulletin, 17* (November 12, 1962), p. 715.

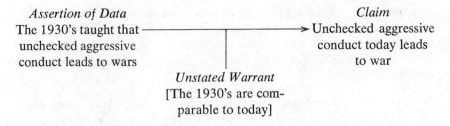

ARGUMENT FROM AUTHORITY

All arguments contain a credibility factor (see Chapter 7) but some arguments, called argument from authority, rest entirely on credibility. Here is an example of such argument again taken from former Vice President Agnew's address on the Media:

". . . As Justice Byron White wrote in his landmark opinion six months ago, it's the right of the viewers and listeners, not the right of the broadcasters which is paramount."[16]

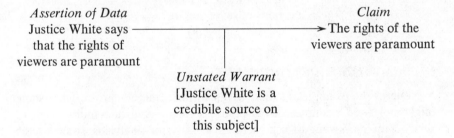

There is another form of argument from authority that might be called a "bandwagon" argument. It rests on the authority of majority action. If someone says that it is okay for him to cheat on his Income Tax because everyone else does, he is making an argument from the authority of the group.

ARGUMENT BY DEFINITION

Argument by definition is a perhaps too often ignored kind of argument. When so much of the content of argument is in its language, in

---

[16] Agnew, p. 45.

semantic shifts and changes, it is essential that definitions be established so that communication can take place. Frequently, whole debates may be taken up in the problem of definition. What is democracy? Truth? God? Here is an example of Senator James L. Buckley of New York arguing by definition.

"We now have a significant opportunity to reshape the politics of this country precisely because the people are searching for new answers, honest answers—answers which substitute common sense for theory, and toughness for soft headedness."[17]

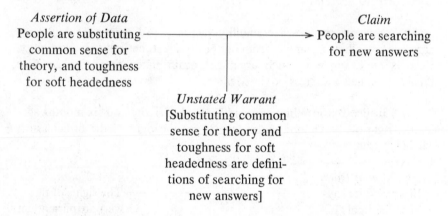

Assertion of Data
People are substituting common sense for theory, and toughness for soft headedness

Claim
People are searching for new answers

Unstated Warrant
[Substituting common sense for theory and toughness for soft headedness are definitions of searching for new answers]

INTERMIXTURE OF ARGUMENTS

None of the examples of these seven forms of argument are what some might call *good* examples of reasoning. Someone will find faults in all of them. You may want to use them as a basis for analyzing some of the problems of argument discussed later in the chapter. But these are not *good* examples precisely because they are *real* ones. Thousands, and in some cases millions, of people believed these arguments. They cannot be viewed in isolation, of course. They must be judged in terms of the social climate and issues that generated them and the audience to which they were addressed and they have to be seen in the context of the other arguments to which they link. Later, in Chapter 8, we will examine Case Building, which is the process of putting together a series of arguments in defense of a particular position. For now we should note that issues rarely exist in isolation. Some of the ones that we have already looked at are combinations of arguments. The fact that we could use one paragraph from Edmund Muskie's speech to illustrate two different kinds of argu-

[17] James L. Buckley, "The New Politics," Devlin, p. 150.

ments is proof of that. You may also note that the Agnew quotation on page 82 contains, in addition to generalization by statistics, arguments from testimony and by analogy, and President Kennedy's short argument by analogy about the experience of the 1930's is also a generalization from a single example.

Thus, arguments are intermixed, sometimes in the same statement, and it is not always possible to know the particular form of argument being used. Since so much of argument depends on what is left out or left unsaid, the critic of argument must be especially careful that he is not misconstruing the argument. And it goes without saying that the arguer who wishes to be understood should put enough into his statement to make his intention clear to his receivers.

CHAIN OF REASONING

Arguments may come in any combination and most frequently there will be multiple arguments tied together. It is probably important that we look briefly at one particular phenomenon of this grouping of arguments. It is a special, though not unusual case, which needs to be understood: the *chain of reasoning*. In chains of arguments, the individual arguments are more than just related to each other; they are dependent on each other. One could argue that fluoridation of water is good for children's health and also good for the parents' pocketbook. But although related to the common theme of the advantage of fluoridation, these two arguments are not part of a chain. If we were to say that smog is a threat to health and that automobiles are the main cause of smog, we would have begun a chain of reasoning that could lead to a number of solutions. Let's diagram that in its simplest form.

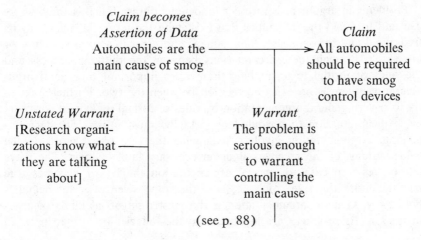

Claim becomes
Assertion of Data   *Claim*
Automobiles are the ─────────────────► All automobiles
main cause of smog   should be required
to have smog
control devices

Unstated Warrant   *Warrant*
[Research organi-   The problem is
zations know what ─────   serious enough
they are talking   to warrant
about]   controlling the
main cause

(see p. 88)

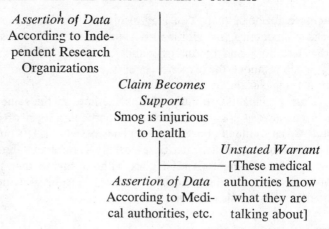

Assertion of Data
According to Inde-
pendent Research
Organizations

Claim Becomes
Support
Smog is injurious
to health

Unstated Warrant
[These medical
Assertion of Data   authorities know
According to Medi-   what they are
cal authorities, etc.   talking about]

Of course, you know that this problem is far more complex than this diagram shows and, therefore, you can see how full diagramming of a complex argument would be nearly impossible. But in this simple way we can illustrate how arguments are combined to provide a rational link from one to the other. Two arguments by authority are used to establish, first, the assertion of data and second, the warrant of the central argument. Chain reasoning has its advantages in that one can establish a continual rational explanation that brings all the materials of the argument together and shows how they relate. It's chief weakness is that it is as vulnerable as its weakest single argument.

PROBLEMS IN ARGUMENT

Problems in argument is a rather innocuous phrase but it is the best we can find to avoid the difficulties that exist with the term "fallacies." In its traditional and formal sense, fallacy means an error in logical structure or material. Although there are relations between the thinking process and the rules of formal logic, making these rules important to general argumentation, there is no exact correlation between the two. Furthermore, to try to govern general argumentation by rules of formal logic is to construct an artifical situation that would not yield the most satisfactory decision-making. Argumentation involves judgments that are based more on the value systems of the receivers than on arbitrary laws of logic. The more one moves into cases of special argumentation the less it becomes true and the more the rules of logic, law, theology, science or mathematics hold sway. General argumentation is the least rigid of all kinds of argumentation. Its problems are analogous to the fallacies of formal logic. In the examination of arguments we look for ways in which these arguments violate social conventions, including a preference for formal logical rules, and we note how to find these in our opponents' arguments and avoid them in our own.

NON-SEQUITUR ARGUMENT

"It does not follow," or in the latin term, *nonsequitur*, is probably the most commonly cited problem in general argumentation. Does it follow that if we flouridate the water in Carbondale, Illinois, there will be less tooth decay among small children? Does it follow that a well-armed America will remain at peace? Does it follow that giving additional stipends to poor people will help them to improve their health care? Does it follow that a cloudy day means that it will rain? Quite clearly, all of these questions will have varying levels of adherence for different persons. Even as you read this you can probably differentiate certain questions that you would clearly identify as *non-sequitur* arguments and most of your friends would also. At the same time you can see how others might have a different priority than you and your friends. It might depend on what part of the country you come from to determine truth value of the sign argument that clouds mean rain. And the other arguments would turn on your particular social background and beliefs. The level of commitment that people are willing to give to an argument would determine how much one would have to prove in order to convince them that their argument does not follow.

CIRCULAR REASONING

Circular reasoning is the process by which one argues that A is true because of B, and B is true because of A. Sometimes such circularity can go in long circles involving a whole series of connections but essentially, no matter how many connections, the problem involved is that one ends up by using as proof the very claim with which he began.

IRRELEVANT ARGUMENT

One of the most common means of rejecting an argument is to argue that it is irelevant. Of course, the difficulty is in determining what is relevant and what is irrelevant. For instance, it is generally considered that attacks on personality are irrelevant arguments in a policy debate. If you say, for instance, that Edward Kennedy should not be President of the United States because of the incident at Chappaquiddick, you may be accused of engaging in an irrelevant argument. You may be told that a man's personal life is not germane to whether or not he can govern the nation. But others will say that this is perfectly relevant because knowing the way a man acts in his private life reveals what kind of a national leader he will be. At what point such questions of personal character become central in determining relevancy, we cannot say. President Grover Cleveland, in a much more conservative time, was elected to the Presidency despite the public knowledge that he had fathered an illegitimate child. Certainly we do tend to have less confidence in people who do not conform to our own moral standards. But the extent to which this is more important to us than other items of credibility, position on the issues, and values is not readily known.

Is it relevant to use the fact that some students cheat in college as a basis for objecting to public higher education? We would guess that most people would say that this irrelevant. One can imagine a scale in standards of irrelevancy depending on subject, times, and audience. Such a scale requires that each arguer look carefully at his arguments and see to what extent they will be judged as irrelevant by his audience and prepare himself, therefore, either to make do without such "irrelevant" arguments or to support them and prove their relevancy.

IGNORING THE OPPOSITE

Even in a debate situation where an opponent is physically present and his arguments are heard by all, arguers will frequently ignore his arguments and simply repeat their own. In the technical terms of intercollegiate debate, this is called failure to advance the debate. One who argues that the United States should intervene in a Latin American country to protect the property of American citizens may be challenged by someone else because this action will bring America much international ill-will. In such a case, the author of the original argument will have essentially two alternatives in dealing with the opposition argument. He may argue that it will not bring ill-will or that what ill-will is created will be worth sustaining for the benefits gained. But such an arguer may also choose to ignore the ill-will argument and simply return to his original argument about American property. This is a risk he should take only in the event of overwhelming concern on the part of his auditors for American property. Otherwise he can be accused effectively of ignoring the opposite.

SHIFTING THE BURDEN

Shifting the burden may be charged against an arguer who takes a position and makes a claim and then demands that someone else prove that he is wrong. "There is a God and I challenge anyone to prove to me that there isn't." By his first statement, the arguer makes his claim and then immediately begs off any responsibility for proving his claim. His success frequently depends on the willingness of someone else in the group to take up the challenge rather than saying, "You made the claim, you prove it."

OVERSTATING A CLAIM

Of considerable interest to federal agencies dealing with advertisements is the problem of companies which overstate the claim. Are there really more vitamins in this food product than in any other? Does the dog food advertised really contain more meat? Will the toothpaste actually control cavities? Essentially in overstated claims we ask ourselves to what extent the claim is supported by the evidence system developed. Overstated claim is frequently used as a source of humor, as when American flags, rockets, Fourth of July celebrations and pompous orators are shown extolling the virtues of a particular gasoline. Volkswagon, recognizing something about the saturation of the American public with overstating claims developed a whole advertising campaign on its opposite, "Think Small."

HASTY GENERALIZATION

Where the examples are inadequate in number or unrepresentative of the area to be generalized, an arguer may be charged with hasty generalization. We have discussed this problem in some greater detail in Chapter 5 in our discussion of specific instances, as we have also discussed a number of the problems of statistical argument and testimony.

INSUFFICIENT CAUSE

A charge that is fundamental to any causal argument is the claim that an insufficient cause has been presented. If we argue that cigarette smoking causes lung cancer, we must develop, as the Surgeon General's office has, an extensive body of data to convince people that we have found a sufficient cause, one to which ⋅ is worth giving adherence. For what is the difference between the statement: "Cigarette smoking causes lung cancer," and the statement: "Toads cause warts?" If I pick up a toad and two days later a wart begins to develop on my hand, I may start the process of establishing a causal link and for some persons this will be adequate, but for many, we will need greater support for the cause.

A common version of insufficient cause goes under the impressve Latin designation, *"Post hoc, ergo propter hoc,"* or "after this, therefore because of this." It is illustrated by the toad example. I picked up the toad, then I got a wart, therefore, the toad was the cause of the wart. There is, of course, a time sequence factor that is essential in all cause to effect reasoning. If something is to cause something else, it must take place, or exist, before the something else happens. But before I got the wart I also washed my hands, drank a glass of milk, and did innumerable other things. To determine which one caused the wart requires much more evidence than I have provided myself with in making the innocent toad into the guilty wart-maker!

INADEQUATE SIGN

Inadequate sign is a problem akin to insufficient cause. We can operate with reasonable certainty that a For Sale sign in a front yard indicates that that house is for sale, but to what extent can we judge an increasing divorce rate, for instance, to be a sign of lower morality, or length of hair to be a sign of social rebellion. Inadequate sign will be one of those arguments that is quite closely related to the social values.

INADEQUATE ANALOGIES

Inadequate analogies are also tied in very directly with questions of immediate audience understanding and social values. Once again, the older distinctions between a literal and a figurative analogy are meaningless in the present context. All analogies are figurative and they base their truth value on the extent to which they established for receivers the impression that they are literal. In other words, there must be a sufficient number of similarities on important characteristics to lead one to believe that, in the argument under consideration, the claim is warranted.

ALLNESS

The problem of allness is, of course, the problem rooted in formal logic and the tests of the syllogism. If one is to reason enthymematically, he needs statements that will have a degree of universal application. To say that some, or a few, or even quite a few adult birds fly does not assert very much confidence in the conclusion that bird X flies. Therefore, we have ways of providing the universal application psychologically. Probabilities are fundamental to general argumentation and most of what we know we are not "certain" about. But the mind has a tendency to close around warrants and to accept claims as if the warrants on which they were based were certain. We vote the straight Democratic ticket even though we know that not all Democrats are fit for office, that not all Democrats are better than all Republicans, or American Independents or Socialist Laborites, or what have you. We may even break discipline and vote for a Republican now and again but that is a special case with a special series of arguments to justify it that does not dampen our enthusiasm for the general warrant, unstated and denied if anyone states it, that all Democrats are superior to all Republicans. This allness characteristic, of accepting warrants as being universally true and treating them as such even though we do not believe or acknowledge that they are, is an essential characteristic in argumentative decision making. There is a point at which a person must accept his arguments as being true and live with it. If we did not, we would be confused by a catalog of continual changing premises that would yield confusion and frustration but would yield no decision.

Yet this very fact makes a vast number of our arguments susceptible to the charge that we are falling into the trap of accepting as universally correct (certain) something which is less so and of demanding that a reservation be placed on our argument. The allness tendency too often leads us to put aside reservations and ignore rather obvious exceptions. If left uncontrolled, it can have a very negative influence on the decision making process. If one closes on an allness warrant before he has adequately considered the reservations to it, he may find himself making decisions on the basis of unlimited claim that will not serve as well as some other, perhaps modified, claim.

CONCLUSIONS

Argumentation is not a single rational system of decision making. Different systems frequently work from quite contrary notions of what good argument is. But there are some general notions about the characteristics of argument that we can study. These notions have been developed over the years from the general standards of rationality set in our society. They are particularly influenced by the standards of formal logic, although those standards cannot be directly applied to testing reasoning in general argumentation.

The best method for understanding argument is by a modification of Stephen Toulmin's scheme. In this model we can chart how people argue for claims by linking them to data (in the form of assertions about the data) and making the claim legitimate by means of a warrant.

The types of arguments that are most useful for our purposes are: enthymematic, generalization, causal, sign, analogy, authority and definition. These arguments will frequently be found mixed together in single paragraphs, even sentences, and will sometimes be found in chains of reasoning.

Serious students of argumentation will concern themselves with some of the problems of argument (a term adopted to avoid the rigid interpretations of the term fallacy). Such awareness will help to make one's own arguments less vulnerable to attack and reveal some of the weaknesses in opposition arguments. Most useful for our examination are the following: *non-sequitur*, circular, irrelevancy, ignoring the opposite, shifting the burden, overstatement, hasty generalization, insufficient cause, inadequate sign, inadequate analogy, and allness.

PROJECTS

1. Read some of the literature cited in this chapter on the relation between the human thought process and formal logic. Conduct a class discussion with others in your class who have done the same. To what extent do you believe formal logic relates to the thought process? To what extent do either relate to the decision making process as we have discussed it in this book?

2. With others in your class divide up the types of arguments and each person bring in an example of one type of argument found in a contemporary publication. Explain the nature of the argument (perhaps diagramming it on the board) and explain the potential problems you see in it.

3. Conduct a class discussion on the subject of the problems found in the argument following Chapter 3 (pp. 65–71). What problems would seem obvious to the majority of Americans? What problems exist for specialized audiences, such as younger people, lawyers, or policemen?

4. Engage in direct clash debates in class where one person advances a specific argument and another responds to it. What are the main disagreements? What problems does each person identify in the other's arguments?

5. Prepare a short speech of a minute or two in which you support a single claim of fact or value. Make it as convincing as possible but embody in it one of the problems of argument. See if your classmates can detect the problem.

5

Support:

Evidence

The simplest and most frequent argumentation situation is the statement advanced by one person and adhered to by another without development. It is an assertion: "It's a hot day today," "he's a lousy cook," "don't trust her with your car," "Russia is a menace." The authors of all these assertions and the persons who receive them and give them adherence could support them with reasons. But sometimes the receivers do not give adherence; they ask questions or pose counter claims: "Not as hot as yesterday," "Really?", "Why not?", "That's an old wornout theory." When that happens, arguments *must* be developed. They may be developed by linking them to other arguments and they may be developed by adding supporting material.

The support of arguments is the subject of this chapter and the two chapters to follow. In this chapter we will examine those forms of support that have been traditionally considered more substantial: specific instances, statistics, and testimony. In Chapter 6 we will examine the social value systems that support argument and in Chapter 7 we will consider how credibility supports an argument.

Because we begin with instances, statistics and testimony, call them evidence, and acknowledge that they are traditionally considered more substantial, we do not mean to imply that they are more important than social values and credibility in gaining the adherence of listeners. They are

97

a traditional starting point in the study of support. Experimental studies on the subject of the effectiveness of evidence are mixed in their results but there are enough positive data to make evidence worthy of careful attention.[1]

FORMS OF EVIDENCE

For purposes of this chapter, *evidence* refers to *specific instances, statistics* and *testimony* as they support a claim in such a way as to cause the receiver to give adherence to that claim.

Evidence need not be a part of the spoken or written argument in order to contribute to adherence. By looking again at the simplest form of argument we can see how support is frequently provided by the person receiving the argument. "He's a lousy cook" may receive instant adherence because of meals one has eaten. Experience provides the support. No arguer can ignore the evidence, the specific instances in this case in the mind of the receiver that may strengthen an argument, perhaps even make additional evidence unnecessary. Neither can he ignore evidence in the mind of the listener, which runs counter to his argument. A listener's unstated negative evidence must be met as surely as the evidence of an active opponent. Although the emphasis in this chapter is on the way in which persons may strengthen arguments through the use of evidence, audience held, but unstated, evidence should always be considered.

SPECIFIC INSTANCES

Specific instances are used whenever an argument involves the giving of examples and illustrations. These terms—examples and illustrations—are found more frequently in contemporary usage than specific instances but they are used to mean essentially the same thing. They refer to both the development of an argument by generalization and the illustration of a

[1] Loren J. Anderson and Kenneth E. Andersen, "Research on the Relationship of Reasoning and Evidence to Message Acceptance," unpub. paper presented to the Speech Association of American Convention, New York, December, 1969; John A. Kline, "Interaction of Evidence and Readers' Intelligence on the Effects of Silent Message," *Quarterly Journal of Speech 55* (December 1969), pp. 407–413; and James C. McCroskey, "A Summary of Experimental Research on the Effects of Evidence in Persuasive Communication, *Quarterly Journal of Speech 55* (April 1969), pp. 169–176.

general principle once established.[2] Either word, example or illustration, could substitute for specific instance in the following statement: "The years 1950 to the present are specific instances that prove that vegetable prices in the market rise every December." Whatever term is used, the phenomenon that we are interested in here will constitute support only when so perceived by the receiver. Specific instances, whether previously known to the receiver or provided as a part of the argument, constitute backing for the argument. *U.S. News and World Report*, in a report on the June 21, 1973 U.S. Supreme Court decision that obscenity would be judged by local standards and be covered by a stricter definition of obscenity, generalized that:

"A survey by 'U.S. News and World Report' staff-members indicates that such [increased state and local] activities are rapidly increasing in many areas. Among their findings: New York—*Police raided a production center for "blue movies" and confiscated thousands of prints valued at more than $750,000. . . .* Austin, Tex.—*Sex-movie theaters have closed down or switched to soft-core films. . . .* Chicago—*A Cook County grand jury indicted six theater executives on charges of obscenity for showing an erotic movie, "Deep Throat". . . .* New Orleans—*Two adult movie theaters have been closed, and a bookstore has agreed to stop selling prurient material. . . .* Washington, D.C.—*Dealers in erotic publications are voluntarily cleaning their shelves of sexually explicit picture books and replacing them mainly with traditional "girlie" magazines. . . .* Detroit—*Four "topless" and "bottomless" go-go dancers employed at three metropolitan-area bars have been found guilty of indecent exposure. . . .* Los Angeles—*It's business as usual for most pornography shops here. Dozens of stores and theaters still sell sex-oriented films and books and admissions to movies containing actual sex acts."*[3]

Six of the seven cities served as examples to support the generalization that local activity was increasing. Anyone using these examples would do so because they intend that they will be regarded as real examples. The statements about each city are meant to stand as specific instances that will be perceived as factual statements.

There is a special kind of specific instance that we shall call the *hypo-*

---

[2] Perelman argues that "whereas an example is designed to establish a rule, the role of illustration is to strengthen adherence to a known and accepted rule." Chaim Perelman and L. Olbrechts-Tyteca, *The New Rhetoric* (Notre Dame, Indiana: University of Notre Dame Press, 1969), p. 357.

[3] "Crackdown on Smut," Copyright *U.S. News & World Report, Inc., 75* (July 1973), p. 26.

thetical example, which is used where real examples are not available. It illustrates a principle to the extent that it is perceived as a real instance. A speaker is using hypothetical examples when he argues for conservation as follows:

> The person who gives his old newspapers to the Boy Scouts is a conservationist.
>
> The woman who takes her bottles to a recycling center is a conservationist.
>
> The man who turns the heat down at his home and his office is a conservationist.

And, by the way, the examples we have just given are hypothethical examples.

STATISTICS

Statistics are basically a compacting of specific instances. Statistics provide us a means for talking about a large number of specific instances without citing every one. No one would think of naming every one of the 140,000 workers, most of them women, who collectively were owed more than $72 million in violation of the Equal Pay Act since it was passed in 1963.[4] The need here is to know the number of persons who were owed and the statistics serve the purpose. They function in argument only because receivers believe, however, that there are specific persons and specific amounts of money behind the statements.

Statistics have come to mean more than raw data—statistical measures are also applied to such data to give a basis of comparison and a measure of significance. Some might want to know that the amount owed under the law was $14.8 million in fiscal 1971 and $18 million in 1972.[5]

Measures such as percentage are used as a basis of comparison. In 1973, the Environmental Protection Agency could define the persentage of a body of water's shore line that failed to meet minimum standards and compare one body of water to another on the basis of percentage of miles of water polluted. Here are the top dozen according to their 1973 figures, reprinted from *U.S. News & World Report*.[6]

---

[4] "Flexing a Muscle," *The Wall Street Journal* (August 22, 1973), p. 1.
[5] "Flexing a Muscle."
[6] "New Hurdles in the Drive Against Pollution," Copyright *U.S. News and World Report, Inc.* 75 (July 30, 1973), p. 34.

Tampa Bay	66%
Cuyahoga River (O)	58%
Monongahela River (Pa., W. Va.)	55%
Savannah River	49%
Ohio River	46%
Lake Ontario	46%
Lake Erie, western shore	45%
Mobile Bay	43%
Niagara River	40%
Lower Hudson River	36%
Green River (Wyo.)	33%
Lower Colorado River	31%

Whole systems of analysis are necessary to define some statistical evidence. When the U.S. Department of Labor says that wholesale prices rose 0.3% between August and November 1971. 6.9% between November 1971 and January 1973, and 24.4% between January and June 1973, they not only are using a comparative measure, percentages, but it is based on a specialized recording system and a selected list of wholesale prices to be examined. Thus, statistics vary from raw data to complex measures that become arguments in themselves.

TESTIMONY

Testimony is the third form of evidence that we will discuss in this chapter. If you recall, it also can stand alone as argument by authority. Just as argument by authority relies on the credibility of the source cited, so the primary strength of testimony as support is its capacity to add credibility to the argument.

There are two types of testimony: *testimony of fact* and the *testimony of opinion*. In the one, a writer or speaker uses the credibility of another to support an argument through statements about the "facts" of the situation. Of course, it does not prove anything about what the facts are but it provides a duplication of perception that will help gain adherence for the claimed fact. In the second, he calls on another for his opinions about the situation. Two examples from an article by Emma Rothschild, "What is the 'Energy Crisis'?" will illustrate:

"Testimony of Fact. *Another indication of the complexity of these questions was given in the press briefing that followed the presidential energy message. Deputy Secretary of the Treasury William Simon complained that 'at present there are no new (U.S.) refineries underway,' and that 'this is in a period where all the refineries are operating at 100 percent of their effective capacities.' Later, Mr. Simon was asked to explain the new regulations that allow extra imports of crude oil.*

"Q. If the refiners are at 100 percent capacity, of what value and what will happen to the new crude oil that comes in here for refining?

"Mr. Simon: There are refineries inland that are not operating at 100 percent.

"Q. So your 100 percent was a very vague number?

"Mr. Simon: No, it wasn't vague. A great majority of them are functioning at 100 percent.

Testimony of Opinion. *A study of energy use in* Scientific American *comments that the shortage of liquid fuels now presents 'no real technological problem . . . along the distribution chain,' and that 'it is easier than keeping grocery shelves stocked." Even supplying a satisfactory 'mix' of petroleum products—heating oil in the winter, or industrial fuels, or gasoline in the summer 'driving season'—is comparable to the challenge grocery stores face when they supply lemonade in July and turkeys in the fall."*[7]

The distinction between fact and opinion is not so great as some would like to make it. Mr. Simon's statement certainly supports the idea that the questions are complex and it seems to provide "factual" information while the *Scientific American* is clearly expressing an opinion. But Mr. Simon's statement is also an opinion of sorts that he wants his reader to share.

The distinction between fact and opinion testimony is a very important distinction to certain specialized forms of argumentation such as the Law. Some of the biases of these specialized forms have been incorporated into our practices in general argumentation. For this reason we test factual testimony by asking about the experience of the testifier, his access to direct perception of the facts, his expertise on the matter at hand and the scope of the statement he makes. In general, good factual testimony comes from an expert source, with direct knowledge, and who makes a careful delineation of the fact to which he testifies. Even so, we must remember that he is only testifying about facts as he observes them. He is not giving facts and any time a person is involved, opinion must be close by.

[7] Emma Rothschild, "What is the 'Energy Crisis'?" *The New York Review of Books*, 20 (July 19, 1973), p. 24.

GENERAL PRINCIPLES FOR THE USE OF EVIDENCE

It is difficult to set down specific principles for the use of evidence. Since the audience addressed is so important in determining the believability of an argument, specific universal rules are not very useful. There are, of course, many rules that have grown up, which serve as a basis for providing help to the speaker in preparing his argument, but those rules can only serve as general principles that are accepted by most persons in our society. It is in that spirit then, of finding principles, which will meet the standards of the general society, that we look to some general principles in the use of evidence.

1. INSTANCES SHOULD BE REPRESENTATIVE

This is just another way of saying that each communicator should choose the best specific instances available to prove his generalization. In the example cited earlier on the impact of a 1973 Supreme Court obscenity ruling and its effect on local law enforcement, we selected seven cities. Do those cities represent the nation? From knowing what is happening in those seven do we have a fair notion of what is going on nationally? Are enough smaller cities included? Small towns? State police action? All of these questions and more come to mind. In the final analysis, the key question is this: to what extent is a listener or reader willing to believe that these examples are representative, and, therefore, reason enough for him to give his adherence to the claim that state and local law enforcement action has increased since the 1973 ruling?

2. INSTANCES SHOULD BE IN SUFFICIENT NUMBER

In order to form a satisfactory generalization, enough specific instances must be provided to convince the receiver of the argument that it is believable. Again, in the obscenity argument, are seven cities enough to justify the generalization that there is increased local action to enforce obscenity statutes? Even where used for purposes of illustration alone, one must wonder how many examples are necessary for clarity. Perhaps one example will clarify an idea but more may be needed in order to provide clarity for larger numbers of receivers. If we say that pollution is a serious problem in America and use the smog problem in Los Angeles as an example, we may be able to generate a good deal of interest and clarity. However, adding noise pollution in New York and water pollution in the Great Lakes might make pollution clearer to all receivers.

3. NEGATIVE INSTANCES SHOULD BE ACCOUNTED FOR

Particularly with knowledgeable receivers one makes a mistake if he fails to account for negative instances. Speakers or writers who fail to account for negative instances of which a receiver has knowledge will lose credibility. Even with people who do not know the negative instances, some acknowledgement of them may strengthen an argument. In the obscenity generalization the story may seem more trustworthy because the one exception to the generalization, Los Angeles, is included.

4. VALUE CHARACTERISTICS OF INSTANCES SHOULD BE GIVEN

It is important to let the receiver know what value judgments would be placed on the example. Phrases like, "the *best* example I can think of at the moment is . . . ;" "The Viet Nam war is a *good* example of American Imperialism;" or "a *typical* example of the efforts to clear up water pollution is the activity on the Connecticut River," help to give receivers a more specific idea of the value the sender puts on the example.

5. ENOUGH DETAIL SHOULD BE GIVEN TO MAKE ALL INSTANCES SEEM REAL

People tend to give greater adherence to more specific examples.[8] Even hypothetical examples should be given the characteristics of real examples. Suppose one were to speak on the traffic congestion and develop a hypothetical case to explain what it is like. That hypothetical example might look like this: "You might start home tomorrow night and find yourself in a massive traffic jam." But it would be better like this: "Suppose as you leave work at 5:00 tomorrow night you turn onto the freeway on the ramp at Temple Street. All you need is one car out of gas just beyond Silver Lake Boulevard to close down the Hollywood Freeway and there you are, stuck for hours in the sweltering heat."

6. THE EXPERIENCE OF THE AUDIENCE SHOULD BE USED

Although the arguer should provide enough examples and realize the mistake of inadequate support, the other side of that coin needs to be

[8] Kline, p. 412.

remembered. The tedious repetition of examples for audiences who already know them can be injurious to the effectiveness of an argument. Therefore, arguers should remind listeners of what they already know and use that information as much as possible, but there is experimental evidence and common sense tradition to support the idea that the repetition of evidence that is already known does not change attitudes.[9]

7. INSTANCES AND STATISTICAL DATA SHOULD BE CURRENT

It seems obvious that the most up-to-date information is superior to less current information in assessing the present situation. Even for historical study, more current information should be more useful because historical evidence is frequently cumulative. That is, every new piece of information adds to the generalization one is able to make. Also, more recent statistics may be more useful in historical argument because more sophisticated statistical measures have been employed.

8. INSTANCES AND STATISTICAL DATA SHOULD COME FROM THE MOST RELIABLE SOURCES

One of the most serious problems to be guarded against is the bias of the source. This is important, not only because of the danger of not drawing a more accurate generalization, but because such bias, when recognized by receivers, will damage the argument. Even though it is sometimes possible to win adherence through the use of sources that some receivers do not recognize as biased, it is not wise to do so. If others see the source as biased, they will hurt your arguments' adherence by word of mouth. Even information that is not biased but *appears* to be from a biased source is poor evidence because of audience reaction. At the time of this writing, a prominent aspirin company is offering a free booklet that they claim explains about aspirin. We have no way of knowing if the information provided by it is accurate but we are confident that many people would distrust it because it is offered by a biased source.

For each example or statistical study which you take from someone else, ask yourself the extent to which that source is biased and the extent to which it will appear biased to your receiver. The Brookings Institute, the Bureau of Labor Statistics, the Gallup Poll and a host of other sources

[9] McCroskey, p. 175.

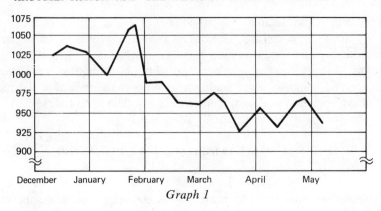

Graph 1

are generally regarded as unbiased. Insurance companies' actuarial statistics, which such companies have reason beyond public service to gather, are generally considered accurate. University research foundations supported by private companies have a variety of levels of confidence attached to them. Company research agencies are usually suspect. These are only some examples to illustrate that a wide variety in bias levels are perceived by receivers. Bias should be carefully considered because it can have a serious influence on the level of adherence one is willing to give an argument.

9. STATISTICAL MEASURE SHOULD BE CAREFULLY CONSIDERED

For our purpose, statistical measures basically answer the question of how typical the examples are. Darrell Huff in the book, *How To Lie With Statistics*, gives many of the problems of statistical argument in layman's language. One could, of course, spend a lifetime of study and become an expert in statistical argument and its errors. For the moment, however, here are a few of the "lies:"[10]

"The Sample With The Built-In Bias."   If you asked your classmates what they thought about euthenasia and they approved it 15 to 5 (that's 3 to 1), that would be impressive, but if 10 others had refused to answer your question, you might have a built-in bias that you were not accounting for. Thus, the potential actual split was 15 to 15 or 25 to 5. The real proportions could thus be as great as 50 to 50 or 5 to 1.

"The Gee-Whiz Graph."   Graphic representation of statistical data can

---

[10] Darrell Huff, *How to Lie With Statistics* (New York: W. W. Norton & Co., Inc., 1954).

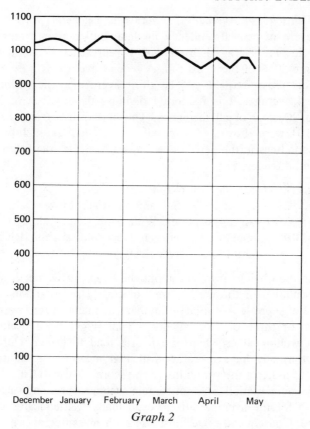

Graph 2

provide a visual clarification. It can also mislead. All graphs should be
carefully examined to be sure that they provide information in a form
that reflects the best interpretation of the data. Here is a graph of the
weekly closing prices of the stock market for one six-month period. They
could be graphed in many ways. Graphs 1 and 2 show two of them.
What these graphs show is dependent on the argument being made and the
level of sophistication of the person to whom it is addressed. Are stock
prices relatively stable as appears to be true in Graph 2? Do they indicate
an erratic market as Graph 1 would seem to imply? Did the stock market
begin a serious decline in February? Does it matter that November 14 of
the previous year was the first closing over 1000? Would prices of a year
earlier help to understand the meaning of these graphs? Remember such
graphs as these are arguments and they are no better than the analysis
and evidence that goes into them.

"The Well Chosen Average."   Average is a general word standing for some measure of central tendency in data, but there are many ways of measuring it. One average is a *median*. It represents the point above and below where 50% of the items fall. A second average is a *mode*, a figure that appears most frequently. The third average is the *mean*. It is an arithmetical average. It is found by dividing the number of items in a series into the total of all the items. The master list, from the examples on page 101 were drawn, of national waters, that as of July 1973 had polluted shorelines in the percentages shown, provides the following measures of central tendency:

Median: 18%—Middle Colorado River.
Mode: 2%—Snake River, Sacramento River, Lower Columbia River.
          3%—Arkansas River, Willamette River, San Joaquin River.
Mean: 21.9%—somewhere between Upper Mississippi River (23%) and Illinois River (21%).

Ignoring the obvious problem about the extent to which these statistics are representative of the nation, we can clearly see that the mode is of little use. But suppose that a large number (as many as ten) were grouped in the two or three percent category. That might be a useful measure because it would tell us where the figures tend to group. Unfortunately, we do not usually have more sophisticated measures, such as standard deviation, to indicate the variability of the scores. Most statistical data used in general argumentation does not contain such measures and such measures are difficult for the average citizen, even many well-educated citizens, to understand. Consequently, we must use such measures as we have available, but we must use them with care.

"Much Ado About Practically Nothing."   On the study of water pollution mentioned earlier, one must decide how much difference is a difference. Obviously, there is a significant difference between Tampa Bay (66%) and the Sacramento River (2%). But should residents along the Illinois River (21%) feel superior to residents along the Upper Mississippi River (23%)? Such a difference is insignificant and might be accounted for by an error in data collecting.

10.   STATISTICS SHOULD BE MADE CLEARER THROUGH COMPARISON

If we live near the Connecticut River, it helps not only to know that twelve percent of its shoreline does not meet the minimum standards, but how does it compare with other Northeastern Rivers, such as the Hudson or the Hoosatanic? And even though it is not a significant comparison, it does increase interest in the problem to know that it takes 81,150 tank carloads of gasoline to meet U.S. needs, and that is enough to "make a train 999 miles in length, long enough to stretch from Washington, D.C. to Kansas City."[11]

11. TESTIMONY IS USUALLY BASED ON CREDIBILITY MEASURES

There is no point here in repeating the information contained in Chapter 7 about credibility. Quite clearly, the purpose of testimony is to provide credibility to an assertion by adding a second person or agency to its support. The trustworthiness and competence of the source of the testimony is essential to its effectiveness.

To strengthen credibility, a more specific source is more valuable than a vague one. Note these citations taken from a 1973 article on food prices:

"Robert Onstead, president of Randal's Supermarkets in Houston, said . . . ."

"Jewel Food Stores in Chicago, the area's largest grocery retailer, reported . . . ."

"Canners in the Southeast say . . . ."

"A San Francisco food chain spokesman said . . . ."[12]

The first two are stronger than the last two because they are more specific, although the third one gains some strength by implying that this is a group opinion.

FIELD DEPENDENCE OF EVIDENCE

There are special cases where evidence, which is considered acceptable in one field, will not be accepted in another. It is called field dependence. In some fields, a kind of credibility has been established for certain message characteristics regardless of the credibility of the sender of the message.

---

[11] "The Gasoline Shortage—When Will It End?" *U.S. News and World Report*, 75 (July 2, 1973), p. 29.

[12] "More Bad News For Food Shoppers," *U.S. News and World Report*, 75 (July 30, 1973), p. 53.

HEARSAY EVIDENCE

Legal practice, for instance, does not give credibility to *heresay* evidence. That is, one person's statement that someone else told him of an event is often not admissable. Only what that person saw himself is admissable. The law makes that provision because only statements from witnesses who can be held responsible are accepted. But in general argumentation the reverse is frequently the case. When a reporter says that the President of the United States (or even a "usually reliable source") told him something, it has a potential for developing a greater adherence to his argument than if he claimed he observed it himself.

ORDINARY AND EXPERT EVIDENCE

A similar situation exists in the difference between an *ordinary* and an *expert* witness. In such argumentative situations as the law court, intercollegiate debate and humanistic scholarship, the expert witness, particularly on a complex problem, is preferred. But in some circles of general argumentation this is not so. The view of a lawmaker is not always better than the ordinary citizen on legislation. It all depends on the perception the receiver has of the credibility of the witness.

Later, we will look at some of the special characteristics of argument, including evidence in different fields.[13] At this point it may be useful to observe that the problem with field dependence in evidence is not merely that some evidence will be accepted in one field and rejected in another, but also, it is a matter of degree.

RELUCTANT EVIDENCE

Reluctant testimony from a witness who is antagonistic to one's purpose is generally considered good evidence in all kinds of argumentation situations.[14] It has long been considered the best evidence in a public debate to use an opponent's statements in opposition to his position.[15]

[13] For an interesting view of difference in evidence in historical, legal, scientific and journalistic argument, see: Russel R. Windes and Arthur Hastings, *Argumentation and Advocacy* (New York: Random House, 1965), pp. 104–156.

[14] Anderson and Andersen, p. 7.

[15] See McCroskey, p. 172, for a study which tends to discredit this theory somewhat.

NEGATIVE EVIDENCE

Negative evidence, or the absence of evidence, is of little use in scientific scholarship but quite proper in historical scholarship.

John Kaplan, in his defense of the Warren Commission Report on the Assassination of President Kennedy, uses negative evidence to reject the charge of New Orleans District Attorney Garrison that Clay Shaw of that city was part of a conspiracy with Lee Harvey Oswald to assassinate the President.

"But even if the charge that Clay Shaw agreed with Oswald to assassinate the President were taken as true, the voluminous newspaper coverage indicates that it is hard to connect this agreement with the actual killing. First, there is no indication that the alleged agreement to have more than one person participate in the killing was followed. Moreover, at the time of the plot there was no way to know that President Kennedy would go to Dallas, where Oswald lived. And Oswald's job at the Texas School Book Depository was secured through means clearly unrelated to a conspiracy at a time when there was no indication that even if the President came to Dallas his route would take him past the depository."[16]

WRITTEN EVIDENCE

There is a clear bias in law for written over unwritten evidence. Senator Sam Ervin was fond of quoting Lord Coke on the subject during the 1973 Senate Hearings into the breakin of the Democratic National Headquarters at Watergate, "One scratch of the pen is worth more than the slippery memory of a multitude of witnesses." This bias for written evidence is not as strong in general argumentation as it is in legal and historical scholarship, but it probably has some general validity.

Thus, each field will have its own interpretation of the degree of reliance that can be put on evidence: "expert" or "ordinary," "original" or "hearsay," "willing" or "reluctant," "positive" or "negative," "written" or "unwritten." There may be some general bias for one or the other in each of these pairs. The arguer will do best to think clearly about the standards of the field in which he undertakes to argue before he forms rules for good or poor evidence.

[16] John Kaplan, "The Assassins," *The Historian as Detective*, Robin W. Winks, ed., (New York: Harper and Row, 1968), p. 411.

CONCLUSIONS

Arguments that need support to gain the adherence of those to whom they are addressed may be supported by using evidence, values and credibility. Evidence, the traditional term for specific instances, statistics and testimony, is the subject of this chapter.

Specific instances may be used to develop a generalization or illustrate a general principle. They can be real instances or hypothetical ones. Statistics provide a means for compacting examples, for talking about a large number of specific instances at one time. Statistical measures provide the basis for averaging and comparisons with a wide variety of sophistication. Testimony is a means of adding credibility to a message. It may be testimony about fact or about opinion.

There are a number of general principles by which we may be guided in using specific instance, statistics and testimony. All are based on the position of the audience, but they provide general guidelines.

1. Instances should be representative.
2. Instances should be in sufficient number.
3. Negative instances should be accounted for.
4. Value characteristics of instances should be given.
5. Enough detail should be given to make all instances seem real.
6. The experience of the audience should be used.
7. Instances and statistical data should be current.
8. Instances and statistical data should come from the most reliable sources.
9. Statistical measures should be carefully considered.
   a. Avoid "the sample with the built in bias."
   b. Avoid "the gee-whiz graph."
   c. Avoid "the well-chosen average."
   d. Avoid "much ado about practically nothing."
10. Statistics should be made clearer through comparison.
11. Testimony is usually based on credibility measures.

Some forms of evidence are field dependent; that is, they have different values depending on the field in which they are used. Hearsay evidence is suspect in a court of law but quite acceptable in general argumentation. Many fields regard the expert witness as superior to the ordinary witness but this is not always so in general argumentation. Reluctant testimony depends for its value on the extent to which the author of it is clearly perceived to be reluctant. Negative evidence is useful in historical but not in scientific argument.

PROJECTS

1. Develop a single argument either in writing or orally in which you support it with specific instances, statistics and testimony.

2. Make a careful observation of about ten television commercials. To what extent do they use support as we have discussed it here? Are there differences among commercials? Which are more convincing to you? Why? (Remember the supporting materials discussed in this chapter are not the only causes of adherence.)

3. Write a short paper evaluating the support in a contemporary argumentative essay or speech.

6

Support:

Values

In our study of the decision making process we have seen how giving reasons is a natural characteristic of, at least, western man and how this is an essential condition for the practice of argumentation. Fundamental to this reason giving activity are the values held by the persons receiving the arguments. These values, when attached to arguments, are vital in gaining adherence. In Chapter 3 we observed that from the earliest point in decision making, when we attempt to identify a claim from a "feeling of doubt," we arrange the values in receiver oriented hierarchies and use them, along with the facts, truths and presumptions, to narrow the possible alternatives and select the claim. Once claims are selected, these value hierarchies provide a basis for finding the issues. In Chapter 4 we have observed how values are essential to every argument. They function from one time to another as claim, data, backing, and, particularly, warrant. There can be no doubt that values are essential supports in any argumentation situation and that their careful study is mandatory.

WHAT ARE VALUES?

"A Value," says anthropologist Clyde Kluckhohn, "is a conception, explicit or implicit, distinctive of an individual or characteristic of a group,

115

of the desirable that influences the selection from available modes, means and ends of action."[1] This definition is a working basis for understanding how values function in argumentation. A value is a conception, abstracted from what people say and do, from which arguments may be built. It need not be explicitly stated. It may be, and frequently (perhaps most frequently) is implied. It serves as a standard for what is good or bad and is used by individuals to select the way they will act and speak.

There is no such thing as a valueless statement. Even the scientist's careful statement about what he observes to be true has behind it the values of careful observation and a desire to reflect nature. Thus, values are important even to claims of fact. Values constitute, along with source credibility and "evidence," the interactive material on which people judge arguments to be worthy of adherence.

Values do not usually appear alone in arguments. Usually they appear in value systems, that is, as a set of linked claims.[2] We hear people argue for better treatment of American Indians, not on the basis of a single value of justice or mercy, but on the basis of a series of values that link together and reflect a unified system wherein each value will be perceived as compatible with every other. Indeed, one of our major arguments over values is over the compatability of values that are frequently linked together. We hear people questioned who argue for freedom as a primary value and discriminate against minorities. We know of those who wonder how someone can oppose legalized marijuana and still get drunk on Saturday night.We know that some people consider it inconsistent for someone to argue for morality and still say he does not believe in God. All these are examples of arguments about the consistency of values in a given system. They come about because values do not stand alone. They work in integrated systems.

VALUES AND DRIVES, NEEDS, WANTS, AND DESIRES

In explaining argumentation we have described a system for understanding human behavior that seems to ignore some long accepted terms for describing that behavior. Under a variety of labels (needs, wants,

---

[1] Clyde Kluckhohn, "Values and Value-Orientations in the Theory of Action," *Toward a General Theory of Action*, Talcott Parsons and Edward A. Shils, eds., (New York: Harper and Row, 1951), p. 395.

[2] Clyde Kluckhohn, calls these "value orientations." "A Value Orientation may be defined as a generalized and organized conception, influencing behavior, of nature, of man's place in it, of man's relation to man and of the desirable and nondesirable as they may relate to man-environment and interhuman relations," p. 411.

desires, drives), the needs of individuals have been considered a motivation for human action. Are these now to be considered nonexistent? Do we have a process, which does not involve them, and if so, how can that be? If there are basic needs that motivate people to act, may we ignore these in developing an understanding of argument?

Although needs, wants, desires and drives are defined differently by different writers, they all are, at least in part, an attempt to find a replacement for the discredited notion of instincts.[3] Drives and needs are terms that particularly draw on physiological origins. Drives for self-preservation, sex, satisfaction of hunger and thirst, and safety are used to explain human behavior and they all are closely tied to the physiological. In time the concept of drives and needs was expanded to include less physiological ones such as ego expansion, sociality, and financial well-being. Terms like wants and desires are more applicable to these socially oriented motivations.[4]

One would be foolish to argue that there are no basic human needs. Obviously, in a situation of extreme hunger, the desire for food will cause persons to violate the most basic value systems of the society such as lying, cheating, stealing and even murder. Thus, in extreme cases these drives will frequently take over and dominate. But they are also mediated by social values. In times of great distress, people have given up food and water, even their lives, for others. The best we can say is that there are basic physiological needs, which influence the development of value systems, and that some needs are developed through values. Values both rise from and create needs.[5]

The primary reason why we will not deal with needs in this book is that argumentation depends much more on the value systems. In a reason giving activity where the argument seldom deals with people under serious deprivation of physiological needs, the operative value system becomes much more important and the needs become adjuncts of the value system. Furthermore, too much attention to needs will tend to distort the value analysis, put too much emphasis on the physiological, and lose the reality of argumentation as primarily a social phenomenon.

[3] For an interesting attempt at the revival of the instinct theory see Robert Ardrey, *The Territorial Imperative*, (New York: Dell Publishing Co., 1972).

[4] Anthropologist Dorothy Lee makes the interesting point that as new needs were discovered it just led to expanding the list. She argues that much of our use of the term need is in itself a reflection of our values. She says that other cultures do not have "needs" in the same sense we do. Dorothy Lee, "Are Basic Needs Ultimate?" *Journal of Abnormal and Social Psychology, 43* (1948), pp. 391–395.

[5] Lee.

VALUES, BELIEFS, AND ATTITUDES

Two other terms that we are likely to find, particularly in the psychological literature, which seem related to values, are beliefs and attitudes. Milton Rokeach has summarized the literature to show that the concept of attitudes is ambiguous to the extent where some have suggested that the term be abandoned.[6] He argues against such a solution to the problem and asks instead for a more careful definition of the terms. He defines an attitude as "a relatively enduring organization of beliefs around an object or situation predisposing one to respond in some preferential manner,"[7] "and a belief as any simple proposition, conscious or unconscious, inferred from what a person says or does and capable of being preceded by the phrase, 'I believe that . . .' "[8] Values, for Rokeach, are "abstract ideals, positive or negative, not tied to any specific attitude, object or situation, representing a person's beliefs about ideal modes of conduct and ideal terminal goals."[9] This definition is congruent with Kluckhohn's definition that we cited earlier.

A belief, then, is the smallest unit. Any simple statement like, "I believe ice cream is good," "I believe the world is round," or "I believe women should be given equal rights," will qualify as a belief. An attitude must be directed at a specific object, person or idea. It is "relatively enduring" like the attitude Blacks may have toward religion or the attitude of American Indians toward property laws or an attitude students have toward school. Attitudes are, therefore, beliefs which are organized and lasting and directed toward a specific object. Values, then, are the general conceptions that a person or group has, which he or they use as criteria to make decisions. They are both more basic than an attitude and more general.

"An adult," says Rokeach, "probably has tens or hundreds of thousands of beliefs, thousands of attitudes but only dozens of values."[10] Thus, while attitude measurement is useful for psychological research, value is more useful in argumentation. We are concerned about the values that people use to select claims and support them. Certainly, their applica-

---

[6] Milton Rokeach, *Beliefs, Attitudes and Values*, (San Francisco: Jossey-Bass, Inc., 1968), pp. 110–111.

[7] Rokeach, p. 112.

[8] Rokeach, p. 113. His classification of beliefs corresponds to the classes of claims discussed on pages 110–113. They are "descriptive or existential belief" (fact), "evaluative belief" (value), and a "prescriptive or exhortatory belief" (policy).

[9] Rokeach, p. 124.

[10] Rokeach, p. 124.

tion will result in specific attitudes that people will have from hearing the argumentation, and there may be an intermediate step in securing adherence, but values are the elements that are directly associated with the arguments.

In addition, values are more useful because they can be identified with specific behavioral phenomena. Because values and value systems have special vocabularies,[11] they reveal themselves through the language of argument and hidden value warrants and may be revealed by diagramming arguments as explained in Chapter 4.[12]

NATURE AND CLASSIFICATION OF VALUES

The theoretical and experimental literature supports the idea that there is a relatively limited and distinct group of value systems that can be identified. There are a large number of potential value patterns that might be found, Rokeach says, but the number will be limited because of the social factors involved.[13] Charles Morris, in an extensive study of the value systems across cultures, found a dominant pattern of American value systems although they were different from other cultures.[14]

[11] Clyde Kluckhohn, p. 406.

[12] Rokeach gives three reasons why values are better bases for studying human behavior than attitudes. "First, value seems to be a more dynamic concept since it has a strong motivational component as well as cognitive, affective, and behavioral components. Second, while attitude and value are both widely assumed to be determinants of social behavior, value is a determinant of attitude as well as behavior. Third, if we further assume that a person possesses considerably fewer values than attitudes, then the value concept provides us with a more economical analytic tool for describing and explaining similarities and differences between persons, groups, nations and cultures," pp. 157–158.

[13] Rokeach, p. 161. cf. Florence Rockwood Kluckhohn, "Dominant and Substitute Profiles of Cultural Orientations: Their Significance for the Analysis of Social Stratification," *Social Forces*, 28 (May 1950), p. 376; Clyde Kluckhohn, "An Anthropologist Looks at the United States," *Mirror For Man*, (New York: McGraw-Hill Book Co., Inc., 1949), pp. 228–261; Mary McEdwards, "American Values: Circa 1920–1970," *Quarterly Journal of Speech*, 57 (April 1971), pp. 173–180; Charles Morris, *Varieties of Human Values*, (Chicago: University of Chicago Press, 1956), p. 185; Jurgen Ruesch, "Communication and American Values: A Psychological Approach," *Communication: The Social Matrix of Psychiatry*, by Ruesch and Gregory Bateson, (New York: W. W. Norton, 1951), pp. 94–134; Edward D. Steele and W. Charles Redding, "The American Value System: Premises for Persuasion," *Western Speech*, 26 (Spring 1962), pp. 83–91; Richard Weaver, "Ultimate Terms in Contemporary Rhetoric," *The Ethics of Rhetoric*, (Chicago: Henry Regnery Co., 1953), pp. 211–232; Robin M. Williams, Jr., *American Society*, 3rd ed. (New York: Alfred A. Knopf, 1970), p. 438.

[14] Morris, p. 44.

LIMITATIONS ON VALUE SYSTEMS

How then do we come by such limited lists of value systems by which we order our lives and which serve so extensively in our argumentation? A number of factors limit the values that are operative in any situation. *Time* is a limit. Values, which today are dominant, may tomorrow be less high in our hierarchy.[15] Some, like parental approval, which were important to us as children, are retained when we become adults, but are less important. There are also *physical* factors that change and limit our hierarchy of values. How we feel on a particular day may change our valuation for activity and so make playing tennis less appealing. Likewise, the particular *psychological* state in which we find ourselves may change our value hierarchy. The most important factor, however, is the *social*. Morris found that the differences between cultures were the most significant ones.[16] We have already observed how physiological needs are potentially strong enough to push all other needs and social values into the background (such as a man dying of starvation), but that such a case is rare and, therefore, not important to argumentation. "The average American citizen," says Maslow, "is experiencing appetite [a value] when he says, 'I am hungry.' " Thus, even when a need seems to be operative, it is a socially determined value.[17]

MOTIVATION AND VALUES

Sometimes persons will have the value system necessary to give adherence to a particular claim but lack the *motivation*. The person in extreme thirst has great motivation. But the receiver of an argumentative message may not. Martin Fishbein observes "that motivation to comply with the norms" is a major determinant of behavior.[18] Thus, even though values indicate something about the cognitive state of the receiver, they do not necessarily predict action.[19]

[15] Morris, p. 68.
[16] Morris, p. 186.
[17] Abraham Maslow, *Motivation and Personality*, (New York: Harper and Row, 1954), p. 38.
[18] Martin Fishbein, "Attitudes and the Prediction of Behavior," *Readings in Attitude Theory and Measurement*, (New York: John Wiley & Sons, Inc., 1967), p. 490.
[19] Although the behavioral study of values has produced little study of this phenomenon there is considerable evidence in the study of attitudes which is applicable to values. Allan W. Wicker, "Attitude vs Action: The Relationship of Verbal and Overt Behavioral Responses to Attitude Objects," *Journal of Social Issues*, 25 (Autumn 1969), pp. 41–78.

It is not enough to find values that most clearly relate issue and audience. Values do not operate independently but in hierarchies. A number of factors may interfere to change that hierarchy: *personal factors* like competing values and motives ("I want to apply for the job but it would interfere with my fishing trip"); *situational factors* ("I would say 'yes' to your proposal to go downtown but my father is in the room and he wouldn't approve"); *specificity of the object* ("when I said 'no' to the blinddate I didn't realize you meant her"); *unforseen extraneous events* ("I agreed to mow the lawn but then Bob got tickets to the ballgame and I forgot it"); and *expected consequences* of the act ("I know I should serve my country, but they shoot at guys in the army").[20]

Thus, even well-chosen values can fail to gain adherence for a claim because of interfering factors which weaken motivation. Arguers need to consider not only the presence of certain values but their intensities. Even stated adherence may not predict behavior. The salesman knows that a customer's desire for a product will most frequently diminish when the salesman is not there and other values, like saving money, will become higher on the hierarchy and inertia will keep the person of low motivation from buying, even when he both desires and can afford the product.

TYPES OF VALUES

There are two types of values, "instrumental" and "terminal."[21] Instrumental values only make a statement of what is valuable: "I think democracy is the best form of government." Terminal values direct people toward end states: "Economic security is worth striving for."[22] It seems clear that terminal values are more influential in getting a level of adherence for which receivers will change behavior. They do a better job of predicting action. However, as we noted in the discussion of claims of policy, it is considerably more difficult to gain adherence for what a person's terminal action should be than it is for a statement of instrumental acquiesence. It would be pleasant to give a simple solution to this problem, but there is none. Every arguer must try to achieve his objective, but he also must understand that, for a variety of reasons apart from the message prepared and its value system, people will sometimes fail to give adherence to a value and, more frequently, fail to act on them.

[20] These are adapted from Wicker's analysis of values, pp. 67–74.

[21] Rokeach, p. 160. cf. Morris, pp. 9–12, "operative values" and "concerned values."

[22] Morris also adds a third type, object values, which refer to that which is desirable even if it is not seen as valuable or a basis of a preferred action. Such a value is a diet which one follows regardless of his liking for it; because without it he will die. In our discussion, such a value is subsumed under the other two.

DOMINANT AND LESS DOMINANT VALUES

Accepting this very real limitation on the success of an argumentation, we must still go forward with an attempt to differentiate more dominant from less dominant values in any particular culture, sub-culture or group. Williams gives four factors that help to identify the dominant values: (1) the *extensiveness* of the value—the proportion of the population giving it adherence, (2) the *duration* of the value—the length of time it lasts in the population, (3) the *intensity* of the value—the strength with which it is held, and (4) *the prestige of the persons or organizations who support it*—source credibility.[23] All of these factors will help to determine the place a value will have in a particular hierarchy. Note how source credibility affects values just as values affect source credibility. Once again we observe how in argumentation all the elements must be taken together. Despite the importance of values, they both determine the strength of other factors and are similarly influenced by them. The interaction is thorough and the arguer needs to develop his argumentation with all factors in mind, aiming for the point where all factors are maximized for audience adherence.

FINDING VALUES IN THE COMMUNICATION OF OTHERS

There is no such thing as valueless communication. If you had never heard of argumentation, or values, or looked at this book, you still could not communicate without values. Your study of values in argumentation will not give you some thing new to use but it will hopefully improve your awareness of values in argumentation and assist you to develop arguments more carefully. It should also assist you to better understand the values of other participants in argumentation. With this understanding you can relate your arguments to those of your supporters and refute those of your opponents. There are three essential ways for finding the values in the communication of others: *experimentally*, by carefully constructed tests of the relative significance of various values, through *content analysis*, by the counting of the key value terms in messages,[24] and by taking main arguments and searching for their warrants. The experimental method is not very usable for our purposes because it requires elaborate preparation.

Content analysis is more useful. Rokeach conducted a study with James Morrison using 25,000 word samples of Adolph Hitler, Barry Goldwater, and Nicolai Lenin, and two socialists to compare the uses of the terms

---

[23] Williams, p. 448.
[24] Rokeach, pp. 168–172, used both of these methods successfully.

"freedom" and "equality." In the results shown below, frequency means the number of favorable mentions minus the number of negative, and the rank represents the place the respondent gave to that value in a list of 17 terminal values.[25]

	Socialists		Hitler		Goldwater		Lenin	
	Frequency	Rank	Frequency	Rank	Frequency	Rank	Frequency	Rank
Freedom	+66	1	−48	16	+85	1	−47	17
Equality	+62	2	−71	17	−10	16	+88	1

Although the men were writing at different times, two in foreign countries and on somewhat different subjects, the results are so striking that they serve as a useful illustration. What would you suspect about the response of each to a specific proposal like fluoridation of water or equality of the sexes? Are there perhaps secondary values in the hierarchy that would help you to predict?

In much of argumentation even content analysis is too cumbersome for the kind of analysis needed. The quickest method is to examine the structure of the argument as discussed in Chapter 4. Values function primarily as warrants to claims and are frequently omitted from the actual statement of the argument but they can be identified by looking for the statement that is essential to warrant a move from assertion of data to claim. For instance, let's take a look at the following argument:

Women have been discriminated against in employment and even though there are some improvements, they still constitute less than five percent of the lawyers, dentists, and physicians. This condition must be changed so that women have equal status with men.

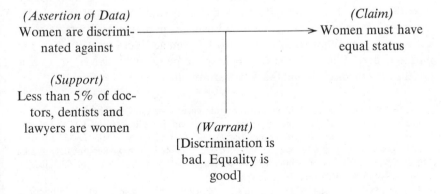

(Assertion of Data)
Women are discriminated against

(Claim)
Women must have equal status

(Support)
Less than 5% of doctors, dentists and lawyers are women

(Warrant)
[Discrimination is bad. Equality is good]

[25] Rokeach, pp. 171–172.

THE AMERICAN VALUE SYSTEMS

Although it is true that individual values can be discovered in the arguments of ourselves and others by such a careful analysis, there is a difficulty that one gets into in attempting to define a whole hierarchy of values for a person or a group. And as difficult as that is, each of us, as a participant in argumentation, should have some concept of the broad systems that most frequently bring together certain values. For this purpose, it is useful for you to have an idea of some of the most commonly acknowledged value systems.

You must approach this study with a great deal of care, however. Because, even though the six basic value systems we are about to define provide a fair view of the standard American value systems, they do not provide convenient pigeon holes into which individuals can be placed. They represent broad social groups. Some individuals (even groups) will be found outside these systems. Many individuals and groups will cross over value systems, picking and choosing from several for their hierarchy. Note how certain words appear as value terms in more than one value system. The purpose of this survey is to provide you with a beginning understanding of standard American values, not a complete catalog.[26]

THE PURITAN-PIONEER-PEASANT VALUE SYSTEM

This value system has been frequently identified as the "puritan morality" or the "Protestant ethic." It has also frequently been miscast because of the excessive emphasis placed, by some observers, on its restrictions on such personal acts as smoking and consuming alcohol.[27] Consequently, over the years, this value system has come to stand for a narrow-minded attempt to interfere in other people's business, particularly if those people are having fun. What truth there is to this image is not important to our purposes here. What is important is how the people who live by this value system view themselves and the world around them.

[26] The following material draws from a wide variety of sources. The following is an illustrative cross section of sources from a variety of disciplines: Virgil I. Baker and Ralph T. Eubanks, *Speech In Personal and Public Affairs*, (New York: David McKay, 1965), pp. 95–102; Clyde Kluckhohn, *Mirror for Man*; Stow Persons, *American Minds*, (New York: Holt, Rinehart and Winston, 1958); Jurgen Ruesch; Richard M. Weaver; Robin M. Williams, Jr., pp. 438–504.

[27] It is ironic that the original American Puritans did not have clear injunctions against such activity.

We have taken the liberty of expanding beyond the strong and perhaps too obvious religious implications of the terms "Puritan" and "Protestant." This value system is what most Americans refer to when they speak of the "pioneer spirit", which in many cases was clearly nonreligious. It also extends, we are convinced, to a strain of value brought to this country by Southern and Eastern European Catholics, Greek Orthodox and Jews who could hardly be held responsible for John Calvin's theology or even the term "Protestant Ethic." Thus, the added word "peasant," which may not be particularly accurate. Despite the great friction that existed between these foreign speaking immigrants from suspect religions and their native Protestant counterparts, they had a great deal in common as their ideological descendants do today. On many occasions after describing the "puritan morality" we have heard a Jewish student say, "that's the way my father thinks," or had a student of Italian or Polish descent say, "my grandmother talks that way all the time."

The Puritan-Pioneer-Peasant value system is rooted in the idea that persons have an obligation to themselves and those around them, and in some cases to their God, to work hard at whatever they do. In this system, man is limited in his abilities and must be prepared to fail. The great benefit is in the striving against an unknowable and frequently hostile universe. They have an obligation to others. They must be selfless. They must not waste. Some believe this is the only way to gain happiness and success. Others see it as a means to salvation. In all cases it takes on a moral orientation. Obviously, one might work hard for a summer in order to buy a new car and not be labeled a "Puritan." In this value system, the selflessness, thrift and hard work take on the characteristics of terminal values in themselves where the work has value beyond what other benefits it can bring one. People who come from this value system frequently have difficulty with retirement, because their meaning in life, indeed their pleasure, came from work.

Likewise, because work, selflessness and thrift are positive value terms in this value system, laziness, selfishness and waste are negative value terms. One can see how some adherents to this value system object to smoking, drinking, dancing, or cardplaying. These are frivolous; they take one's mind off more serious matters and waste time.

Some of the words that are associated with this value system are these:

Positive: Activity, work, thrift, morality, dedication, selflessness, virtue, righteousness, duty, dependability, temperance, sobriety, savings, dignity.

Negative: Waste, immorality, dereliction, dissipation, infidelity, theft, vandalism, hunger, poverty, disgrace, vanity.

THE ENLIGHTENMENT VALUE SYSTEM

America became a nation in the period of the Enlightenment. It happened when a new intellectual era based on the scientific finding of men like Sir Isaac Newton and the philosophical systems of men like John Locke were dominant. The founders of our nation were particularly influenced by such men. The Declaration of Independence is supremely an enlightenment document. In many ways America is an enlightenment nation and if enlightenment is not the predominant value system, it is surely first among equals.

The enlightenment position stems from the belief that we live in an ordered world where all activity is governed by laws similar to the laws of physics. These "natural laws" may or may not come from God depending on the particular orientation of the person examining them, but unlike many religious people in the value system just discussed, the enlightenment man believes that man can discover these laws by himself. Thus, he may worship God for God's greatness, but he finds out about his universe himself. He can do this because he has the power of reason. The laws of nature are harmonious and one can use reason to discover them all. He can also use them to provide for a better life.

Because man is basically good and capable of finding answers, restraints on him from doing what he sees as right must be limited. Occasionally, men do foolish things and must be restrained by society, but only occasionally. Never should a person be restrained in matters of the mind. The reason must be free. Thus, government is an agreement among men to assist the society to protect individual rights. That government is a democracy. Certain rights are inalienable, they may not be abridged; "among these are life, liberty and the pursuit of happiness." Arguments for academic freedom, against wiretaps and for scientific inquiry come from this value system.

Some of the words that are associated with this value system are these:

Positive: Freedom, science, nature, rationality, democracy, fact, liberty, individualism, knowledge, intelligence, reason, natural rights, natural laws, progress.

Negative: Ignorance, inattention, thoughtlessness, error, indecision, irrationality, dictatorship, fascist, bookburning, falsehood, regression.

THE PROGRESSIVE VALUE SYSTEM

Progress was a natural handmaiden of the Enlightenment. If these laws were available and if man had the tool, reason, to discover them and use them to his advantage, then progress would result. Things would continually get better. But although progress, as it has become so important in America, is probably a historical spinoff of the enlightenment, it has become so important on its own that it deserves at times to be seen quite separate from the enlightenment.

Richard Weaver, in 1953, found that "one would not go far wrong in naming progress" the "god term" of that age. It is, he said, the "expression about which all other expressions are ranked as subordinate. . . . Its force imparts to the others their lesser degrees of force, and fixest the scale by which degrees of comparison are understood."[28]

Today, the unmediated use of the progress value system is questioned, but progress is still a fundamental value in America. Most arguments against progress are usually arguments about the definition of progress. They are (as we noted on pages 56 and 57) about what "true progress is."

The following are some of the key words of this value system:

Positive: Practicality, efficiency, change, improvement, science, future, modern, progress, evolution.

Negative: Old fashioned,[29] regressive, impossible, backward.

THE TRANSCENDENTAL VALUE SYSTEM

Another historical spinoff of the Enlightenment system was the development of the transcendental movement of the early nineteenth century. It took from the enlightenment all its optimism about man, freedom and democracy but rejected the emphasis on reason. It argued idealistically that there was a faculty higher than reason; let us call it, as many of them did—intuition. Thus, for the transcendentalist, there is a way of knowing that is better than reason—which *transcends* reason. Consequently, what might seem like the obvious solution to problems is not necessarily so. One must look, on important matters, at least, to the intuition, to the feelings. Like the enlightenment thinker, the transcendentalist believes in a

[28] Weaver, p. 212.

[29] Note that "old fashioned" is frequently positive when we speak of morality and charm but not when we speak of our automobiles.

unified universe governed by natural laws. Thus, every person, by following his intuition will discover these laws and universal harmony will take place. And, of course, little or no government will be necessary. The original American Transcendentalists of the early nineteenth century drew their inspiration from Platonism, German idealism and Oriental mysticism. The idea was also fairly well limited to the intellectuals. By and large, transcendentalism has been the view of a rather small group of people throughout our history. But at times it has been very important. It has always been somewhat more influential among younger people. James Truslow Adams once wrote that everyone should read Ralph Waldo Emerson at sixteen because his writings were a marvel for the buoyantly optimistic person of that age but that his transcendental writings did not have the same luster at twenty-one.[30] In the late 1960's and early 1970's, Henry David Thoreau's *Walden* was the popular reading of campus rebels. The emphasis of antiestablishment youth on oriental mysticism, like Zen, should not be ignored either. The rejection of contemporary society and mores symbolized by what others considered "outlandish dress" and "hippie behavior" with its great emphasis on emotional response and "do your own thing" indicated the adoption of a transcendental value system. Commune living is reminiscent of the transcendental "Brook Farm" experiments that were attempted in the early nineteenth century and described by Nathanial Hawthorne in his novel, *The Blithdale Romance.*

In all of these movements the emphasis on humanitarian values, the centrality of love for others and quiet contemplation over activity has been important. Transcendentalism, thus, rejects the common idea of progress. Inner light and knowledge of one's self is more important than material well-being. There is also some tendency to reject physical well-being because it takes one away from intuitive truth.

It should be noted that not everyone who argues for change is a transcendentalist. The transcendental white campus agitator of the late 1960's discovered that, despite all their concern for replacing racism and war with love and peace, their Black counterparts were highly pragmatic and rationalistic about objectives and means. Black agitators and demonstrators were never "doing their thing" in the intuitive way of many Whites.

It should also be noted that while a full adherence to transcendentalism has been limited to small groups, particularly among intellectuals and youth, many of the ideas are not limited to such persons. One can surely

[30] James Trustlow Adams, "Emerson Re-read," *The Transcendental Revolt*, George F. Whicher, ed., (Boston: D.C. Heath, 1949), pp. 31–39.

find strains of what we have here, for convenience, labeled transcendentalism in the mysticism of some very devout older Roman Catholics, for instance. And perhaps many Americans become transcendental on particular issues, about their country in time of war, for instance.

Here are some of the terms that are characteristic of transcendental thinking:

Positive: Humanitarian, individualism, respect, intuition, truth, equality, sympathetic affection, feeling, love, sensitivity, emotion, personal kindness, compassion, brotherhood, friendship, mysticism.

Negative: Science,[31] reason, mechanical, hate, war, anger, insensitive, coldness, unemotional.

THE PERSONAL SUCCESS VALUE SYSTEM

The least social of the major American value systems is the one that moves people toward personal achievement and success. It can be related as a part of the enlightenment value system but it is more than that because it involves a highly pragmatic concern for the material hapiness of the individual. To call it "selfish" would be to load the terms against it, although there would be some who accept this value system who would say "yes, I'm selfish." "The Lord helps him who helps himself" has always been an acceptable adage by some of the most devout in our nation.

A study published in 1964 may give us a better view of this value system. A group of college students in that year were studied to discover which of twelve values were most important to them. The top five for men were: Career, Family, Economic Security, Identity, and Religion. For women, the top five in order were: Family, Identity, Economic Security, Career, and Religion. Even among men, who placed it first, Career was seen as a means to other things, such as a better life for their families, recreation and so forth.[32] The increased awareness brought about by such movements as Women's Liberation may have changed this order somewhat; career may be stronger and family weaker among women, for instance. Nonetheless, the men and the women had the same top five and only the fifth, religion, could be called a social value. The study confirms the findings of others that "privatism" (the full life with family and

---

[31] It is interesting to note, however, that one of the major organizations in the United States with transcendental origins, the Christian Science Church, combines transcendentalism with science.

[32] Robert Mogar, "Value Orientations of College Students: Preliminary Data and Review of the Literature," *Psychological Reports, 15* (December 1964), pp. 746–748.

friends, with practical thinking about material benefits) is a strong value among the young. We see no reason to believe that this has changed in ten years or that it is limited to younger people. In some ways it appears today as a personal and pragmatic combination of the progressive and transcendental.

Here are some of the terms that tend to be characteristic of the Personal Success value system:

Positive: Career, family, friends, recreation, economic security, identity, health, individualism, affection, respect, enjoyment, dignity, considerateness, fair play, personal, brotherhood.

Negative: Dullness, routine, hunger, poverty, disgrace, coercion, disease.

THE COLLECTIVIST VALUE SYSTEM

Although there are few actual members of various Socialist and Communist groups in the United States, one cannot ignore the strong attachment among some people for collective action. This is in part a product of the influx of social theories from Europe. It is also a natural outgrowth of a perceived need to control the excesses of freedom in a mass society. Its legitimacy is not limited to current history, however. There has always been a value placed on cooperative action. The same person today who would condemn welfare payments to unwed mothers would undoubtedly praise his ancestors for barn raising and taking care of the widow in a frontier community. Much rhetoric about our "pioneer ancestors" has to do with their cooperative action. And anticollectivist Presidents and evangelists talk about "the team." At the same time many fervent advocates of collective action in the society argue vehemently for their freedom and independence. Certainly the civil rights movement constituted a collective action for freedom.

But whether the collectivist value system is used to defend socialist schemes or promote "law and order" there is no doubt but that collectivism is a strong value system in this nation. Like transcendentalism, however, it is probably a value system that, at least in this day and age, cannot work alone.

Here are some of the terms that tend to characterize the collectivist value system:

Positive: cooperation, joint action, unity, brotherhood, together, social good, order, humanitarian aid and comfort, equality.

Negative: disorganization, selfishness, personal greed, inequality.

It is clear that these six value systems do not constitute a complete catalog of all American Value systems. Combinations and reorderings produce different hierarchies. Two values that are common in these systems and sometimes operate alone that we would like to mention briefly are *nature* and *patriotism*. From the beginning of our nation there has been the idea that the natural is good and there for our use and preservation. There has also been since John Winthrop first proclaimed that the New England Puritans would build "a city on the hill" for all the world to see and emulate, the idea that America is a fundamentally great nation, perhaps God-chosen, to lead the world to the true life. This idea may be somewhat tarnished in some quarters today but there is no doubt that it will revive as it has in the past, and linked to other value systems we have discussed, will once more be a theme that will draw the adherence of others to arguments.

SPECIALIZED VALUE SYSTEMS

Although we have described the value systems that account for the predominate values, which will be found in general argumentation in this nation, we must be aware that, particularly where they are isolated from the general culture by geography or social convention, in small communities or in ghetto or barrio, rather distinct value systems are preserved. Clyde Kluckhohn describes the value differences in five cultures (Mormon, Texan, Chicano, Zuni and Navaho) that coexisted in the same region of New Mexico when the study was made by the Laboratory of Social Relations of Harvard University during 1949 to 1954.[33] We can secure a rough statement about those five cultures (although oversimplifying Kluckhohn's analysis) by the following chart of how each culture generally responded to eight polar-opposite value pairs.

The Universe is—	Orderly	Governed by chance
	Mormon	Texan
	Zuni	Chicano
	Navaho	

---

[33] Clyde Kluckhohn, "The Study of Values," *Values in America*, Donald N. Barrett, ed., (Notre Dame, Indiana: University of Notre Dame Press, 1961), pp. 17–45. We have used the more modern term Chicano for Kluckhohn's term Spanish-American. The reader should be aware that some have complained about this study because of the traditional middle class orientation of the language used. We use it here because it is a pioneer study of this kind and the best illustration we can find of our point.

The Universe is—	Unitary	Pluralistic each with
	Mormon	different rules
	Chicano	Texan
	Zuni	Navaho
Priority should be given to—	Group	Individual
	Mormon	Texan
	Chicano	Navaho
	Zuni	
Emphasis should be placed on—	Others	Self
	Mormon	Texan
	Chicano	Zuni
		Navaho
Persons are—	Dependent	Autonomous
	Mormon	Texan
	Chicano	
	Zuni	
	Navaho	
Persons should confront conditions by being—	Active	Acceptant
	Mormon	Chicano
	Texan	
	Zuni	
	Navaho	
Persons should stress—	Discipline	Fulfillment
	Mormon	Texan
	Zuni	Chicano
		Navaho
The culture emphasizes the—	General	Unique
	Mormon	Chicano
	Texan	Zuni
		Navaho

Although the "Texan" probably represents the closest approximation of the most popular general American value system, it is interesting to note that the Mormon, the closest group ethnically, differs in a number of significant ways and the two Indian cultures also have sharp value differences.[34]

In recent years we have become aware of the fact that the largest racial minority in America, the blacks, have a unique value system (perhaps even a whole set of separate value systems) as well as sharing the prevelant ones.

[34] Kluckhohn, p. 43.

There is no space here to examine very carefully those value systems. Many older blacks share the dominant enlightenment progress oriented value system with an enthusiasm that surpasses middle class white expectations and the puritan morality has always been strongly reinforced through the powerful black ministers.

The "Black Revolution" in the past ten years has brought a new awareness, particularly to many younger black people, which has been disturbing to much of the White community. The concept of separatism and Black Nationalism is foreign to the thinking of Whites, even (perhaps mostly) the liberals. The white liberal's notion of equality is shaken, his values are threatened, by blacks who proclaim their difference and demand separation. This looks like a new collectivist values system. It also has overtones of a denial of equality, perhaps even a proclamation of superiority. Nonetheless, it is highly pragmatic, aimed at self help, demanding payment for work already done, and seeking self determination. At least, the arguments of black Americans for the most part reflect the prevailing value system.

What is unique about black value systems can perhaps be understood by reminding ourselves of a few realities in black history. The overwhelming fact of black culture is the slavery experience followed by the semi-slavery existence of the next one hundred years. The almost deliberate breakup of families, the antiliteracy actions, then statutes, the authoritarian rule of those years was so pervasive that it profoundly influenced black values.

The prohibitions against assembly or petition created an oral culture where the only genuine place of group communication was the church where, permitted by whites, blacks developed a code in music and speech that said one thing to the white man and another to each other. In short, the black value system is far more difficult for a white person to define because he can never be sure if the blacks he listens to are jivin' him, or are using the white person's value system to say something quite different to his brothers and sisters. In any event, there can be no doubt that arguments addressed to black audiences require that the speaker have extensive experience with the black culture.[35]

---

[35] For those more interested in the relationship of argumentation to the Black experience see: James L. Golden and Richard D. Rieke, *The Rhetoric of Black Americans*, (Columbus, Ohio: Charles E. Merrill Publishing Co., 1971), pp. 1–49; Arthur L. Smith, *Language, Communication and Rhetoric in Black America*, (New York: Harper and Row, Publishers, 1972); Arthur L. Smith, *Rhetoric of Black Revolution*, (Boston: Allyn and Bacon, Inc., 1969), pp. 1–104.

CHANGES IN VALUES

The political unrest among younger people during the late 1960's and early 1970's combined with their rejection of traditional mores in dress, sex and other social activities has led some people to believe that a major shift in values is taking place and that the less popular transcendental and collectivist values are taking over for the other more traditional puritan, enlightenment value systems. This position was given a full statement in *The Greening of America* by Charles A. Reich, but subsequent studies of a cross section of American youth has thrown serious doubt on that thesis.[36] The news that Richard Nixon got almost as many votes from the first time voters, aged 18 to 24, in 1972 than George McGovern, even though the open and avowed spokesman for the most traditional of values, helps to make *The Greening of America* significantly less eminent than the enthusiastic Mr. Reich led some to believe.[37] This is not to deny change, but we should observe that much change is in conclusions, not values. For instance, younger people favor the legalization of marijuana in larger numbers than older people and to many this seems like the denial of traditional values, but the arguments for legalization one hears are based on traditional values: "Legalization is reasonable;" "illegality increases cost; "Illegality aids crime;" "it is not injurious to health or mental state." These arguments may be good or poor on other counts, but there is no question but that they conform to traditional values.

Values do change, not by overnight revolution, but as in the theory advanced by Florence Kluckhohn:

"Fundamental values alter slowly—in the overwhelming majority of cases. But . . . basic value-shifts occur when external pressures impinge on the already existent variations in the system. The systematic variation always contains the potential for change but remains dormant or latent until environmental events or intensified contacts with other cultures bring a second —or third—order position into dominance. If this be correct, we escape the puzzling mystique of 'emmanent causation.' "[38]

What one finds then is not the overturning of one value system for another but a situation where variation is "both permitted and required." Such

[36] Charles A. Reich, *The Greening of America*, (New York: Bantam Books, 1970); James L. Spates and Jack Levin, *International Social Sciences Journal, 24* #2 (1972), pp. 326–353.

[37] "The Landslide: How and Why?" *Newsweek, 80* (November 13, 1972), p. 30.

[38] Clyde Kluckhohn, "The Study of Values," p. 24.

gradual change comes about due to external and internal pressures by means of a shifting of hierarchies.

THE INTERACTION OF VALUE SYSTEMS

We have already mentioned how various systems interact and how groups and individuals will use one system at one time, another at a second time and a combination on still a third occasion. It is an important concept for we should not permit ourselves to get a static notion about the application of values to argumentation. We must be aware that there are fundamental contradictions in our society that each person and group must resolve. Conflicting values must be balanced so that a person can arrive at a point where he finds his values congruent with one another.

CONCLUSIONS

Essential in the decision making process are the values that a receiver holds. With evidence and source credibility they constitute the support for a claim. Values are a general conception of what is good or bad that may be applied in a wide variety of argumentative situations. Values form a more useful basis for understanding human action than do "needs" because they are more social and less physiological and more likely to be the source of a claim in general argumentation. Values are akin to beliefs and attitudes. Beliefs, the smallest units, are combined into attitudes that in turn are related to a specific object or situation. Value analysis is the most useful because it applies to a much smaller number of abstract ideas that can be applied to many different situations.

Value systems are limited by time, by physical factors, and the psychological state of the person receiving the communication and by that person's motivation. Values may be "instrumental" or "terminal," that is, they may make statements about what is good or bad, or they may make statements about objectives that one should have.

Some values are more dominant than others depending on how many people hold it, the length of time it lasts, the intensity with which it is held and the credibility of its supporters.

Values may be found by experimental quantitative research, content analysis or the analysis of arguments as explained in Chapter 4. The latter method seems like the most practical method in general argumentation.

Even though attempting to identify *the* value systems of America is risky, we can identify six that will, when used with good sense, account for most cases of general argumentation: (1) puritan-pioneer-peasant, (2) enlightenment, (3) progressive, (4) transcendental, (5) personal success, (6) collectivist. In addition, two values that appear in several of the others, nature and patriotism, need to be given special attention.

In this country there are specialized value systems that function as rather distinct value subcultures. The distinctive youth subculture so widely proclaimed a few years ago seems not to have materialized.

PROJECTS

1. Using a speech or essay provided by your instructor, note through content analysis of value terms and by testing arguments as explained in Chapter 4, what the value system of the speaker or writer is.

2. From contemporary magazines collect eight or ten different ads for the same type of product (cigarettes, perfume, liquor, automobiles, etc.) and observe to what extent a single value system emerges.

3. Note the differences between two different magazines that aim at different audiences (*Playboy* and *Field and Stream*, *Ms* and *Ladies Home Journal*).

4. Conduct a debate in class with some of your classmates on a value claim in which the most of the support comes from other value statements. How effective is it? Under what circumstances can values stand alone?

5. The following magazine ad is almost nonverbal. What are its arguments?

Marlboro Illustration, courtesy of *Philip Morris, Inc.*

7

Support:
Credibility

As has already been observed, persons give adherence to arguments in a process that involves the interaction of three factors: their perception that the argument is rational, their perception that the argument employs values that are congruent with their values, and their perception that the argument comes from a credible source. All of these factors need not be consciously present; indeed a person may give adherence despite the absence of one of them. But, an argument is most believable if all are present. An ardent Democrat might accept a Republican President's argument (for additional controls on wages and prices) if the President's argument seemed reasonable and convinced him that the economic health of the nation and himself would result even though he had little personal regard for the President. Likewise, a conservative Republican, for whom the President had great credibility, might accept such a proposal even though the argument was in violation of his strong value orientation toward a free market economy.

Each of these factors interact and influence the adherence a person makes to an argument. This point needs to be stressed because it is too easy to make the mistake of viewing each as separate objective phenomena. Such interaction is undoubtedly the reason why researchers in communication have found it difficult to isolate each for experimental purposes.[1] In actual practice, persons engaged in argumentation will need to treat an argument as a whole thing. In this chapter we will examine as best we can, credibility as a function, which adds or detracts from the adherence a person gives to argument, recognizing that it is not so separable in actual practice.

WHAT IS CREDIBILITY?

When Aristotle first defined credibility as one of the three forms of proof, he used the term *ethos* and it meant that "proof", which was provided to the receiver of the message "by the character of the speaker . . . when the speech is so uttered as to make him worthy of belief."[2] It is easy to see how in the formal public speaking situation listeners' responses are, in part at least, based on their regard for the speaker as well as the acceptability of his message. In private conversations we find some people more believable than others. Even for people we have not known before, our judgment of their character by what they do or say influences the level of adherence that we give to their arguments.

Aristotle's concept of *ethos* was most useful for his times and in many situations in our own times where we wish to look at how one consciously (artistically) designs messages for maximum effect. It is not comprehensive enough, however, to explain the credibility factor in much, though perhaps not most, modern argumentation. Vast changes have come over our society in the past one hundred years that have added new dimensions to all argumentation. Radio and television, complicated print media, complex political, social and economic systems and a host of other factors have complicated the communication process and have consequently complicated our understanding of the application of credibility.

Face to face communication and direct written communication, where the source of the communication is known to the receiver, are still important parts of our communication scene. Extensive new problems associated with a mass society have been added, however. Ghost writers, advertising agencies, actors, hired advocates, artists and a host of others have entered every phase of our communication lives. Thus, while hired advocates (such as lawyers) and ghostwriters are not strictly modern phe-

---

[1] James C. McCroskey and Robert E. Dunham, "Ethos: A Confounding Element in Communication Research," *Speech Monographs, 33* (November 1966), pp. 456–463; Paul D. Holtzman, "Confirmation of Ethos as a Confounding Element in Communication Research," *Speech Monographs, 33* (November 1966), pp. 464–466.

[2] *The Rhetoric of Aristotle*, Lane Cooper, trans., (New York: Appleton-Century-Crofts, Inc., 1932), p. 8.

nomena, their development as pervasive factors in our society is a comparatively recent phenomena and they have become involved in all phases of contemporary life.

Is it the TV star who sells us coffee on TV? Or, is it he and a whole team of production people, script writers and advertising men? And when he tells us to "buy my Instant Maxwell House" he may sincerely believe it is "better than freeze-dried" but it isn't *his* Instant Maxwell House. It is General Foods' Instant Maxwell House. Yet we know that the argument he makes is believable to many people. Is it because of his credibility? The credibility of General Foods? The credibility created by the production people? The script writers? The other actors in the commercial? It is an ironic but probably true observation that, in this sense, a half-hour speech on the floor of the United States Senate has less complex *ethos* than a thirty second television commercial.

Not only does the presence of multiple sources complicate the examination of *ethos*, there is also the problem of the influence of the prior reputation of the source. That part of credibility is beyond Aristotle's concept of *ethos* for it is not a part of what the speaker designed; it is not part of his "artistic proof." Presumably, from the beginning of human communication, a person's reputation has influenced his credibility with listeners and conglomerate sources are, at least, as old as major newspapers. Today, as in earlier times, newspapers such as *The National Observer, The Christian Science Monitor*, and the *New York Times* have credibility for many people beyond that of the individual writers who are published there. Thus, the problems of understanding credibility are compounded a thousandfold by the mass aspects of modern society.

The only solution to the potential confusions of modern mass society when studying argumentation is to look at credibility from the standpoint of the perceived source. In such a system, who designed a message only becomes important if it is perceived by the receiver of the message as important. If receivers give adherence to a message because of the credibility of a certain person that they perceive to be the source when it is a group, or a ghostwriter who actually constructed the message, then we may raise questions about how this comes about but we need not pass judgment. However, we should be concerned if someone responds negatively because of distrust for us or because he perceives us as not having prepared the message ourselves. Credibility may become an issue when someone raises it as in: "How do you know he is telling the truth—he gets paid to say that by the company?" Or, "Why he didn't even write that himself." But, whether challenged or not, credibility is a function of the perception of the receiver. We are not, therefore, assessing the "character" of the source, only the receiver's perception of it.

We might put it in summary form by saying that credibility is the quality that the receiver gives to the image of the source. As citizens and human beings we are deeply concerned about the morality of acts and the essential morality of ourselves and the people with whom we deal. However, as students of argumentation, it is essential that we always be aware that some people can be considered quite credible while advocating what we see as quite immoral acts. To a gang of thugs, a man gains credibility by being willing to kill without remorse.

WHAT KINDS OF CREDIBILITY ARE THERE?

The most obvious kind of credibility is what we shall call *direct credibility*. This is the kind of credibility that one develops by making direct statements about himself. The politician who tells a group of farmers, "I was a farm boy myself," is using direct credibility. Perhaps the most successful practitioner of direct credibility in recent times has been President Richard M. Nixon. The following quotation from his speech in defense of military action in Cambodia on April 31, 1970 will illustrate:

"I have rejected all political considerations in making this decision. Whether my party gains in November is nothing compared to the lives of 400,000 brave Americans fighting for our country and for the cause of peace and freedom in Vietnam.
"Whether I may be a one-term President is insignificant compared to whether by our failure to act in this crisis the United States proves itself to be unworthy to lead the forces of freedom in this critical period in world history.
"I would rather be a one-term President and do what I believe was right than to be a two-term President at the cost of seeing America become a second-rate power and to see this nation accept the first defeat in its proud 190-year history.[3]

A second kind of credibility that we will refer to as *secondary credibility* is quite similar to the first but the source uses another person's credibility as the basis for his argument. "Joe Namath wears Dingle Boots" was a simple printed advertisement that increased the sales of Dingle Boots

[3] Wil A. Linkugel, R. R. Allen, and Richard L. Johannesen, eds., *Contemporary American Speeches*, (Belmont, Calif.: Wadsworth Publishing Co., Inc., 1972), p. 243.

by eight percent. It wasn't necessary for Joe Namath to say a thing, only to permit his name and picture to be used. Secondary credibility encompasses all the area of arguments in which testimony functions. Any testimony used in an argument is automatically a form of secondary credibility. If we argue that the proposed steam-powered electrical generating plant should not be built because the Sierra Club, a wilderness protection society, says that the power plant will damage the environment, then we are adding the credibility of the Sierra Club to our own. The Sierra Club is being used as secondary credibility. It should be observed, of course, that secondary credibility, like all other credibility, can be either positive or negative. The argument against the generating plant would have a negative result if directed at a group that considered the Sierra Club a group of meddling idealists.

In both direct and secondary credibility a communicator influences the believability of his argument by directly indicating his own qualification or by associating his proposal with the qualification of another. There is a third kind of credibility that we shall call *indirect credibility* by which we increase credibility by developing arguments, and supporting them and presenting them in a way that implies credibility to our listeners. The values that we imply in our arguments give listeners certain perceptions about us. Even the medium makes a difference. Receivers will attach credibility to a particular source of communication. All of these characteristics of indirect credibility will be discussed elsewhere in this book for what we are saying is that everything done in an argumentation situation affects credibility. Indirect credibility might be explained by saying that one way a speaker or writer increases credibility is by the quality of the message produced.

With a bit of bending and stretching, the three types of credibility that we have thus far discussed (direct, secondary and indirect) all will fit under Aristotle's term *ethos*. All involve what the source of communication does to increase credibility and consequently increase the adherence to the argument. There is yet a fourth kind of credibility which, while not beyond the sender's control, is beyond what the sender may do in the course of the actual communication. This kind of credibility we shall call *reputation*, referring, of course, to what receivers know about the source in advance of the communication. Much of the preliminary research that has been done on credibility has been in this area and it shows, as would be expected, that we tend to believe those persons whom we perceive as reputable more than those persons who seem to us to be less reputable or disreputable. Reputation is based on what receivers have heard from others or have deduced themselves. It can be enhanced, particularly in a relatively unknown source, by introductions or endorsements to books, plays, or speeches. Reputation will differ in its importance depending on the circumstances.

Certain carefully structured forms of argumentation are designed, in part at least, to decrease the impact of reputation. In the court of law or in the intercollegiate debate tournament, although the reputation of the lawyers or the debater presenting the case can not be entirely eliminated from the decision, such credibility is rather consciously guarded against. In other situations of argumentation, reputation is not protected against. Governmental hearings most frequently involve people who are there because of the reputation they have or the organization that they represent, and persons of little or no reputation, regardless of what valuable argument they might have, are frequently not invited or permitted to testify.

These, then, constitute four types of credibility that receivers ascribe to sources of argumentation: direct, secondary, indirect and reputation.

WHAT ARE THE FACTORS CONTRIBUTING TO SOURCE CREDIBILITY?

In recent years much experimental research has been carried on to determine what the dimensions of source credibility are.[4] A variety of factors have been discovered but essentially there appears to be general agreement on two dimensions that are very strong on all scales. There is some agreement on two other dimensions which, if they exist at all, are substantially weaker than the first two.

The first of the well established dimensions is the *competence* that receivers perceive the source to have. A variety of words have been used since ancient times as a synonym for competence: "sagacity," "reliabil-

[4] Kenneth Andersen and Theodore Clevenger, Jr., "A Summary of Experimental Research in Ethos," *Speech Monographs, 30* (June 1963), pp. 59–78; Kenneth Andersen, *Persuasion: Theory and Practice*, (Boston: Allyn and Bacon, Inc., 1971), pp. 217–263; John W. Bowers and William A. Phillips, "A Note on the Generality of Source-Credibility Scales," *Speech Monographs, 34* (June 1967), pp. 185–186; Kim Giffin, "The Contribution of Studies of Source Credibility to a Theory of Interpersonal Trust in the Communication Process," *Psychological Bulletin, 68* (August 1967), pp. 104–120; James C. McCroskey, *An Introduction to Rhetorical Communication*, 2nd ed. (Englewood Cliffs, N.J.: Prentice-Hall, Inc., 1972), pp. 63–81; David Markham, "The Dimensions of Source Credibility of Television Newscasters," *Journal of Communication, 18* (1968), pp. 57–64; Jack L. Whitehead, "Factors of Source Credibility," *Quarterly Journal of Speech, 54* (February 1968), pp. 59–63; Carl I Hovland, Irving L. Janis, and Harold H. Kelly, *Communication and Persuasion*, (New Haven: Yale University Press, 1953).

ity," "authoritativeness," "expertness," "qualification," "logical." Common sense experience would confirm for us that we find an argument more believable that is advanced by a person that we believe to be competent.

Persons who are perceived by receivers to be *trustworthy* also have high credibility. In the literature since classical times, other words have been used that may help to define the meaning of trustworthiness: "probity," "character," "evaluative," "reliable," and "safety." Again, common sense would tell us that we tend to accept ideas more readily from persons whom we regard as being trustworthy.

These two dimensions—competence and trustworthiness—are agreed to by all writers. The other two factors—each of which is accepted by some and not by others—are the *goodwill*, which the receiver perceives that the source has for him and the *dynamism* that the receiver sees in the source. Terms like "intentions," "openmindedness," "objective," "impartial evaluation," "kind," "friendly," and "personal attractiveness" have been used to characterize this goodwill dimension. *Dynamism*, the only one of the four terms to be strictly modern, has had only one other word associated with it. That word is "showmanship."

It is easy to see how factor analysis might have shown either goodwill or dynamism to be weak or nonexistent as separate dimensions. Goodwill could classify very easily as a subcategory of trustworthiness. That is, we tend to find trustworthy those persons who we perceive to have good will toward us. Likewise, dynamism, when it functions, may very well be a kind of judgment about competence. We know that dynamism in a speaker increases retention and serves as an intensifier.[5] If we are inclined to accept the point of view of the speaker, his dynamism (that is, his physical and vocal activity) will help to intensify the acceptance that we give. One can easily see how greater physical and vocal activity would, under certain circumstances, cause a person to retain more information simply because he would pay more attention to what was being said.

However, dynamism has a serious drawback not possessed by competence and trustworthiness or even goodwill. Dynamism may be perceived negatively. One hardly can imagine a person deciding to give adherence to a particular argument because of a conviction that the person advancing the argument is incompetent, or untrustworthy, or does not have goodwill toward him. But it is a very common phenomenon for a person to reject an argument because the person advancing it is too dynamic. The overly enthusiastic salesman is an easy example of this very problem. Dynamism

[5] William D. Coats and Uldis Smidchens, "Audience Recall as a Function of Speaker Dynamism," *Journal of Educational Psychology, 57* (August 1966), pp. 189–191; Don A Schweitzer, "The Effect of Presentation on Source Evaluation," *Quarterly Journal of Speech, 56* (February 1970), pp. 33–39.

in its positive application appears to be related to competence. In its negative interpretation it appears to be related to trustworthiness.[6]

WHAT DO WE KNOW ABOUT CREDIBILITY?

Much of what we know about credibility is a matter of common sense. But there is a growing body of research on that subject that may be tapped. In the remainder of this chapter we shall examine some of this research and, combined with common sense observations, attempt to define some of the principles that a communicator might use in making his arguments more believable.

Let us first look at what we know about the influence of the reputation of the speaker on his credibility. The reputation of a source has a significant influence on the effectiveness of a message, particularly in the case of identifiable class references; a person will tend to get greater comprehension out of the message from someone who comes from his own socioeconomic class. And the more sensitive a receiver is to the relative credibility of the source, the more susceptible he is to changing his views because of it.[7] It is reasonable to believe that we tend to find most credible those persons who come from the same group as we do. There is also some evidence to suppose that some biases exist in all classes for persons from higher socioeconomic classes.[8] This conclusion needs to be approached with more caution because the study was made of college students who, even if they come from lower socioeconomic classes, tend to see themselves as potential upper class. Nonetheless, it is reasonable to assume that greater credibility would be attached to people who appear to have met all the standard measurements of success, a high value in our society.

A physically attractive person appears to have greater credibility than a

---

[6] Schweitzer and Ginsburg also found a factor, other than dynamic, which was related to a mode of presentation. It included such matters as command of English. For our purposes we shall treat this as a subcategory of competence. Don Schweitzer and Gerald P. Ginsburg, "Factors of Communicator Credibility," *Problems in Social Psychology*, Carl W. Backman and Paul F. Secord, eds., (New York: McGraw-Hill Book Co., 1966), pp. 94–102.

[7] Andersen, p. 220; M. Myers and A. Goldberg, "Group Credibility and Opinion Change," *Journal of Communication, 20* (June 1970), pp. 174–179; Andersen and Clevenger, p. 66; Elliot R. Siegel, Gerald R. Miller, and C. Edward Wotring, "Source Credibility and Credibility Proneness: A New Relationship," *Speech Monographs, 36* (June 1969), pp. 118–125.

[8] Andersen and Clevenger, p. 73.

less attractive person.[9] Although there are indications that in our male oriented society, men are generally considered more credible, an attractive person physically and personally will be considered more credible than an unattractive person whether man or woman.[10]

Some studies seem to show that reputation is effective in adding credibility only in those cases that are relevant to the message. For instance, in one study it was found that the objectively irrelevant factor of Communist affiliation did not affect a communicator's credibility when his message was concerned with the desirability of capital punishment. Such affiliation did affect his ethos when the message concerned federal control of education. Others show that "irrelevant" factors do affect credibility.[11] It seems reasonable to believe that the specific reputation of the speaker, which is subject related, is considerably more important than reputation, which is not. However, common sense confirms the experimental evidence that credibility, while stronger when subject related, is nonetheless operative when not subject related. People buy products because professional athletes advocate them and one is hard pressed to find a standard of competence in the ability to hit a baseball for judging the quality of a cigarette behind a level of competence that ought to apply to almost any cigarette smoker. Politicians have long recognized the desirability of having celebrities endorse their candidacies. We do not know the exact range in which such credibility is effective in causing a person to adhere to an argument but it seems reasonable to assume that nonmessage related credibility is somehow inversely related to the significance of the argument to the receiver. In other words, about a relatively unimportant matter like which toothpaste to buy, which cigarette to smoke, or which hair cream to use, a source whose competence is unrelated to the subject is more likely to influence us than on a subject of greater importance. On more important questions, such unrelated competence only serves to rein-

[9] James O. Whittaker, "Sex Differences and Susceptibility to Interpersonal Persuasion," *Journal of Social Psychology, 66* (June 1965), pp. 91–95; James O. Whittaker and Robert D. Meade, "Sex of Communicator as a Variable in Source Credibility," *Journal of Social Psychology, 72* (June 1967), pp. 27–34.

[10] Andersen and Clevenger, p. 63; Judson Mills and Elliot Aronson, "Opinion Change as a Function of the Communicator's Attractiveness and Desire to Influence," *Journal of Personality and Social Psychology, 1* (1965), pp. 173–177.

[11] Elliot Aronson and Burton W. Golden, "The Effects of Relevant and Irrelevant Aspects of Communicator Credibility on Opinion Change," *Journal of Personality, 30* (June 1962), pp. 135–146; Jean S. Kerrick, "The Effect of Relevant and Non-relevant Sources on Attitude Change," *Journal of Social Psychology, 47* (1958), pp. 15–20; J. W. Koehler, J. C. McCroskey, and W. E. Arnold, "The Effect of Receivers Constancy Expectations in Persuasive Communication," Research Monograph, Department of Speech, Pennsylvania State University, 1966.

force convictions that are already held and not to influence changing attitudes. What Marlon Brando thinks about the plight of the American Indian or John Wayne argues in defending laissez-faire American capitalists will be significant in reinforcing the people who already hold those views and less important in changing beliefs.

There is a problem with this view, of course, in that such unrelated credibility probably has some effect on people who have little personal involvement in the question. Such persons are more susceptible to change than are persons with strong convictions. And even for highly involved receivers, such references are more influential than not mentioning them at all.[12]

Level of involvement is only one way in which the state of the receiver affects credibility. There are many ways in which their beliefs, their views of the problem discussed, of the circumstances under which it takes place and when it takes place will affect the image they have of the source. A phone call at three AM in the morning suggesting a trip to the beach the following weekend is likely to have a less favorable impact on a speaker's credibility than the same suggestion made at seven o'clock in the evening.

In addition to the influence of the prior reputation of a communicator and his behavior and appearance, it is quite clear that the endorsements made by others and the introduction the communicator is given will affect his credibility.[13] There is also a subtler kind of endorsement that only the mass media may provide. The mere fact that out of the millions of bits of information that are culled each evening for the 6 o'clock news, a person might be selected gives him a kind of credibility. Although the image created by the media may create negative credibility for an individual, his mere presence on the media makes him a person of importance. There is no doubt but that many cases of instant credibility were created in the late 1960's as campus agitators found themselves on, or in some cases engineered themselves on, the mass media. One should not doubt that the reputation of a source of an argument is increased because he has been quoted in a book, published an article, been seen in public, and reported in the daily newspaper or appeared on the Johnny Carson show.

[12] Kenneth K. Sereno, "Ego-Involvement, High Source Credibility, and Response to Belief-Discrepant Communication," *Speech Monographs, 35* (November 1968), pp. 476–481; Percy H. Tannenbaum, "Initial Attitude Toward Source and Concept as Factors in Attitude Change Through Communication," *Public Opinion Quarterly, 20* (Summer 1956), pp. 13–25.

[13] Andersen and Clevenger, p. 64; Franklin Haiman, "An Experimental Study of the Effect of Ethos on Public Speaking," *Speech Monographs, 16* (August 1949), pp. 190–202.

In addition to the observations we have made on reputation, there are a number of statements that we can make about the direct, secondary, and indirect credibility that the speaker may develop in the actual presentation of his argumentation. One of the difficult ironies to deal with in a communication situation is the plight of the person who comes to that situation with little credibility. It is not that he is not worthy of credibility necessarily, but only that it is not recognized by auditors. What we have thus far said about reputation would seem to reinforce over and over again a communication principle not too much different from the line from an old song, "the rich get richer and the poor get poorer." A person who comes to an argumentative situation with a substantial and favorable reputation in the area of the argument that he wishes to advance has an enormous advantage over one who does not. Therefore, it is essential that the person who is unknown build his credibility. Hopefully, an introduction explaining his qualifications made by a person who is seen by the group as reputable will strengthen his credibility and lessen the need for the speaker to make overt comments about his own qualifications. But frequently even this is not available and consequently such a person is forced to "toot his own horn." It is not an uncommon characteristic for the source of an argument to introduce statements about himself and it is generally considered that such statements, if not too obvious in the way they are introduced, tend to increase credibility.[14]

Perhaps the most persistently mentioned characteristic of credibility and the one we will hear about in every day discussions of communicators is sincerity. It would seem a simple rule that to add to credibility one should "be sincere." But the evidence is quite clear that sincerity cannot be determined by receivers.[15] Thus, when a person says, "I believe him because he is sincere," that person really means, "I believe him because I believe him to be sincere." It is the appearance of sincerity that receivers are able to judge and there is no basis for believing that it constitutes an accurate statement about the source. This problem with sincerity only reinforces once again the reality of the idea that credibility, like beauty, is in the eye of the beholder.

Perhaps the strongest basis for indirect credibility is the extent to which the speaker identifies with the values of his audience. A more complete

[14] Andersen, p. 228; Terry H. Ostermeier, "Effects of Type and Frequency of Self Reference Upon Perceived Source Credibility and Attitude Change," *Speech Monographs, 34* (June 1967), pp. 137–144.

[15] Andersen and Clevenger; Richard Eisinger and Judson Mills, "Perceptions of the Sincerity and Competence of a Communicator as a Function of the Extremity of His Position," *Journal of Experimental Social Psychology, 4* (April 1968), pp. 224–232.

discussion of social values and their role in argumentation is contained in Chapter 6, but a few points might be made here.

We might suggest that one way to increase credibility is to speak only in favor of those things that the audience likes and to carefully avoid any conflict with audience opinion. But of course, even if desirable, such an approach to argument is virtually impossible. There are many times, if we are concerned about significant issues in our society, when we must take a position not held by our receivers. In such a case it is still essential that we search for common ground with our receivers. Find as many points on which agreement exists, utilize the value systems that are important to our receivers and show that our proposal is in keeping with their values. Construct a hierarchy of values, which shows quite clearly that while our proposal is contrary to some of their values, it is still consistent with others, and that those other values are more important. And that, furthermore, those who would oppose our position have opted for a false hierarchy of values. As a last resort, if it is essential to conflict directly with vital value systems of our audience, do so with tact in such a way as to make possible change as little threatening as possible. We know that there is a "boomerang effect."[16] Even persons of high credibility lose some of that credibility when they associate it with lower value materials. Every communicator should be prepared to invest some of his credibility at times in raising the estimation that receivers have of his proposal, but he cannot do it too often or recklessly or he will lose all of his credibility.

The kind of value that is introduced can influence adherence. For instance, while making fear appeals may be influential in some situations, they will be accepted only from a high credibility source. Strong fear appeals will boomerang when they come from a low credibility source.[17]

Arguers should take care to avoid obvious indications that they mean to manipulate the receivers.[18] Where one has a bias and it is known, a clear and honest identification of it may actually help credibility. People tend, we believe, to put greater trust in the person who openly admits that he has a bias. It is the receivers' discovery of covert bias that is most damaging to credibility.[19]

Evidence appears to strengthen the credibility particularly of a low credibility source, and particularly if the evidence is not known to the

[16] Andersen, p. 240; Andersen and Clevenger, p. 69.

[17] Murray A. Hewgill and Gerald R. Miller, "Source Credibility and Response to Fear-Arousing Communications," *Speech Monographs, 32* (June 1965), pp. 95–101; McCroskey, p. 75.

[18] Hovland, Janis, and Kelly, p. 86.

[19] Mills and Aronson.

receiver.[20] Such findings are easy enough to understand. A highly credible source is much more likely to be effective using assertion argument than is a lower credibility source. People are less critical of him. They are less likely to wonder, "where did you get that idea?" or "how do you know that is true?" Consequently, evidence becomes considerably more important in strengthening the credibility of a low credibility source and anyone who chooses to argue from a position of low credibility must give this principle serious attention.

There are many studies, which show that an authoritative source connected to an argument, will make that argument more believable, and one, which shows that an authoritative group has higher credibility than an authoritative individual.[21] There is an interesting phenomenon known as a "sleeper effect" in the use of authoritative sources as secondary credibility. A high credibility source tends to produce a substantial initial change in people's views. But as time goes on that initial change weakens and a low source gains.[22] This would lead one to believe that the credibility of the source has immediate impact but for long range adherence the quality of the argument and the evidence take on greater significance.

Well organized speeches appear not to increase credibility, but disorganized speeches clearly weaken credibility especially for low credible sources, and showing disorganization with cues like, "I should have mentioned this earlier" hurts the speaker's perceived ability to organize.[23]

In a speaking situation more fluent delivery increases the credibility of

[20] James C. McCroskey, "A Summary of Experimental Research on the Effects of Evidence in Persuasive Communication," *Quarterly Journal of Speech, 55* (April 1969), p. 175.

[21] Andersen and Clevenger, p. 71; Robert S. Cathcart, "An Experimental Study of the Relative Effectiveness of Four Methods of Presenting Evidence," *Speech Monographs, 22* (August 1955), pp. 227–233; Terry H. Ostemeier, "Effects of Type and Frequency of Self Reference Upon Perceived Source Credibility and Attitude Change," *Speech Monographs, 34* (June 1967), pp. 137–144; Irving D. Warren, "The Effect of Credibility in Sources of Testimony on Audience Attitudes Toward Speaker and Message," *Speech Monographs, 36* (November 1969), pp. 456–458; Myers and Goldberg.

[22] Andersen and Clevenger, p. 67; McCroskey, *An Introduction to Rhetorical Communication*, p. 80.

[23] James C. McCroskey and R. Samuel Mehrley, "The Effects of Disorganization and Nonfluency on Attitude Change and Source Credibility," *Speech Monographs, 36* (March 1969), pp. 13–21; Harry Sharp, Jr. and Thomas McClung, "Effects of Organization on the Speaker's *Ethos*," *Speech Monographs, 33* (June 1966), pp. 182–183; Eldon E. Baker, "The Immediate Effects of Perceived Speaker Disorganization on Speaker Credibility and Audience Attitude Change in Persuasive Speaking," *Western Speech Journal, 29* (Summer 1965), pp. 148–161.

people.[24] One might also observe a similar phenomenon with grammar or in written communication with spelling. Unconventional spelling and grammar have a negative effect on credibility in influential segments of our society. But all delivery and grammatical factors are undoubtedly a social dimension. One study has shown, for instance, that a quiet delivery has two interpretations attached to it (unsure and very confident) and that these are related to the receiver's social attitude.[25] Thus, one receiver may find a quiet delivery a sign of confidence or unconventional grammar a sign of camaraderie.

A final aspect of credibility that is worthy of note is its relation to language. Studies, which have been made, show, for instance, that militant and opinionated language tends to be counterproductive. That is, it decreases the credibility of the source. Obscenity for a general American audience tends to decrease all categories of credibility except dynamism.[26] One finding about language and credibility, which would seem to be in conflict with common sense opinion, is that unfamiliar words tend to increase credibility.[27] The experiment that produced this result was conducted among college students who may have responded with their own concept of what the investigator wanted. For many college students, "big words" are better words, not because they necessarily believe it but

[24] Erwin P. Bettinghaus, "The Operation of Congruity in an Oral Communication Situation," *Speech Monographs*, 28 (August 1961), pp. 131–142; Gerald R. Miller and Murray A. Hewgill, "The Effect of Variations in Nonfluency on Audience Ratings of Source Credibility," *Quarterly Journal of Speech*, 50 (February 1964), pp. 36–44; McCroskey, "A Summary . . . ," p. 173; W. Barnett Pearce and Bernard J. Brommel, "Vocalic Communication in Persuasion," *Quarterly Journal of Speech*, 58 (October 1972), pp. 298–306. Cf. Kenneth K. Sereno and Gary J. Hawkins, "The Effect of Variations in Speakers' Nonfluency Upon Audience Ratings and Attitude Toward The Speech Topic and Speakers' Credibility," *Speech Monographs*, 34 (March 1967), pp. 58–64.

[25] W. Barnett Pearce, "The Effect of Vocal Cues on Credibility and Attitude Change," *Western Speech*, 35 (Summer 1971), pp. 176–184.

[26] McCroskey, *An Introduction to Rhetorical Communication*, p. 75; William McEwen and Bradley S. Greenberg, "The Effects of Message Intensity on Receiver Evaluations of Source, Message and Topic," *Journal of Communication*, 20 (December 1970), pp. 340–350; Gerald K. Miller and John Basehart, "Source Trustworthiness, Opinionated Statements and Responses to Persuasive Communication," *Speech Monographs*, 36 (March 1969), pp. 1–7; Gerald Miller and J. Lobe, "Opinionated Language, Open- and Closed Mindedness and Response to Persuasive Communication," *Journal of Communication*, 17 (December 1967), pp. 333–341; Velma J. (Wenzlaff) Lashbrook, "Source Credibility: A Summary of Experimental Research," Paper presented to the Speech Communication Association Convention, San Francisco, December 1971, p. 8.

[27] E. R. Carlson, "Word Familiarity as a Factor in Forming Impressions," *Psychological Reports*, 7 (August 1960), p. 18.

because they feel they are expected to respond this way. They have been taught that people who use "big words" are more competent. Although they respond that way in public, they do not necessarily so respond among their peers. In our society we suspect that the complexity of the language is less important then the reputation of the speaker. The speaker would do well, however, to put his arguments in the language that the listener can understand and readily follow. To a large extent, speaking the language of one's receivers establishes common ground with them that is important in dealing with audience values.

CREDIBILITY AS A DYNAMIC PROCESS

There has been some tendency in recent years to see credibility as the central factor in communication. One can see how this would come about when one subsumes under credibility the quality of the argument and the value system used by the source of the communication. We have seen how the nature of the message affects credibility and there is considerable evidence that credibility is related to subject matter.[28] Common sense would tell us that most people would judge a person's competence in relation to a particular argument or area of argumentation to be more critical than his general competence.

We are tempted to say that those who have decided that credibility is the central factor in communication have arbitrarily taken that position and have designated other aspects as secondary factors. If that were the case, it would be no more serious a fault than those who found the rational aspects of argument or the values and motives of receivers central. There is, of course, considerable experimental evidence and common sense experience that shows credibility to be a vital factor in argument. To ignore it as part of the study of argumentation, as has too frequently been done in the past, is to seriously handicap the arguer.

For a most effective development of argumentation we must realize, as we have noted elsewhere in this book, and specifically, at the beginning of this chapter, that the process of argumentation is dynamic. Factors of credibility, value, evidence, and argument, interact, and decisions are made by receivers of arguments to reject or lend adherence to those arguments on the basis of a wide variety of such factors both internal to the argument itself and outside it. Credibility, likewise, is a dynamic process.

[28] Milton Rokeach and Gilbert Rothman, "The Principles of Belief Congruence and the Congruity Principle as a Model of Cognitive Interaction," *Psychological Review, 72* (March 1965), pp. 128–142.

Sources that are accepted as trustworthy may also be regarded as incompetent and vice versa. Receivers are not given neat little choices between highly competent and trustworthy sources who show goodwill and are dynamic and their opposites. Thus, the element of credibility is a composite of responses to the dimensions and it may change even as the message is being received. A reader may know nothing of an author but as he reads a book he develops a great appreciation for the author's competence based on what he has read. Similarly, experience with a communicator can change the trustworthiness dimension. To complicate matters still further, there is reason to believe that for a given audience, low credibility is not just the opposite of high credibility but a new configuration of dimensions.[29]

The whole process of decision making from the highest level down through the single minor argument is constantly changing in an interaction process among the elements that make it up. What we see as students of argumentation when we talk about particular functions are arbitrarily frozen bits of information. What receivers see is a generalization, a movement, a trend in argument where all the factors are seen together. The same is true of the dimensions of credibility. They must always be seen in terms of a particular argument, time, receiver and circumstance.

It would be an error, however, to think that the principle of changing credibility with changing times, circumstance and problem means that every situation of argumentation is completely different from every other. There are general principles of credibility that exist within each society like the social values, the conventions of evidence, reasoning and language. There are certain attributes of personality that are admired by substantial majorities of the people. There are also attributes that are admired rather universally within specific identifiable groups. Credibility is not a haphazard factor in the argumentation situation. The arguer can increase the believability of his argument by a conscious attention to those aspects of his character and image that might influence his credibility with a particular group of receivers.

CONCLUSIONS

People give adherence to arguments because they perceive them to be rational, to employ values with which they agree, and to come from a credible source. Credibility is an important factor in argumentation. There are four kinds of credibility. Direct credibility is being used when the

---

[29] Schweitzer and Ginsburg.

speaker makes direct statements about himself designed to increase his credibility. Secondary credibility comes from associating the credibility of another with the argumentation. Indirect credibility is that credibility, which comes indirectly because the arguer develops his argument in such a way as to make him more believable. Reputation refers to the credibility that comes from what the receiver knows about the source before the particular argumentation begins. All influence adherence but only the first three can be directly controlled by the speaker or writer at the time of the particular argumentation.

Observation over centuries and experimental research have isolated two primary factors in source credibility: competence and trustworthiness. We tend to believe those persons whom we perceive as competent and trustworthy. There are two other factors that are perhaps present and possibly subcategories of the other two. One is the goodwill that a speaker seems to show for his listener. A second is the dynamism of the speaker. Dynamism, unlike the other three, can be a negative quality if someone feels it is excessive.

A summary of contemporary research and theory shows that we know a good deal about the nature of credibility.

1. The reputation of a source has a significant influence on the believability of the message.

2. Persons from the same socio-economic class are more believable than others, although there is some tendency for all classes to see greater credibility in persons from the upper class.

3. Physically attractive persons are more credible than less physically attractive ones.

4. Men are generally perceived to be more credible than women, although a physically and mentally attractive woman is more credible than a less attractive man.

5. Reputation is more effective if it is relevant to the message, although irrelevant factors do count.

6. The endorsements of others and favorable introductions by others of reputation influence credibility.

7. Statements made about oneself, if not too obvious, increase credibility.

8. Listeners cannot judge sincerity but the appearance of sincerity is quite important.

9. The strongest basis of indirect credibility is the extent to which the speaker identifies with the values of the audience.

10. Evidence strengthens credibility, particularly for low credible sources and if the evidence is not known.

11. More authoritative sources for evidence increase credibility.

12. Disorganization decreases credibility.

13. More fluent delivery and use of conventional grammar frequently increase credibility.

14. Militant and opinionated language will decrease credibility. Obscene language increases only the dynamism category.

Credibility, like all of argumentation, is dynamic. These are not neat categories. A credible source may, for some people, appear less trustworthy and vice-versa. In each case, the arguer should pay close attention to his audience and measure carefully the specific impact that he and his secondary sources will have on the audience.

PROJECTS

1. Examine a speech of personal defense such as Richard Nixon's Fund Defense Speech, Edward Kennedy's Chappiquiddick Speech, or Spiro Agnew's Resignation Speech. What kinds of credibility does the speaker use? How does he develop them? Which are most important? Compare what you found on your speech with what others found examining a different speech.

2. Develop a written argument in which your support for your claim comes from associating your own and others' credibility with it.

3. Discuss with a small group of classmates some prominent public person. What do you think of his reputation? What would he have to do to become a credibile speaker for you?

4. Using athletes or entertainers in television and print media commercials is apparently considered effective by advertising agencies. Write a short paper in which you analyze a series of ads and try to discover the reasoning by which one would go from the commercial to buying the product.

8

Building Cases

The culmination of argumentation in all but the most informal of situations is a case, or an overall plan, for winning adherence through the strategic selection and organization of arguments. Howard H. Martin and Kenneth E. Andersen's use of the term "strategy" in persuasion is particularly appropriate to the concept of the argumentative case:

"Strategy, in the original military sense of the word, meant a grand design framed to accomplish stated objectives by means of intelligent deployment of a host of resources. Strategic decisions involved knowledge of available alternatives and the judgment and 'art' to bring all of one's available resources to bear in the most advantageous and economic way. This seems exactly the task of the persuasive speaker or writer."[1]

From all the potential issues and arguments relevant to a particular claim and audience, a case is selected by those who will seek adherence.

In Chapter 3 we discussed how specific agrumentative claims might be found from a broad "feeling of doubt," and then how such a claim would

[1] Howard H. Martin and Kenneth E. Andersen, "Communication Strategies," in H. Martin and K. Andersen, eds., *Speech Communication* (Boston: Allyn and Bacon, Inc., 1968), p. 126.

be analyzed to discover specific issues. Our study clearly revealed, contrary to much popular notion, that argumentative situations do not involve just two sides. For most claims there will be a variety of cases that could be, and often are, advanced. Except in the most formal of situations, such as a criminal trial, the question will not be whether a particular case should be accepted or not. It will, instead, be what, if any, of the various cases presented or potential, will deserve adherence.

There is a close interrelationship between analysis as discussed in Chapter 3 and case building. We said then that analysis is not just a matter of acquiring knowledge; it is a process whereby all the constituents of the argumentation situation are related, one to the other, in such a way that what needs to be argued and what it will take to make those arguments convincing is known so that the arguer may more effectively develop his arguments, evidence, values, credibility and language. When these elements of argumentation become more clear, various alternatives by which they can be combined to form a strategy or case will emerge. Obviously, the strength of the analysis will directly determine the variety and quality of case ideas.

THE BRIEF

Certainly there are many different occasions for preparing an argumentative case or presentation. Some of them will be on less significant claims so that the time available will not warrant as much preparation as will others. For our explanation, we will suggest the fullest possible preparation, and expect that some adjustments downward will sometimes be made. The start, then, of a case is the preparation of a full brief. A brief, contrary to the implication of its name, is an attempt to outline all the essential materials in an argumentative situation built around a single claim. The basic format is suggested below:

1. Statement of the claim for which adherence is sought,
2. Statement of any definitions necessary,
3. Statement of material which virtually all those involved with the claim agree upon, including shared values,
4. Statement of potential issues,
5. Outline of each issue with claims and support for *both* sides.

Number 1 is self-explanatory, and the second item is probably clear—it means that within any claim there may be specialized words and phrases that need special definition to be sure that all are using them the same way. The third statement is particularly important, for from this material come the starting points on which a case may be built. In any agrument, a case begins where the audience is. In law, it is common to state in a brief admitted matter, or that body of assertions over which no argument will occur. We mean to include much more. Regardless of the claim under study, those involved must share many values and agree on many "facts" or argumentation would not be possible. Thus, it becomes vital to case building to take stock of these points of agreement in a systematic way. That is to say, do not simply guess at them, obtain them empirically. For example, in law the values of courts may be obtained by examination of previous decisions, and the values of opposing parties may be learned through the exchange of written or oral interrogatories or questions. In close-knit business organizations, co-workers should continually assess the values and decision tendencies of each other. In face-to-face argumentation, one may simply ask the others whether or not they agree with this point or accept that value. You probably find yourself doing that informally already. In political decision making, public opinion polls are now quite common, and formal questions may be put to others involved in the argument. The general study of values inherent in the group concerned with the claim, as suggested in Chapter 6, will be helpful in this. Furthermore, points of agreement on credible sources should also be included. In other words, this is an unusually important portion of the full brief.

The procedure for finding item number 4 in the brief is clearly explained in Chapter 3 and the fifth statement is fairly clear. In this step, the brief maker seeks to evaluate the potential for argument on both sides of each issue, not with a view toward arguing both sides, but to form an opinion as to those issues most likely to serve the needs of the case.

To illustrate the process of writing a full brief, consider the example of the development and deployment of antiballistic missiles throughout the United States.

1. Policy Claim: Congress should authorize and provide funds for development and deployment of antiballistic missiles throughout the United States.

2. Definitions: An "antiballistic missile" is a device that can intercept and destroy enemy missiles before they reach their target; to deploy "throughout the United States" means that selected strategic areas such as Washington, D.C., military installations, and major cities, will have a ring of A.B.M. sites established.

3. Shared Values, Facts, Credibilities:
    a.   All involved wish to avoid a war with the Soviet Union or China.

    b. All tend to give general credence to intelligence reports produced by the combined agencies of the U.S.

    c. All believe the United States could afford an A.B.M. system if it is truly necessary.

    d. All believe money should not be spent unnecessarily.

    e. Other points of agreement could be mentioned, but will not.

4. Potential Issues:

    a. Is the Soviet Union developing a first-strike potential?

    b. Is present U.S. defense susceptible to first-strike destruction?

    c. Have U.S. diplomatic accords with the U.S.S.R. and China failed to deter the threat of war?

    d. Is the A.B.M. system a significant breakthrough in the arms race?

    e. Is the arms race merely an expensive, but futile, effort?

    f. Is there an inherent antagonism between capitalist and communist countries?

    g. Would an A.B.M. system effectively deter a missile attack?

    h. Does present technology permit construction of an A.B.M. system?

    i. Could defense of the U.S. best be entrusted to an A.B.M. system?

    j. Many, many more potential issues could be listed, but will not.

5. Outline of Issues, Argument, and Support: (Only one will be given for illustrative purposes).

I. The Soviet Union is developing a first strike potential.	I. The Soviet Union is *not* developing a first strike potential.
A. Intelligence reports confirm this.	A. Intelligence reports do not confirm this.
1. The President has been briefed by the C.I.A.	1. Leading Senators have been briefed by intelligence agencies.
2. The Sec. of Defense has been briefed by the Defense intelligence agency.	2. The citations by the President and Secretary of Defense are vague and unreliable.
B. The Soviet Union retains its commitment to conquer the U.S.	B. The Soviet Union does not retain its commitment to conquest.
1. Communist ideology demands it according to Marx, Lenin, Stalin, Khrushchev.	1. Communist ideology has changed in the past few years —current leaders reject war with the U.S.

Notice that this example of a brief is unrealistic in a number of ways: the kinds of support are only suggested, not clearly and specifically cited; the lists of agreements and potential issues are incomplete and stated in general terms too often; and the parallel of arguments in step five is too great. It is not to be expected that each argument will parallel exactly with an opposing one, but the example should serve the purposes of this chapter.

Notice also that when arguments are cast in brief form we have used the more traditional outline structure rather than the Toulmin layout introduced in Chapter 4 (see page 77). There, the Toulmin model that we have adapted to our use is an analytical tool useful before or after the actual written or oral argument is prepared. That layout, however, was not devised to serve as a communicative structure and our observation of argumentation suggests that typically the traditional outline method is used in both written and oral argumentation. Of course even our outline format does not conform to outlining used to show the constituents of some narrative. It is instead a communicative plan in which the audience is first told the claim to be made, then they are given the support for the claim. Such outlining principles as that, which demands a "2" if there is a "1," are irrelevant.

THE AUDIENCE ORIENTATION OF THE CASE

Once a full brief is prepared, it is necessary to examine the specific audience to which the case will be presented. As you can see, the points of agreement (or potential starting points of argument) are stated in general terms in the example above. But in the course of argument for a certain claim, it is likely that cases would be presented to several audiences. For example, on the A.B.M. example, one Senator could be expected to present his case to a variety of audiences among his constituency, to an audience of members of a Congressional committee, and to fellow Senators during formal debate. Each of these audiences is a bit different and would call for the selection of a slightly different case.

You will recall from Chapter 3 the importance in analysis of presumption. It is no less important in case building because it is essential that the arguer make a careful assessment of which side has, for the specific audience, preoccupied the ground. In law, a formal and artifical presumption is made in favor of one accused of a crime. In court, presumption merely means that in the absence of a clear and convincing preponderance of evidence beyond reasonable doubt, the accused will be set free. Otherwise, what would the court do when it becomes clear that neither side had an adequate case? In nonlegal questions the concept of presumption suggests the momentum of the decision makers. How are they tending? Where do they seem inclined to go if no counter argument intervenes? Traditionally, it has been presumed that the audience will always favor rejection of new policies—a presumption in favor of the status quo. This, of course, simply does not work in practice, any more than juries truly assume innocence on the part of those accused of crimes. In fact, empirical data on legislative decision making suggests that many potentially controversial measures pass without much dissent at all:

". . . in almost every policy domain, however contentious some measure may be, numerous noncontentious measures quietly receive unanimous and near-unanimous approval. The formal record does not show how, if at all, they differ in content from the more contentious measures on the same subject."[2]

For some reason, presumption clearly favored these new policy proposals. Often, within a decision making body such as a legislature or even a club, the group is tired, or they have just spent a great deal of time debating a measure and are talked out, or they are anxious to go home, or no one has taken the responsibility to oppose. But for whatever reason, major motions are passed with virtually no discussion or opposition. Scheduling meetings so that major items come up just before mealtime is an old tactic to reach this kind of consensus. A Utah legislator was asked why a bill was passed to limit faculty salary increases at state universities to five percent and he replied, "It came up at the end of the session and no one seemed very interested in it. If anyone had spoken out against it, we would have killed the bill."

To conclude, the traditional concept of presumption, that the proposer of new policy always bears the burden of proof, is an unreliable gauge in case preparation. In fact, by a careful reading of the momentum of the audience, the best case for a claim may be total silence. In the instances cited above, if the proposer had insisted on taking the time to present a full argument, it might possibly have generated that negative response to trigger controversy and possible defeat that might not have otherwise occurred. Burden of proof, then, is not arbitrary; it merely defines what the audience demands of the arguer. If you argue for an antiballistic missile system, what will this specific audience demand that you prove or will they demand nothing of you but give a burden of proof to your op-

---

[2] John C. Wahlke, "Policy Determinants and Legislative Decisions," in S. Sidney Ulmer, ed., *Political Decision-Making* (New York: Van Nostrand-Reinhold Co., 1970), p. 95.

ponents? On any given claim a wide variety of burdens may be assigned. Sometimes audiences will even set up demands for proof that no amount of argument could satisfy.

Another useful concept in understanding the role of the audience in case building is the concept of a *prima facie* case. It refers to the case, which, if the decision maker grants adherence, will bring about the action desired. One might easily have a case that meets a burden of proof that will do what the audience demands of it, but will soon be found faulty because it will not bring about the action desired. Sometimes because of poor analysis and case construction, the decision maker may accept everything you say, but still not agree it leads to the goal being sought. For example, some negotiators among students have demanded reforms in the university with the ultimate goal of strengthening student control but have been frustrated when the reforms could be granted *in toto* without any change in the locus of power. Their problem was in the case they built.

Cases, then, are selected in terms of the audiences to whom they will be presented, and they are constructed from materials derived from the interaction of the claim and the audience. Cases built without regard for the specific audience often lead to disaster. Notice some of the considerations. Momentum has already been mentioned—if the situation suggests it, remain silent or summarize your case in a single sentence. Special rules may need to be followed—an argument prepared for court would be out of place at a political rally. All former college debaters discover that many of the protocols they learned in educational debate are irrelevant, or even damaging when debating in other contexts. Time will sometimes be the most important rule—no case that requires more than 15 minutes to present will be accepted by some groups, and lawyers accustomed to the more leisurely pace of the court often find it difficult to adjust. The particular claim may require the presentation of the case over and over again in the form of a persuasive campaign before full adherence can be achieved.

Cases may need to be adjusted to a variety of audiences and media of communication ranging from a full hour presentation to one minute on television. The format in which the case is to be given will vary and the advocate must be prepared. Sometimes a formal debate context is used, and uninterrupted presentations can be made. Often, as in a hearing or presentation, the decision makers will freely interrupt the advocate with questions that must be answered immediately regardless of the place they should fall in the case. Sometimes opposing advocates are permitted to cross examine the speaker, or even interrupt with brief speeches of counter argument. On television, the media officials may create a debate by filming brief statements from various people and then editing them together to give the appearance of answering one another. The advocate must adjust the case for such situations.

It is difficult to suggest specific tools with which to perform this audience analysis. If time and situation permits, it would be useful to administer some form of paper and pencil test to a sample of your audience. An attitude test, a semantic differential, or simply a public opinion survey would provide important insights into the audience's potential reaction to your case. If possible, extended personal interviews with sample members of the audience could reveal their response to your argumentation. In many situations this occurs spontaneously in the form of luncheon meetings with officers of the company who will participate in deciding your proposals, or lobbying sessions with members of the decision making body. Such face-to-face interviews with as many members of the potential audience as possible serve at least two functions. First, they give you valuable information as to the state of mind and momentum of the audience, and second, they allow you to try out case elements so that decision makers have time to grow familiar and comfortable with them prior to the formal presentation of the case. If the situation permits you to employ the paper and pencil instruments of audience analysis, it would be important to seek the advice of a testing specialist who can direct the selection of the sample, the construction and administration of the tests, and the analysis of the data gathered. Such a specialist may be useful in the interview process as well as if a large sample is to be used. However, in most situations, the presenter of the case and a few immediate colleagues will have only limited access to the audience. Here, it is wise to become a sensitive listener in informal conversations. Finally, in some select situations, professional assistance for audience analysis will be readily available. In politics, it is easy to secure the services of an opinion sampling firm. In law, there are firms that specialize in gathering data about potential jurors. In business, there are consultants who stand ready to assess the decision making climate of a target group. Whenever these formal aids are available, their use will increase significantly the quality of cases developed.

COUNTER ARGUMENT

No matter what the format in which a case is to be used, it must be prepared in the expectation of counter argument. Sometimes case writers permit themselves the delusion that their carefully built arguments will be considered by decision makers in their originial form. This rarely happens. Before the case is finally considered, it must typically endure attacks from those advocating other points of view. Even unstated counter arguments can be damaging to the case if permitted to remain in the decision maker's mind unchallenged. Counter arguments are often presented, however, and they often change the character of a case from that originally planned. The best plan in case building is to do so in the expectation of attack and the test of a case will be not only its basic integrity but its ability to withstand and endure attack as well.

What factors should be considered in determining whether a case will "defend" well? First, the availability of support, as discussed in earlier chapters, is critical. Support is needed both for the initial presentation and for rebuttals that follow. Elements in a case that have some support for the basic argument but none to back up in response to rebuttal are dangerous. Some effort can be spent on asking oneself where an opponent is likely to make the most vigorous attacks on the case (this is one reason for the preparation of the full brief). If the central attack is liable to come at a point lacking in secondary support, the case may need to be changed. Among some debaters it is popular to "sandbag," or layout the case originally with thin support, and hold in reserve massive amounts of support to be used in rebuttal. This is a strategem frowned on by many and appropriate only to a few situations, such as educational debate, and some criminal trials. In general, however, a case without secondary support will be difficult to defend.

THE GENERAL ORIENTATION OF THE CASE

Typically an argumentative case is thought of as a highly partisan, one-sided presentation. However, in recent years empirical studies have suggested the value of a two-sided approach in which the arguer considers arguments of various kinds with relative impartiality, and then concludes in favor of one position. Early research tended to show that the one-sided case is most effective in limited situations, and the two-sided approach should be more effective with decision makers who are educated beyond the high school level, are likely to be exposed to presentations in opposition to the original case, or who are initially opposed to the position taken in the case.[3] More recent investigations have led to the conclusion that "the two-sided speech was either just as effective or more

[3] C. I. Hovland, C. I. Lumsdaine, and A. A. Sheffield, *Experiments on Mass Communication* (Princeton: Princeton University Press, 1949); and A. A. Lumsdaine and I. L. Janis, "Resistance to 'Counter-propaganda' Produced by One-Sided and Two-Sided 'Propaganda' Presentations," *Public Opinion Quarterly*, 17 (1953), pp. 311–318.

effective in every instance except one: where listeners heard a one-sided speech of opposition a week after having heard a one-sided speech advocating a change in public policy."[4]

Both the initial perception as well as the ability of a case to withstand opposition are enhanced through the two-sided approach except where the decision maker is highly ego involved in the decision. The more ego involved an individual is, the more variations of opinion he will reject. If the case falls clearly outside that range of positions acceptable or at least not committed on by the decision maker, it will tend to be perceived as even more distinct than the arguers intended it to be. "The greater the commitment or dedication of an individual to his stand on an issue, the greater the displacement of a discrepant message away from the bounds of his acceptance."[5] On the other hand, if the case is perceived as within the decision maker's latitude of acceptance, it will tend to be seen as in greater agreement with his own position than the arguer intended. It has been asserted that whether an argument is labeled reasonable or not is more a function of the position and perception of the decision maker than any intrinsic characteristics of the argument: as a case is seen in disagreement with one's own position, "it is dubbed *at the same time* as unreasonable, propagandistic, false, and even obnoxious."[6] Of course, in the ordinary course of argument it is impossible to control the amount of ego-involvement in the topic on the part of the decision maker. But it is possible to increase the number of possible interpretations of the topic in relation to a specific case through a two-sided or even multisided approach, and this will increase the probability of change toward the advocated position.[7]

THE SEQUENCE OF ARGUMENTS

Inevitably, a case will consist of some arguments that will be seen as stronger by some decision makers than the other elements in the case. This will vary from audience to audience and is difficult to determine in relation to any particular judge or other decision maker. However, if it is

---

[4] J. W. Koehler, "Effects on Audience Opinion of One-Sided and Two-Sided Speeches Supporting and Opposing a Proposition," in Thomas D. Beisecker and Donn W. Parson, eds., *The Process of Social Influence* (Englewood Cliffs: Prentice-Hall, Inc., 1972), pp. 351–369.

[5] Carolyn W. Sherif, Muzafer Sherif, and Roger E. Nebergall, *Attitude and Attitude Change* (Philadelphia: W. B. Saunders Co., 1965), p. 226.

[6] Sherif, Sherif, and Nebergall, p. 227.

[7] Sherif, Sherif, and Nebergall, p. 244.

possible to make a determination that for a given audience one of the case elements is stronger than others, the question comes as to where in the sequence of the case it should be placed. Research results in this area are not clear, but generally speaking, if the decision makers are likely to be antagonistic to the case, or even uninterested in it, the strongest arguments should be presented first. If the audience is highly ego involved in the claim, it is wise to present those arguments most congruent with those of the decision makers first.[8]

OBLIGATIONS OF A CASE

Much literature on the theory of persuasion speaks of changing beliefs, attitudes, or position regarding a topic. Many studies have been performed to observe the situations under which various forms of persuasion generate *some* amount of change in an audience. An argumentative case has more precise obligations than this. Certainly, as with any other kind of persuasion, the case is built to change or reinforce positions to the extent possible, but unless it can secure the adherence of the relevant decision makers, it has failed. For example, a case made in a legislative body for a public policy, which brings many to its support, and still fails to achieve a majority vote, fails at least for that time. A presentation to the chairman of a committee with which he can sympathize but not support, is a failure. A legal case that convinces many of the quality of its position, but the lawyer's client still loses the suit is a failure. These situations are about as satisfying to the professional advocates as is the statement by a debate judge that a college debate team is clearly better than the opponents but the opponents won the debate.

Even more, much research in persuasion notes that after the passage of a few weeks the effects of a persuasive message may disappear, but an argumentative case must sustain its support over the passage of weeks and months. Many persuasive situations are such that immediate effects are sufficient—selling some products, winning votes that cannot be taken back, moving people to write their Congressman, or convincing a group to go on strike. But almost no important decision is made in which an immediate and irrevocable choice results from the single presentation of argumentative cases. In law, an elaborate and complicated system of appeals requires all decisions be subject to several reviews that may ultimately occupy several years. In legislatures there are commonly rules for committee consideration as well as two or more debates on the floor and final

[8] Martin and Andersen, p. 129.

approval by an executive. In complex organizations, such as business, military, educational, and government, there are usually several levels of administration through which a claim and its accompanying cases must pass before action is taken. A chief obligation of an argumentative case is to win and *sustain* adherence over time.

Sustaining a case raises certain necessary characteristics that must be considered. In educational debate as well as some persuasive situations, use is made of the ignorance or naivete of the decision maker. "Trick" cases that catch opponents off guard long enough to win a debate have been used. In advertising, misleading references to evidence are made in the thought the audience will never check it out. For example, one pain killer says it contains the "ingredient doctors recommend." Of course that ingredient is aspirin, which can be obtained more easily and less expensively in other products, but few members of the audience bother to explore the claim. In educational debate evidence is sometimes quoted out of context or manufactured altogether in the expectation that the judge or opposition will not be able to prove the error until the debate is over. But these are not representative argumentative situations, for in important decision making, time is taken for advocates to check out opponents' evidence and other strategies. Trickery simply is not a practical approach to the case.

Of all the obligations of a case, providing an appropriate justification for the claim is the most important. Remember it is not enough (sometimes not even necessary) for a case to change the mental state of the decision makers. The case must provide them with bases acceptable within the context in which the case is presented for adherence to the claim. For example, many have spoken persuasively against inadequacies in welfare, mental health institutions, education, economic control, transportation, ecology, and a host of other issues. But they are often dissatisfied by the failure of government to provide the support to make corrections. It is one thing to agree that poverty should be eliminated, but another to provide justification to legislators to take money from other areas in order to launch a "Marshall Plan" for the poor. It is one thing to agree that our children should have the finest education available, but another to provide justification to increase budgets for schools and universities in the face of diminishing enrollments. Even though the decision makers feel strongly that something should be done in the direction advocated, they will not, perhaps cannot, adhere to the policies until they are satisfied they can justify the action to their constitutents, their fellow legislators, or any other significant group. Providing this justification is a singular function of the argumentative case.

Furthermore, justification satisfactory in one context may not serve another. A Senate committee may be satisfied, and say so in its report, that government officials are guilty of crimes. But the materials on which they justify that position might be rejected in a court of law or a political meeting. A justification for expenditure of billions of dollars for space exploration may be satisfactory in Congress, but be rejected by groups representing the poor. A justification for establishing a new line of production may satisfy the marketing unit of a company but be insufficient for the Board of Directors. Cases must be constructed in such a way as to provide sufficient justification for the adherence of all decision makers.

OCCASIONS FOR CASE BUILDING

Because cases are so much associated with legal argument, it is easy to believe that only in formal debate is it appropriate to take the time to build one. In fact, case building in various forms occurs in many different situations daily.

LAW

Chapter 11 will discuss legal argument in detail. It is sufficient here to mention that lawyers not only use cases during the ordinary trial, they also prepare them regularly in the form of memoranda to clients arguing a position on a legal question, presentations to regulatory agencies, investigative bodies, and quasi-judicial groups such as the Federal Communications Commission, National Labor Relations Board, or the Securities and Exchange Commission. When a lawyer represents a client in any kind of decision making situation, he will need to prepare some kind of case.

LEGISLATION

Much has already been said about the case used in policy questions. Let it be said that policy making bodies from city and county commissions to the Congress engage in extensive hearings pursuant to legislating and those who testify before them advance cases just as much as those who debate before the formal assembly. Not only lawyers and legislators testify before such committees. Many representatives from private organizations who will be affected by proposed legislation also testify. Those who are associated with special interest groups, such as the League of Women Voters, Common Cause, Sierra Club, etc., will also be invited to testify. They must all advance a case effectively if they want to have influence.

PRESENTATIONS

In a vast number of organizations, including businesses, governments, military, civic, charitable, and action organizations, policy making is done by select committees before whom presentations are made. The presentation, sometimes called simply a briefing in less formal situations, is a concept most common to business, government, and military decision making. It is an extraordinary form of a case designed to secure approval of a plan of action. Most often, they are carefully prepared and even scripted by members within the organization, and in modern practice they often involve the use of many media of communication including visual support, recordings, charts, graphs, models, as well as the verbal presentation. Ordinarily, a presentation will be prepared only on the request of an employer or supervisor to achieve a specific goal such as securing a policy decision within the organization, or securing the commitment of an outside person or group to a contractual or other association with the home group. When an advertising agency seeks a new client, they make a presentation to show what they can do. When an engineering or architectural firm seeks a client, they make a presentation. The same is true of other manufacturing and service organizations. Thus, a presentation usually does not represent the views of the one person giving it, but rather gives the position of an entire organization. There are five characteristics of this form of case building:

1. They are prepared for repeated use;
2. they are impersonal and feature a spokesman, not a speaker;
3. they have programmed visual and/or audio accompaniment;
4. they are problem oriented;
5. they are planned carefully and receive top management approval.[9]

More than usual space has been taken to describe this occasion for case building because it is so pervasive in modern society, and because it often is not perceived as an occasion for case development.

INFORMAL OCCASIONS

Whenever an individual or small group invites an outside party to speak in relation to a decision, it is appropriate to prepare some kind of case. If

[9] David L. Woods, "Presentations: A Semantic Illusion?" Unpublished paper provided by the Navy Department Speech Bureau.

a faculty committee is considering a petition to waive a requirement and invites the student making the request to come before it, the student should prepare a case. If an employer is considering a request for a raise and asks the employee to come in to talk about it, he should come with a case. If an accrediting agency is examining a program to see if it deserves a license or other form of accreditation, they should be given a case in your behalf by a spokesman. Minicases are even appropriate when a husband wants approval from a wife for a camping trip, or a wife is seeking approval to accept an office in an organization, or if children are seeking parental approval for a two-week trip to Florida. The more important the decision is to you, the more painful a denial of adherence to your proposal would be, the more reason you have for building a case.

FORMATS FOR CASE BUILDING

No one or few proper or correct procedures for building cases exists. The best format for a case is the one best suited to the decision making group to which it is to be presented. Thus, case building begins with the audience. As suggested earlier, the best case may be a simple assertion: "I think we should do this." If those involved say they agree, the case has won. Of course, one must never forget the need to sustain the case, and simple assertions tend not to go very far.

To illustrate the process of case building, it is possible to describe a few formats that have been used frequently with success. Remember the case structure employed is a communicative one that resembles the traditional outline, and not the analytical adoption of the Toulmin model. This list does not exhaust the subject; it is illustrative.

PROBLEM-SOLUTION

Probably the most common approach to case building is one based on a problem-solution approach. It is characteristic of journalistic writing and can be found in essays, special interest publications, or virtually any issue of the *Reader's Digest*. The format is as follows:

I.   There is a serious problem.
    A.   The problem exists and is growing.
       (Appropriate support is given.)
    B.   The problem is serious.
       (Support)

    C.   Present methods cannot cope with the problem.
        (Support)

II. There is a solution to the problem.

    A.   The solution is practical.
        (Support)

    B.   The solution is desirable.
        (Support)

    C.   We can implement the solution.
        (Support)

The argumentative rationale of this case format is reasoning from cause to effect and from effect to cause. This line of argument is discussed in Chapter 4 (see p. 83), and it can be illustrated analytically in this way:

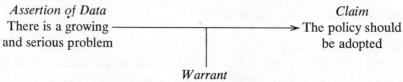

Assertion of Data	*Claim*
There is a growing and serious problem	The policy should be adopted

Warrant
Since X is the cause of the problem,
and our proposed policy will eliminate
the cause; and since to eliminate a
cause is to eliminate its effect.

That is to say, a great many people in the United States and similar cultures accept the idea that most events or phenomena have one or a few factors that cause or account for them. Thus, if some evil exists, there must be a cause for it, and any proposal that will ameliorate or eliminate that cause should provide relief from the evil. In educational debate this is called a "Need, Plan, Advantage" case, and elsewhere it is referred to as a rational-deductive or synoptic case.[10] It suggests a complete analysis of the present state of affairs, the discovery of evils inherent within the present policies (inherent means a characteristic inextricably bound up with the policy and correctable only by changing the policy), an analysis of alternative solutions, and finally a demonstration of the preferred solution. This is an extremely common format for a case and will therefore be familiar to most audiences. It is difficult to defend against a strong counter agrument because it is increasingly difficult to justify a notion of discrete causes and inherent evils.

[10] David Braybrooke and Charles E. Lindblom, *A Strategy of Decision* (New York: The Free Press of Glencoe, 1963), pp. 37–57.

COMPARATIVE ADVANTAGES

To cope with the rhetorical difficulties in sustaining a problem-solution case, policy makers as well as other debaters have adopted in many instances what is called a comparative advantage or incremental approach. David Braybooke and Charles E. Lindblom suggest that an observation of the way policies are considered and enacted reveals that typically it is not done by seeking full knowledge of the present system and the proposed alternative, and then deciding to substitute one for the other. This requires, they say, dealing with more uncertainty of consequences and risking more disruption of the system than policy makers are willing to do. Instead, policies are changed by repetitive, small changes in relatively unimportant variables, or relatively unimportant changes in important variables. Social change that

"largely repeats (with respect to the elements altered and with respect to the character and scope of the changes) frequent previous change . . . . Changes in interest rates, tax rates, severity of court sentences, school curricula, budget allocations to various public services, or traffic regulations achieve changes of this kind."[11]

These changes are called increments and come from society's willingness to try small improvements on the current policies, test them, try some more improvements, and thereby move gradually from status to status. These are the "decisions of ordinary political life, even if they rarely solve problems but merely stave them off or nibble at them, often making headway but sometimes retrogressing."[12] These policies are adopted not out of a rejection of present policies but from a desire to improve them within margins of predictable consequences.

The basic format of the comparative advantages or incremental case is this:

I.   Adoption of the proposal would be advantageous in way 1.
   A.   The present policy does not now enjoy this advantage. (Support)
   B.   The proposal would provide the advantage. (Support)
II.   Adoption of the proposal would be advantageous in way 2.
   A.   The present policy does not now enjoy this advantage. (Support)

[11] Braybrooke and Lindblom, pp. 64–65.
[12] Braybrooke and Lindblom, p. 71.

B.   The proposal would provide the advantage. (Support)
(Additional advantages may be claimed.)

An example of incremental change contrasted with the problem-solution approach is in public policy regarding medical care in the United States. For many years debaters have advanced a problem-solution case against the private practice of medicine and have proposed a national health service in its place. Opponents have been quite successful in challenging these cases. But during the same years, debaters have made out comparative advantages cases against selected elements of the private medical system. For example, the lack of care for the poor was attacked, the lack of sufficient medical schools was challenged, the lack of enough hospitals was noted, the problems of medical care for the aged was argued, the problem of insuring the average citizen against the costs of medical care was suggested, and so on. Each of these proposed advantages, that is, where private medicine had not provided a service or advantage and it was proposed that the government should do so, have been adopted. Today, when the adoption of a national health service is discussed, debaters may be able to suggest it will not be a change in an entire system but merely another increment in the constantly changing medical policy. Whatever happens, the successful cases in this debate have been those of comparative advantages.

The argumentative rationale of this case is reasoning from lesser to greater or *a fortiori* in classical terms. If the present policy is good, think how much better it would be with the addition of this advantage, is the line of reasoning. By building on the known, argumentation into a relatively restricted unknown is made easier.

A schematic illustration of this rationale is shown in the Toulmin format in this way:

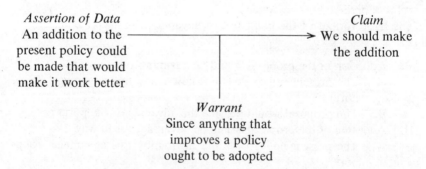

Assertion of Data
An addition to the
present policy could
be made that would
make it work better

Claim
We should make
the addition

Warrant
Since anything that
improves a policy
ought to be adopted

There is a parallel between this line of thought and the enthymematic argument discussed in Chapter 4 (see p. 41).

CRITERIA

In some argumentative situations, particularly those not directly involving policy making, the use of criteria as the basis of case building is popular. This case is directly related to the discussion of the analysis of claims of fact and value in Chapter 3. It will be particularly noted in legal argument where statutory or case law provides the criteria on which a case can be built. For example, in debating diplomatic recognition of the People's Republic of China debaters argued that three criteria must be met before a nation deserves recognition: (1) the government must in fact be in control of the nation; (2) the government must be able to speak for a majority of the citizens; and (3) the government must be prepared to meet its responsibilities in the international community of nations. Opponents argued that the only true criterion for diplomatic recognition was whether or not the action would be politically and militarily advantageous to the country contemplating the action.

The basic format of the criteria case is this:

I.   The criteria necessary to warrant the proposal are these:
  A.   Criterion 1
      (Support)
  B.   Criterion 2
      (Support)
  (Additional criteria as desired may be argued.)
II. The proposal meets all the necessary criteria.
  A.   It meets criterion 1.
      (Support)
  B.   It meets criterion 2.
      (Support)

The argumentative rationale for the criteria case is reasoning from definition. In criminal trials and some civil cases it is possible to say in advance what must be done for a case to be *prima facie* and this will be particularly influential in winning adherence to the case. In nonlegal contexts, it is sometimes possible to derive criteria from the practice of the organization or system in which the case is to be made. In general, it is often a successful approach to achieve adherence to criteria, and then use that adherence as a starting point from which to advance a further claim.

Argument from definition is discussed in Chapter 4 (see pages 85–86). In a Toulmin layout the case would be in this form.

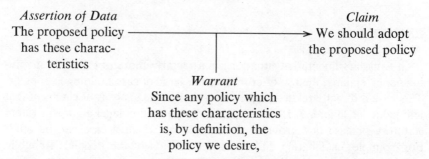

Assertion of Data
The proposed policy
has these charac-
teristics

Warrant
Since any policy which
has these characteristics
is, by definition, the
policy we desire,

Claim
We should adopt
the proposed policy

In recent years, the concept of a "criteria" case has been employed to designate a specific form of case used in intercollegiate debate. This will be discussed in greater detail in Chapter 13, but it might be useful to describe it briefly here. Essentially, this form of criteria case deals with values as much or more than actual proposed policies. The affirmative argues in favor of adherence to a set of values, which when adopted, will lead to the adoption of the affirmative policy proposal. Once again, the acceptance of criteria is used as a starting point for argument in favor of a policy. The difference is that sometimes it is more difficult to secure consensus on the criteria.

CHAIN OF REASONING

Often a successful case requires moving more gradually from points of agreement to adherence to the new proposal so that a case takes on the characteristic of a step-by-step progression. Regardless of the logical model used for this, it can be called generally a chain of reasoning case. This format is particularly suited to proposals that may generate strong disagreement or trigger ego-involved contrast effects that would increase polarization between the debater and the decision maker. To establish as much common ground as possible and thereby stave off the more violent reactions, the debater begins by claiming what he is relatively sure the decision makers will accept. Then, an added claim will be attached to the first that moves the adherence a bit further toward the claim, and finally, the claim itself is advanced.

The format for a chain of reasoning case is basically that of any one of a number of logical forms. The syllogism is quite commonly used:

Major premise: "We can agree upon this general statement"
Minor premise: "This specific claim can be readily accepted"
  (Support)
Conclusion: "The claim follows logically from these premises."
  (Support)

Sometimes it is necessary to advance support for the major premise, but often a sufficiently universal generalization can be found that support is unnecessary. Most important, the major premise should embody values shared by the decision makers and arguer, strongly held, and instrumental to the claim to be advanced.

Other forms of the syllogism may also serve for this format. The hypothetical syllogism would function in this way:

> If a particular claim is accepted, then the proposed claim should be adopted.
> (Support)
> The claim should be accepted.
> (Support)
> The proposed claim should be adopted.

Use could be made of the disjunctive form of the syllogism:

> Either the former claim or the proposed claim must be accepted.
> (Support)
> The former claim cannot be accepted.
> (Support)
> Thus, the proposed claim must be accepted.

Debaters have also tried the Toulmin layout of argument to create a case. The difference here would be a clear separation of Data, Warrant, Backing, and Claim. Finally, an inductive format may be employed in a chain of reasoning case.

> Claim 1 should be accepted as fact.
> (Support)
> Claim 2 should be accepted as fact.
> (Support)
> (State as many such claims as desired.)
> If these claims are all accepted, then it follows the proposed claim should be accepted as a consequence.
> (Support)

In the latter format, the proposed claim remains undisclosed from the decision makers until the entire argument is complete. In this way, maximum opportunity can be taken to establish common ground and prevent negative ego-involved reactions.

The essential rationale of the chain of reasoning case, however, can be shown in the Toulmin layout by indicating that one argument establishes a claim, and then that claim becomes data for another argument, and so on until the critical claim is reached.

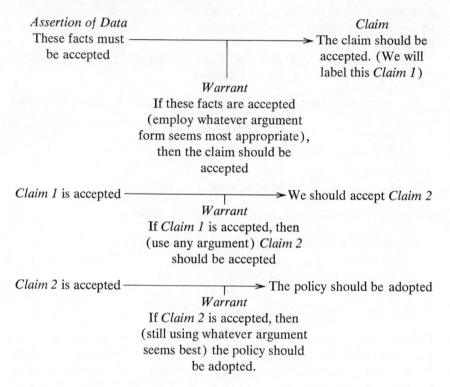

Assertion of Data
These facts must
be accepted

Claim
The claim should be
accepted. (We will
label this *Claim 1*)

Warrant
If these facts are accepted
(employ whatever argument
form seems most appropriate),
then the claim should be
accepted

Claim 1 is accepted ────────→ We should accept *Claim 2*
Warrant
If *Claim 1* is accepted, then
(use any argument) *Claim 2*
should be accepted

Claim 2 is accepted ────────→ The policy should be adopted
Warrant
If *Claim 2* is accepted, then
(still using whatever argument
seems best) the policy should
be adopted.

For a thorough discussion of the chain of reasoning form of argument, go back to Chapter 4 and examine pages 87–88.

RESIDUES

Similar to the chain of reasoning case is the one that uses the method of residues. This is a particularly analytical approach and if the first claim —that a distinct number of alternatives is open—is accepted, argument for the proposed claim becomes much easier. The format is this:

I.   X (state the number), and only X alternatives may be chosen. (Support)

II. X minus 1 alternatives (all but the proposed claim) are unacceptable.

III. Only the proposed claim remains to be selected.

This format resembles the disjunctive approach, and differs only in that it serves to eliminate as many alternatives as seem available. Physicians and scholars are prone to this case format. In diagnosing an illness, for example, the physician may note from symptoms that only a certain number of ailments create those particular reactions. Then he systematically eliminates them until only one remains. The reasoning of fictional detectives such as Sherlock Holmes, called deduction, is of this variety. In a certain number of policy situations, when a limited range of decisions is open, the method of residues may prove to be a particularly appropriate case format to use.

From an analytical point of view, the method of residues has this appearance.

Assertion of Data   *Claim*
The proposed policy is ———————————————— We should adopt
workable and alterna-   the proposed
tives 2, 3, 4, and 5   policy
are not workable

Warrant
Since these are the only five possible
policies, and since only number one is
workable, and since we should adopt
the only workable policy,

SYSTEMS

Some decision makers are unwilling to accept the more standard assumptions of causal relationships or the ability of an arguer to analyze a problem as if it were a frozen state of affairs. Instead, they demand the recognition that all that we deal with is in a constant state or process, cannot be measured in a finite way, and is necessarily in part a function of the judgments of human beings.[13] If the audience is of this mind, a unique approach to case building is required. One that approaches decision making from the point of view of systems theory can serve in this situation. Cases using this format arose during and after World War II and have been variously called systems analysis or operations research. Instead of speaking of problems and their solutions, the case speaks of interrelationships of elements forming a system and the potential impact on the system as new elements are introduced. The case builder must establish a

---

[13] For an excellent discussion of this concept see David H. Smith, "Communication Research and the Idea of Process," *Speech Monographs*, *39* (August 1972), pp. 174–182.

model (preferably mathematical) that serves as a simplified representation of the operation or system under discussion, and which focuses on those elements of the system with which he wants to deal. Next, the case builder must advance some measure of effectiveness to show the extent to which the operation or system is attaining its goal. "A *consistent* statement of the fundamental goals of the operation is essential to the mathematical logic of the model."[14] Finally, a demonstration of the necessity of decision and the relative merits of alternatives is presented. The format could be set forth in this way:

I.   The present system has these constituents.
     (Support, primarily by means of a model.)
II. The goals of the present system are these.
     (Support)
III. To modify the system to maximize goals, these alternatives are available.
     (Support)
IV. This alternative should be chosen.
     (Support)

Similarly, the case can be set out using one of the case formats already mentioned, but including these elements: (1) Goals of the present system; (2) Relationship of the system to achievement of goals; (3) Impact of the present system's progress toward goals; (4) Relationship of the claim to the present system; (5) Impact of addition of the claim to the system in relation to goals.[15]

The argumentative rationale of the systems case is the process character of reality and the need to deal with it systematically. Winning of adherence to such cases has often come from the ability to present much of the support in the form of computer simulation of the system and selection mathematically from alternatives. Robert McNamara who was Secretary of Defense under Presidents Kennedy and Johnson introduced this type of case into Congressional Committee Hearings and often won his argument by the weight of data he could bring to bear on the question.

A systems approach is difficult to illustrate schematically, but in a simplified form it would take the following appearance in a Toulmin layout.

[14] Cyril C. Herrmann and John F. Magee, "Operations Research for Management," in Abe Shuchman, ed., *Scientific Decision Making in Business* (New York: Holt, Rinehart and Winston, Inc., 1963), p. 27.

[15] For a particularly thorough discussion of these elements see Bernard L. Brock et al., *Public Policy Decision-Making: Systems Analysis and Comparative Advantages Debate* (New York: Harper & Row, Publishers, 1973), pp. 85–109.

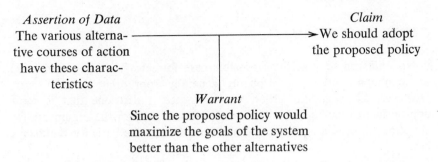

Assertion of Data
The various alternative courses of action have these characteristics

Claim
We should adopt the proposed policy

Warrant
Since the proposed policy would maximize the goals of the system better than the other alternatives

PUBLIC INTEREST AND OPINION

In the justification of public policy decisions, administrators and legislators often employ a case centered around a determination of the public interest or opinion. This case is similar to the criteria case but is more specifically aimed at the argumentative rationale that what the people believe and want ought to be done. Although lawyers and debaters engaged in the educational debate often scorn the use of polls and other opinion measurements, politicians do not. The format is quite simple.

I.   The public opinion and interest demand this claim.
     (Support)
II. Therefore the claim should be adopted.

When the debater takes the initiative to set out such a case, it tends to force opponents to take the philosophical position that the people do not know what is good for them—a claim that may be popular within small circles but which is difficult to advance to the public at large. Of course, the case is not particularly useful if the support for stating what the public wants is not strong. A single opinion poll probably will not suffice—it is too easily refuted. However, when the first contention can be based on a combination of past and present polls and generally held beliefs of the public interest, the case can be a strong one.

In the analytical schematic, this case format has these elements.

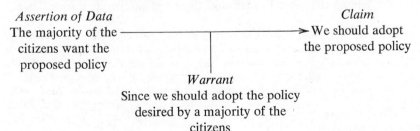

Assertion of Data
The majority of the citizens want the proposed policy

Claim
We should adopt the proposed policy

Warrant
Since we should adopt the policy desired by a majority of the citizens

OTHER CASE FORMATS

No limit can be placed on possible case formats. The ones mentioned are commonly used and probably generally appropriate to audiences. However, as suggested earlier, the best case is that one that is most appropriate to the specific situation. Essentially, any of the argumentative structures discussed in Chapter 4 might be used as the basis for building a case.

When advancing a case that must gain adherence over time and to many different audiences, the case takes on the characteristics of a campaign. Then the arguer may wish to formulate cases along lines of persuasive designs, such as the stimulus-response design, the motivational design, the social design, the personality design, or the cognitive design that is most closely associated with the traditional case structure.[16] At such a point, it would be useful to refer to references on the theories of persuasion.[17]

CONCLUSIONS

The case constitutes an overall strategy for securing adherence through argumentative justification. Analysis and brief construction constitute the start of case building, and the focal point is the specific audience to which it is to be presented. A case is more than a basic presentation. It must be able to withstand counter argument, and it should be prepared with attention to how well it can be defended. Argumentative cases have greater obligations than persuasion generally. They must win that adherence necessary to secure a favorable decision, and they must be able to sustain that adherence over time and through a number of levels of review.

There are many occasions for the construction of cases. Situations such as legal argument, legislative argument, and the organizational presentation are among the most formal, and there are numerous informal situa-

[16] For a full discussion of these persuasive designs, see Otto Lerbinger, *Designs for Persuasive Communication* (Englewood Cliffs: Prentice-Hall, Inc., 1972), pp. 53–112.

[17] In addition to Martin and Andersen, and Beisecker and Parson already cited, the reader may wish to refer to other sources on persuasion theory such as Wallace C. Fotheringham, *Perspectives on Persuasion* (Boston: Allyn and Bacon, Inc., 1966); Dan Nimmo, *The Political Persuaders* (Englewood Cliffs: Prentice-Hall, Inc., 1970); and Milton Rokeach, *Beliefs, Attitudes, and Values* (San Francisco: Jossey-Bass, Inc., Publishers, 1968).

tions for which a case should be prepared. There are a number of possible case formats. They include the problem-solution, comparative advantages, criteria, chain of reasoning, residues, systems, and public interest and opinion. But the best case format of all is the one most appropriate to the audience to which it is to be presented.

PROJECTS

1. On a number of cases selected from law, politics, business, school debate, etc., describe the argumentative rationale.

2. On a subject of interest to you, prepare a case for presentation to the rest of the class.

3. Exchange cases with other class members and write a critique on the one you receive.

4. Prepare a basic case for a claim using one of the formats discussed in this chapter where several others in the class used a different format on the same claim. Compare your methods and discuss the relative advantages of each.

5. Write a short essay (no more than three pages) explaining how a case you are preparing to use before the class would need to be changed if delivered before a quite different audience.

9

Refutation

Argumentation implies at least the possibility that others may criticize the statements an arguer makes. Such critics will sometimes be advocates of alternate positions who must deny adherence to other points of view in order to gain it for their own. Other critics function simply to test the arguments of others so that adherence, if given, will be based on a thorough understanding of the issues. There is a general belief in our nation that arguments subjected to close examination by critics somehow lead to "better" decisions than those which are not. Therefore, the role of the critic is invaluable to the process of argumentation and that role is dependent on the skills of refutation.

THE PROCESS OF REFUTATION

Various terms are used to refer to what is called here the process of refutation. Some writers distinguish between *refutation* and *rebuttal*. For them, refutation embodies the attacking of others' arguments, while rebuttal suggests a broader effort to criticize opponents' reasons while defending one's own arguments from their attacks. Of course, in such contexts as law and educational debate, "rebuttal" is a word used to designate the entire portion of the presentation that follows the construc-

185

tive arguments, and is devoted exclusively to attack and defense. For this chapter, "refutation" will be used to designate both attacking others' arguments and defending one's own.

The need for refutation comes from the decision makers. Some writers on argumentation speak of a "burden of rebuttal" in reference to the logical requirements inherent in the interplay of arguments pro and con. In highly specialized decision situations, particularly in educational debate, the decision makers are charged with the responsibility of keeping notes on all that is said, and the debaters have a corresponding duty to make *some* reply to every attack on their position. Sometimes, failure to comment on an attack, however trivial, may bring the loss of the debate. But this is primarily a learning situation, and presumably the reason for it is to teach the young debaters to be alert to attacks. In most argumentative situations, the burden of rebuttal comes only from those whose adherence is sought. As we noted in the chapter on case building, silence may be the most effective strategy. One should determine how much refutation to engage in depending on how much decision makers demand it.

If an opponent is presenting a case to a highly antagonistic audience, the listeners may generate sufficient criticism in their own minds to reject it. At such a time, it may be wise for the critic to summarize as briefly as possible the attacks he believes to be in the minds of the decision makers. It might be a mistake to protest too much. On the contrary, a case presented to a favorable audience may be immune to criticism, and its refutation may then prove to be a long and frustrating endeavor.

Ability in refutation is a key aspect of the total effort in argumentation. Don Faules experimentally investigated the relation between effectiveness in refutation and general effectiveness as a debater. He concluded that those who scored high on a test of refutation skill were also likely to be rated as excellent debaters by trained observers.[1] Faules also found that those who produced the best arguments in refutation also tend to produce more total arguments than others not rated as highly.

RELATION OF REFUTATION TO LOGIC

Curiously, although most analysts today do not subscribe to the notion that argument derives its strength from its approximation to formal logical models, they still inconsistently tend to recommend the application of logical tests in refutation. That is to say, even those who recognize the

---

[1] Don Faules, "Measuring Refutation Skill: An Exploratory Study," *The Journal of the American Forensic Association*, 4 (Spring 1967), pp. 47–52.

essentially rhetorical nature of argumentation—that validity is derived from the adherence of relevant decision makers—often describe refutation largely in terms of logical inadequacies. W. Ward Fearnside and William B. Holther state the case for formal logic in the extreme when they say that they believe the ". . . triumph of rhetoric is like the spread of a virus infection." They decry mistakes in logic as well as premises which ". . . are frauds, snares, delusions," as well as the tricks used to bring people to accept such premises. What they call for, in preparing to refute such arguments, is the development of "a serum against some forms of persuasion." And the serum comes from logic, which is the "defense against trickery." Fallacies are faulty reasoning processes and specious persuasions, and the application of logical thought will reveal them.[2] C.L. Hamblin defines a fallacious argument, "as almost every account from Aristotle onwards tells you, . . . [as] one that *seems to be valid* but *is not so*,"[3] even though in a later chapter he observes that dialectical rules derive their authority from the participants of each dialogue.[4]

Once again, even writers who recognize that the arguments that human beings deal with regularly cannot be subjected to the rigor of formal logic, tend to describe refutation as a process of raising the level of discourse by exposing logical errors. Again, the error, for such writers, is inherent in the argument and remains only to be pointed out to the audience. Rather than seeking to observe how human beings *actually* engage in criticism of argument, such writers presume to know how they *ought* to do so, and the model is typically formal logic. Howard Kahane suggests that his book is a response to the low level of most political argument. He notes that there are cases in which persuasion is successful when it ought not to be, and his book is "an attempt to raise the level of political argument and reasoning by acquainting students with the devices and ploys that drag that level down."[5] He defines a fallacy as an "argument which *should not* persuade a rational person to accept its conclusion. . . ."[6] It does not matter to this author whether the argument does, indeed, persuade. It is inherently fallacious, and therefore ought not to be worthy of adherence.

Clearly, such theories of refutation are predicated on a notion of correctness and a "rational" man such as that described in Chapter 2. The

[2] W. Ward Fearnside and William B. Holther, *Fallacy The Counterfeit of Argument* (Englewood Cliffs: Prentice-Hall, Inc., 1959), pp. 1–3.

[3] C. L. Hamblin, *Fallacies* (London: Methuen & Co., Ltd., 1970), p. 12.

[4] Hamblin, p. 283.

[5] Howard Kahane, *Logic and Contemporary Rhetoric* (Belmont, California: Wadsworth Publishing Co., Inc., 1971), p. xi.

[6] Kahane, p. 1.

critic can, if sufficiently well educated and analytical, find what are the "errors" within any line of reasoning. Then, as in the Platonic approach to argument discussed in Chapter 1, the process of refutation is an effort to help others see, as the critic does, the errors. Such an approach also lends itself to outlines of "errors" of argument that frequently occur. Fearnside and Holther, for example, outline 51 different fallacies common to contemporary argument, ranging from such material fallacies as hasty generalization and faulty cause, through psychological fallacies such as misusing authority and rationalization, and to the logical fallacies of *non sequitur* and undistributed middle term.[7]

Other contemporary writers on argumentation and debate take a middle ground—not dismissing the value of logic in exposing weaknesses of argument, but recognizing as well that in the final analysis the test of argument is in its ability to win adherence of those to whom it is addressed. Such a theory is still related to formal logic as was discussed in Chapter 3. But logic's role is better illustrated by C. David Mortensen and Ray L. Anderson when they say that while they reject the "deadly notion that there is a logic for every argument," they recognize in discourse "some overall fabric of reasoned force."

"The claims of any argumentative discourse hang together in some sequence and fit into a coalescence of views that exhibits attributes of form and force. And it is this coarser anatomy of argument, the gestalt force, which is always present and is always to be accounted for, and never something merely to be assumed."[8]

For these reasons, they suggest that refutation of argumentative discourse is more on the form of rhetorical criticism than logical analysis—that is, the refutation is less oriented to testing the validity or truth value of particular arguments, and more oriented to the communicative characteristics of style, coherence, completeness, evaluative terms, supporting materials, metaphor, etc.[9] This is the position adopted in this book.

THE APPROACH TO REFUTATION

In formal debate situations, there are assigned positions of advocacy. Legal argument includes prosecutor and defense or plaintiff and defend-

---

[7] Fearnside and Holther.

[8] C. David Mortensen and Ray L. Anderson, "The Limits of Logic," *The Journal of the American Forensic Association*, 7 (Spring 1970), pp. 71–78.

[9] Mortensen and Anderson, p. 78.

ant. Educational debate assigns a team to the affirmative and one to the negative. Political situations typically involve party membership that tends to establish opposing sides on policy questions, but not necessarily so. Many other argumentative situations permit opposition to emerge rather than formally assigning it.

Whether the situation features assigned advocates or not, the question of engaging in refutation is one that must be considered with regard to each claim under discussion. The question must always be, "Will I advance my position regarding the claim if I attack others' arguments?" In law, it is often wise not to put on a defense if by so doing the client will be better served. In politics the same is true.

Even if the decision is made to refute, this does not necessarily mean that one must oppose directly. In some theories of self-defense, participants are instructed not to meet an enemy head-on, but to use his own momentum to defeat him. If he lunges at you, push him further in the same direction. So it is in refutation—if you disagree with someone's argument, you may achieve your goal by urging him further in the same direction than by trying to destroy what he has said. In politics this is common. Opponents may amend a bill to make it even more comprehensive than intended, and by so doing, they destroy its chances of garnering a majority. On the other hand, by moving an opponent in the very direction he is tending you may sometimes gradually move him close enough to your own position that further opposition is unnecessary. In any event, once the decision to refute is made, a decision on how to approach that refutation should be based on a careful analysis of the constituents of the argumentative situation.

ANALYZE THE CLAIM

To determine the approach to refutation, a reference to the analysis of the claim must be made. In Chapter 3 we noted that analysis involves a thorough understanding of all points of view regarding a claim. No one is prepared to defend his own position or attack another until he knows as much about the arguments and issues as possible. For this reason, the building of a full brief, as described in Chapter 8, is particularly important. Knowledge of potential arguments is critical not only to analysis and case building, but to refutation as well.

ANALYZE THE OPPONENTS

Once you are informed about the various points of view that could be taken with regard to the claim, study to the extent possible the opponents with whom you will actually be involved. In law, discovery procedures often permit advance knowledge of what opponents will argue. In politics, there is opportunity for face-to-face interaction with prospective opponents as well as newspaper reports, television reports and the like. In most argumentative situations, it is possible and wise to use interpersonal and group communication, as in the conference or interview, to learn as much as possible about the approaches to argument by others.

ANALYZE THE DECISION MAKERS

Then bring this detailed knowledge of the claim and potential opponents to the analysis of those to whom the arguments will be addressed. Of course, in many conference situations, this will be, at least in part, the opponents themselves. Some assessment must be made of the impact of opponents' arguments on the decision makers before any careful approach to refutation can be selected. Just as in the process of building constructive arguments and cases, it is necessary to know the values, credibility standards, and ideas about evidence of the decision makers. The approach to refutation, in the final analysis, is determined by the impact of opponents' arguments on the audience, not some hypothetical truth standard.

SELECT A POSTURE FOR REFUTATION

There are a variety of perspectives or postures from which to refute another's arguments. Carelessly responding to an argument may lead to more damage to your own position than your opponent's. A characteristic of unsophisticated arguers is the tendency to say anything negative about an opponent's argument that comes to mind—they may criticize everything from grammar to analysis; they may attack and defend indiscriminately. Mature debaters have learned to refute only when it is to their maximum advantage, and remain silent on other openings even though they might score a "point" for their side in a game sense. Let us look at five possible postures.

Direct Refutation. A common posture for refutation is point-by-point or *direct* refutation. As the designation suggests, in this posture the arguer considers opponent's arguments individually, and comments critically on each—sometimes attacking its relevance, or support, or whatever special method, as described later in this chapter, seems appropriate. At the same time, it is common to *defend* an alternative position. Thus, one speaks negatively of others while defending one's own position, although some merely attack without defending an alternate proposal. This may be effective but it may also be turned against the arguer because he is "only destructive."

Compromise. In educational debate, "defense of the status quo with minor repairs," is an appropriate posture. This amounts to a compromise. Here, a criticism of competing proposals is combined with an effort to modify one's own so as to make it more attractive to decision makers. In this approach to refutation, rather than denying the qualities of opposing arguments, one simply adopts them to his own advantage. This is a two-way process, however, and the danger is that the opponent will take advantage of these admissions merely to strengthen his own position.

Counterproposal. In educational debate, counterplan is an approach to refutation in which an improved version of the opponents' proposal is advanced to replace it. Such a posture is chosen only when the overall goals of the opponents' position is appealing but their specific plan for accomplishing them is unacceptable.

Denial. In some specialized argumentative situations, for instance, when an accusation has been made such as charges of criminal behavior, charges of incompetency or inefficiency in an organization, or charges of failure in an operation, a posture of pure *denial* may be an effective refutation. It will generally be effective, however, only when the decision makers seem disinclined to accept the charges and they are requiring a full "burden of proof" of those making the charges. By refusing to take any specific issue, or comment specifically on any particular point, the arguer denies opponents any help in fulfilling their burden. Such obstinacy may not win popularity contests, but it often denies others the justification they need to make their charges stick.

Even-if. Finally, it is common to adopt an *even-if* posture in refutation. That is, to avoid appearance of inconsistency, one may attack an opponent's charges of evils or needs for their policy while at the same time suggesting that their proposal would not remove the evils, even if they existed. Such apparently inconsistent positions are taken by criminal defense lawyers when they plead that their client is not guilty of a crime, and not guilty by reason of insanity. What they say is this: the accused did not commit the crime, but *even if* he did, he is insane and ought not to be held accountable.

PREPARING TO REFUTE

Refutation is not a "shoot from the hip" operation. Although people may put each other down or score an occasional "gotcha" on friends, when serious argument is involved, refutation is carefully prepared for. Typically, the results of all the analysis of the claim, opponents and decision makers should be systematically combined into refutational units called blocks.

BLOCKING ARGUMENTS

To block an argument is to put down on paper the statement of an argument an opponent is likely to make along with the support to be used and the likely impact of the argument on the decision makers. Then, alternatives to refutation are considered, and the best is put down on the same paper. When that argument is actually advanced, it will be possible to glance at the paper and have the benefit of calm and deliberate choice as to the approach to refutation. This will counteract some of the emotional effects of being engaged in argument—often cognitive processes function poorly under stress, and such notes will help. A simple diagram of such a block is given below; its form is that of a Toulmin layout that was discussed in Chapter 4.

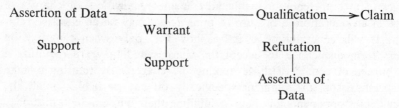

Example:

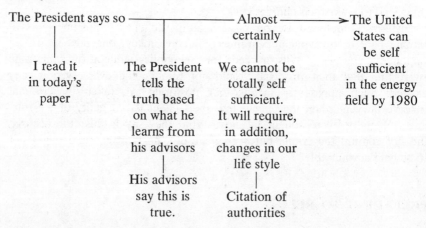

Note that in blocking this particular refutation to an argument we have chosen *a* refutation, not *the* refutation. We might have said, "you misread the paper," "he didn't say that," "his advisors do not say that," "the President does not tell the truth," and a host of others. We have selected a basis of refutation and blocked it out so that we know what to do should that argument come up.

Depending on the importance of the argumentation, the preparation of refutation may involve blocking only major arguments or it may include the preparation of a block for virtually every imaginable argument an opponent could use. When actually engaging in argumentation, though, the over-use of blocks could lead to sterility of refutation. Sometimes inexperienced debaters use the blocks as substitutes for thinking during a debate. They merely read their block in reply to each argument. Mature debaters look on the block as a foundation for refutation. They know that they have a basic position prepared and are, therefore, free to concentrate on the argument and search for more spontaneous and relevant refutation. If no original thoughts come, nothing is lost—they can employ the block. However, it is that spontaneous analysis of argument that most often leads to the best refutation, and then the block can be ignored.

PROBING OPPONENTS

To discover weaknesses in opponents' arguments, it is often possible to look to the opponents themselves. There are various ways to probe opponents' positions. The most common is simply to launch a light but general refutation of everything that has been said with a view toward drawing out the defense. As in football, the offensive team may run a series of plays at various points to see where the weaknesses are, so in argument, a series of refutations may draw out the points at which support for arguments is thin, or analysis is not thorough, or areas the opposition simply is not prepared to argue. Then, the concerted refutation can be aimed at these weak points. As suggested above, it is sometimes possible to probe by means of formal interrogation, either written or oral. In law, it is common to pose interrogatories to the opposition, or to take pretrial depositions from key witnesses. In other argumentative situations, letters may be written asking potential opponents to describe their positions, or face-to-face communication can, by way of interview or negotiation, review prior to argument how the other side will construct their arguments, and where weaknesses may lie. In educational debate, the process of cross-examination is particularly well suited to such probing. This is a procedure, in less formal structure, that may be used in a great many argumentative situations.

Perhaps the most important aspect of probing, however, is done by means of careful note-taking—or studying the *flow* of argument. Unless the arguer has kept careful notice of what originally was said by the opposition, and how they responded to interrogation or cross-examination, or probing refutation, it will be virtually impossible to take advantage of discoveries. Keeping an analysis of the flow of argument basically involves writing down, for each issue or subargument, the original position, the refutation given, and the responses. So that in the course of a full debate or conference or negotiation, before major refutation is undertaken, note can be made of the points of strength and weakness as they have emerged. Obviously, such notes must include arguments given on all sides of any issue, preferably in parallel format. How the notes are actually kept— whether on large sketch pads as in educational debate, or in computers —is largely a matter of individual taste and habit. The important factor is that at any time the arguer can see how the arguments are progressing —how the opponents have defended, or failed to defend, their position.

For the beginner at argumentation a simple flow chart such as the following might be useful (paper size, at least $8\frac{1}{2}'' \times 11''$).

My Arguments	My Opponent's Refutation	My Refutation

The smallest column is the one for the opening arguments. Because you know these in advance you can outline them in advance. Then as you hear your opponent, you will put in his comments opposite your own arguments to which they refer and then your refutation next to that. Thus, you have a capsule of the issues flowing across the page and a convenient basis from which to speak. For more elaborate argumentation situations using more speeches of refutation, a more elaborate chart is necessary.

STUDY THE DYNAMICS OF THE AUDIENCE

Although it is usually done less formally than keeping a flow sheet, experienced debaters keep note of the "flow" of the audience or decision makers. That is to say, they keep in mind the stages of decision making as discussed in Chapter 2, and try to assess the point at which their particular judge or colleagues happen to be. What impact did the last arguments have on the thinking of the decision makers? Are the decision makers still at a point of objective seeking of information, or are they moving toward decision and beginning dissonance-reduction or reinforcement of the decision they are tending toward? In educational debate, one asks, "Are we ahead or behind in this debate?"

Of course, if the audience or judge is in a posture of uncommunicativeness, the assessment of the dynamics of decision making is based on pure judgment and the reading of any nonverbal cues that are available. But this is not so common. In most situations, it is possible to interact with those who will ultimately decide, and then a probing of their tendencies is possible.

SELECT STRATEGY OF REFUTATION

Only after the maximum of preparation has been done should the strategy of refutation be selected. Then, the points to be attacked, and the manner of attacking them should be a function of first, where is the decision maker: what has been the reaction to opponents' arguments and at what point in the decision making process is he? Second, of all the points that could be attacked, which will accomplish the greatest damage to the opponents' position? For example, attacking some of the evidence cited may result in the simple supplying of second-line evidence, with the result of little or no harm done. On the other hand, challenging the basic analysis of opponents, or the values to which they subscribe, may be more difficult, but if successful will do greater damage. In other words, in any refutation, it is necessary to establish some priority of attack. Too many arguers set forth each attack with the same vigor as every other. The decision maker is confronted with a vast series of arguments, all apparently equal in force, and is left to choose among them. A wiser approach would be to give emphasis and priority to the refutations as they are presented. Finally, and accordingly, selection of refutation strategy must be in part a function of what can be most effectively communicated to the decision makers. It may be that a refutation is available that would do much damage to an opponent, but if it is too complex to explain in the time available, or requires knowledge on the part of the judge that is not possessed, it might be wiser to select another attack. Arguers who complain that the decision makers were too stupid to understand their points are revealing their own stupidity: it is the responsibility of those making the refutation to communicate it.

COMMUNICATING REFUTATION

Although any communication event is unique and must be evaluated independently, some general procedures of refutation can be stated. First, it is important that you perceive the opponents' case in the same way the decision makers do. If you are attacking an issue or argument that the decision makers do not see as important, or even a part of the opposition case, the refutation will be wasted. Therefore, it is important to learn, if possible, how the decision makers understand the opposition case. If this is not possible, then it is important for you to communicate the organization that you see in the opposition case. Sometimes, when the opponent is not particularly effective in communication, it is necessary for you to create an organization for someone else's case.

Once you are reasonably confident you and the audience see the case similarly, the typical format for successful refutation consists of these steps:

1. State the point in the opponents' case to be refuted.
2. State the refutation to be made.
3. Communicate the refutation.
4. Communicate the impact of the refutation on the entire position of the opposition.

Point four is a too frequently overlooked point. Too many debaters simply stop with the attack, and the ultimate effect of what they have done escapes the decision maker.

Equally important is the need to preserve or "pull through" the attacks previously made. In the course of a long conference or debate, it is easy for participants to forget the telling points made earlier. The effective arguer recapitulates these points regularly, just as those who are engaged in defense continually remind others of their points that have *not* been challenged.

TIMING REFUTATION

Refutation is most often thought of as following an attack. In some formal debate situations, such a procedure is more or less dictated. However, there is a body of data emerging to suggest that if conditions permit, refutation, which comes *before* the attack, is significantly more effective.

In the biological sciences, it has long been accepted that in some conditions, preexposure to weakened forms of virus may cause the system to generate sufficient defense to prevent contracting a serious disease. Thus, most of us have been inoculated against disease and can be said to have an immunity to them that was induced by preexposure to the virus. An analogy from this to persuasion has been made by some investigators. The theory is similar in that preexposure to weakened forms of arguments can generate an immunity in decision makers so that they will reject the attack that subsequently comes. Admittedly, to date these studies have dealt with "cultural truisms" such as the value of brushing teeth, and may not be generalizable to many other topics for argument. But there is enough support to warrant consideration.

William J. McGuire and his colleagues, in a series of experiments have concluded that preexposure to refutation, which suggest attacks that might be made and then shows their weaknesses, can increase the resistance of decision makers to those and other similar attacks to which they are subsequently exposed.[10] Although the refutation in advance worked best when it specifically rejected the arguments the decision makers heard later, it worked almost as well in generating resistance to new attacks. Although merely making arguments in support of the policies to be defended did little to increase resistance to attacks on them, when this support is combined with a refutation such as is described above, it makes resistance stronger still. It was discovered that presenting the inoculation to the decision makers rather than requiring them to create their own defenses was superior in inducing resistance. And the persistence of the immunity ranged from two days to a week, suggesting that if possible, prerefutation should come in this time period.

Again, the data are far from conclusive. But secondary support coming from the series of Tannenbaum studies reported below is strong enough to warrant the conclusion that sometimes, when circumstances permit, refutation should precede the attack against which it is directed.

[10] William J. McGuire, "Inducing Resistance to Persuasion: Some Contemporary Approaches," in Thomas D. Beisecker and Donn W. Parson, eds., *The Process of Social Influence* (Englewood Cliffs: Prentice-Hall, Inc., 1972), pp. 197–218.

SPECIAL METHODS OF REFUTATION

There are, of course, no correct methods of engaging in refutation. When the theory presumes that successful refutation is a function of adherence, the parameters of formal logic no longer serve to guide the process. There are some special methods that can be discussed that have been employed by those engaged in argumentation for years and which seem likely to succeed. There are, as well, some methods that have been empirically tested.

EMPIRICALLY TESTED METHODS

In a series of experimental studies, Percy H. Tannenbaum examined four different special methods of refutation singly and in combination: (1) Denial; (2) Source Derogation; (3) Point-by-Point Refutation; and (4) Supportive Refutation.[11]

Denial. In the denial approach, the refutation sought to reduce the impact of an opponent's argument by using the same sources to reject the point. For example, if the opposition has quoted the noted economist Dr. J. Fred Muggs as saying wage and price controls have proved to be failures in preventing inflation, refutation by denial would involve finding a statement by the same Dr. Muggs saying *specifically* that he had not made that statement and in fact felt wage and price controls to have been successful in fighting inflation. Specificity is necessary for denial to be an effective mode of refutation, says Tannenbaum.[12]

Source Derogation. A common procedure is one in which refutation proceeds by challenging the credibility of sources used by the opposition. In this instance, one might seek to show that Dr. Muggs is not qualified to comment on wage and price controls. Again, to be effective, the derogation must be specific—showing Dr. Muggs to be personally unqualified in the area quoted.

Point-By-Point Refutation. When each individual argument of the opposition is considered and counter-arguments are made, it is called point-by-point refutation. This proved to be the best method under all con-

---

[11] Percy H. Tannenbaum, "The Congruity Principle Revisited: Studies in the Reduction, Induction, and Generalization of Persuasion," in Leonard Berkowitz, ed., *Advances in Experimental Social Psychology* (New York: Academic Press, 1967), pp. 272–320.

[12] Tannenbaum, p. 279.

ditions, according to Tannenbaum.[13] Here, it should be noted that in six replications, the point-by-point not only proved to be superior to the other three forms of refutation, it was typically stronger when it came *before* the attack, in the immunization format, than when it followed it. Before or after the attack, point-by-point refutation is effective.

Supportive Refutation. Defensive arguments are frequently used in support of the object of the opponent's attack. Here, the debater may argue that while Dr. Muggs is not strong on wage and price controls, the following three other authorities are, and then list them. Support would, of course, include other kinds of support than testimony. This method, along with the other three, was found to be an effective technique of refutation.

In most situations, arguers do not rely on a single approach to refutation. Instead, they will use a combination. Tannenbaum examined combinations, and found the point-by-point method, when combined with source derogation, to be the superior technique. In fact, point-by-point refutation can be effectively combined with all other methods and source derogation can be used with supportive refutation. Obviously, it is not effective to challenge a source and then seek to use the same source to counteract a point.

Curiously, supportive refutation, wherein defense of the position attacked occurs, proved to be the least effective technique in the Tannenbaum studies. When combined with point-by-point, the effectiveness was no better than when point-by-point refutation is used alone.[14] In fact, it is worth noting that in all the experiments, point–by–point refutation was superior: "It is clear that the [point–by–point] refutation condition . . . substantially alters the force of the assertion."[15]

Another technique was suggested by the Tannenbaum studies, but not tested. Consistent with the theory of cognitive dissonance or congruity, if the decision maker is confronted with differences between sources and testimony, there will be a need to deal with it psychologically. Thus, it may be effective to show that sources with low credibility for the judge are in agreement with the sources used to support the opponents' claim. Such negative source agreement might work this way. When Dr. Muggs is quoted by the opposition, rather than challenge him, simply show that a number of sources with no credibility are saying the same thing. To quote, for example, Herbert Hoover saying there will never be another depression.

[13] Tannenbaum, p. 282.
[14] Tannenbaum, p. 290.
[15] Tannenbaum, p. 304.

TRADITIONAL METHODS OF REFUTATION

Arthur Schopenhauer, in his classic essay on *The Art of Controversy*, reasons that refutation can take two different paths—either to attack the quality or "truth" of the opponents' arguments, or to show that the opponents have been inconsistent with themselves. The first method is more familiar, and has been discussed above.

Inconsistency. The latter method is probably more common in legal contexts. There, it is possible to confront a witness with contradictions between pretrial testimony and that given in court. In political situations a similar approach is possible by making a careful compilation of all the assertations made by opponents and their authorities, and then comparing them with the assertions made during the argument. If it is possible to confront the decision makers with a series of self-contradictions by opponents, the effectiveness of the refutation can be great in reducing their credibility. An experienced trial lawyer says this:

"There is such a thing as momentum of contradiction. As the witness is forced repeatedly to retract his answers, the effect upon the jury is increased disproportionately. Each succeeding defeat registers more deeply because of the accumulated impact."[16]

Overthrowing Evidence. To overthrow evidence by showing it is unqualified, out of date, or irrelevant is quite a common form of refutation. In this, as well as many other traditional methods of refutation, to obtain specific clues as to procedure, turn back to the discussion of modes of support, notice what is necessary to make them effective, and potential methods of refutation emerge.

Counter Evidence. It is also common to present *counter evidence* designed to reduce or eliminate the impact of opposition efforts. Because this is probably the most obvious and easy method of refutation, it regularly comes to mind first. But, as suggested earlier, it is also the least damaging to opponents—they can produce second line evidence of their own, and probably return their case to its original strength with little effort. Because of this, it is unwise to rest an entire refutation on attacking evidence.

Attacking Reasoning. Attacking warrants or other forms of reasoning is also a common method of refutation. Here, to the extent the decision makers employ logical models, logical tests and the exposing of fallacies

---

[16] Louis Nizer, *My Life in Court* (New York: Pyramid Books, 1961), p. 114.

may prove effective. Again, the test for discovering the problems with arguments as discussed in Chapter 4 can be used to suggest approaches to refutation. Remember, exposing of reasoning problems may not be effective since judges are not bound to be logical in selecting claims to which to adhere, and they may refuse to accept the assertion that their thinking is fallacious. But, to destroy a major warrant or line of reason may produce more lasting and widespread damage to another's case.

Dilemma. Demonstrating a dilemma is often a recommended approach to refutation. Here, the method is to show that either of two possible interpretations are possible and equally damaging to the opposition. For example, when Richard M. Nixon was accused of involvement in the Watergate conspiracy, two explanations were advanced: either Nixon was involved, and is therefore to be condemned, or he was ignorant of criminal activities going on under his nose and is therefore to be condemned. If the dilemma is credible, it puts the opponent in a most difficult position.

Reductio ad absurdum.   An often misunderstood technique, borrowed from formal logic, is *reductio ad absurdum*. Often debaters confuse this with ridicule. In fact, it is a particularly common and effective refutational process in which the opponents' own line of reasoning is extended to the point that errors within it become magnified and thereby obvious. For example, a national organization proposes complete freedom for citizens in their choice of medicines. They claim no one should interfere with this right by setting up restrictions on access to drugs. By carrying this line of reasoning to its extreme, anyone who wanted to could prescribe medication to the point of killing themselves. When audiences are asked if they approve the right to suicide, the support of the position might diminish. (Note, this does not typically dissuade supporters.)

Residues.   The method of residues has been discussed in Chapter 8 on case building. The process can also be used as a refutational technique. It is similar to the dilemma method, but differs in suggesting a limited number of alternatives or explanations, and then systematically eliminating all those that are favorable, leaving only a negative interpretation of the opponents' case. For example, one could ask why did the Committee to Re-elect the President in 1972 give substantial sums of money to the convicted Watergate burglars? It could have been for humanitarian purposes—they wanted to help those less fortunate than themselves; or they were engaging in a program of rehabilitating criminals; or they thought they were giving the money to someone else; or they wanted to buy their silence. If it is possible to eliminate all but the last alternative, by the method of residue, the Committee is indicted for misbehavior.

In the broader sense, there may be many techniques in which a refutation may be communicated. Certainly there are more ways than those suggested here. Perhaps the most important thing that can be said, in closing, about the process of refutation is this: the sum total of refutation must equal denial of adherence by the deciding group, or it has failed for the time. Surely, in some cases, such as a dissent by a Justice of the Supreme Court of the United States, a strong but unsuccessful refutation may serve ultimately to win a majority, even if many years must pass. Even then, however, it fails unless it ultimately wins adherence.

In watching informal arguments, and educational debates, one may feel that decisions are made by summing the total number of successful points made by each side and voting for the winner in a numeric sense. This does not appear to be the case, even in these informal situations. On the contrary, judges or other decision makers typically proceed in the manner described in Chapter 2 in the discussion of conference. Decisions emerge gradually and are the product of many influences. In refutation, it is always essential to examine the overall definition of the claim and the opponents' analysis of it. Commonly, in setting up their argument, case builders will point to many evils and claim many advantages that they simply cannot show their specific proposal bringing to pass. To refute such cases, it is more important to ask the decision maker to keep in mind, (1) what does the case seek to accomplish? and (2) can it be accomplished within the policy or proposal that has been advanced? Opponents may show that they can meet restricted goals that are set up later in the argument, but in refutation it is usually valuable to return the decision makers' attention back to the broader claims made earlier in the argument. It is at this level of higher analysis that the most successful refutation occurs.

CONCLUSIONS

The process of refutation has been defined and its rhetorical rather than logical nature has been described. In approaching refutation, it is advisable to analyze the claim, the opponents, and the decision makers. A variety of postures for refutation exist. Direct refutation, defense of other proposals, compromise, counterproposals, and pure denial are among those available. In preparing to refute, it is important to "block" the potential arguments so as to have maximum opportunity for original thinking during the heat of the argument. Before selecting an actual strategy of refutation, it is often valuable to probe opponents by tentative attacks, direct and cross examination, and most important, through a careful set of notes showing the flow of argument.

In any argument, there will be changes in the reaction of the audience or other decision makers. For refutation to be successful, it must constantly be responsive to the current status of the audience. Major factors to consider in selecting strategies are the extent of damage they will do to the opposing case and the ease with which they can be communicated to the decision makers. Because of new studies in refutation, the timing has become an important factor to consider. Inoculation theories, which would call for refutation to preceed the main attack, have received considerable support. Finally, a series of special methods of refutation, some of them supported by empirical evidence, and others supported by traditional usage, are useful to the participant in argumentation.

PROJECTS

1. Prepare in writing a set of refutational blocks for a case you prepared to use in class.

2. Exchange cases with other class members and prepare in writing a refutation of the case.

3. Observe arguments in both informal and formal settings to see and describe the approaches to refutation employed.

4. Choose a policy claim on which to debate and divide the class into two teams—one affirmative and one negative. Each team should be in numbered order. The first affirmative should advance an argument to which the first negative must agree or disagree. Should he agree, then he would propose an argument to which the second negative must either agree or disagree. As soon as one party disagrees, all argument goes back and forth in the designated order until the judge (your instructor?) rules that that point has been won. At that point a new argument is begun. All admitted and "won" arguments must be considered in subsequent clashes. (This is called direct clash debating and its emphasis is on quality of refutation.)

10
The Language of Argumentation

Language is fundamental to any argument. It is the stuff of which arguments are made. Consequently, we have been discussing language in all that we have said so far. Differing arguments require different language. Whether we refer to ourselves as "we" or "I" can have an impact on credibility. Arguments from analogy are related to the language function of metaphor, and the choice of words such as "progress," "freedom," or "nature" reflect the value systems of the arguer and the receiver.

In order to avoid confusion we treat language here in quite a narrow sense. We shall generally deal with language in the limited sense of style, that is, "the selection and arrangement of those linguistic features that are open to choice. . . . Where there is choice there is style; where there is none there is grammar."[1] Style will be practically limited in this chapter to those things that are not specifically covered by the other chapters in this book.

Before we begin to examine these four areas, a word or two of caution is necessary. Although among the oldest studies in western culture, the amount of evidence confirming rules of effective language usage is limited. There is a good deal of normative research to tell us how lan-

---

[1] Joseph DeVito, "Style and Stylistics: An Attempt at Definition," *Quarterly Journal of Speech, 53* (October 1967), pp. 249–251.

guage functions and how words are joined together in the normal language, but there is limited experimental evidence of audience responses to language. Consequently, many of the rules of language usage must come from the conventions passed down from one generation to another. Such conventions have been preserved by educated persons with a high degree of language sophistication who generally have been more interested in literary writing than in spoken or written argument. Consequently, the natural language of spoken, or even written, general argumentation may not conform to those conventions. We have tried in this chapter to modify those conventions where recent research and experience seems to call for it.

A second caution pertains to the significance of these language factors in the total process of argumentation. Although important, they are not as important as some other factors. John Waite Bowers has noted that:

"Within the range of "standard English (for example, excluding obscenity) language and para language variables have less effect than many content and extra-message variables. What a speaker says and what conditions he says it under seems to be more important, in general, than how he says it."[2]

We would probably not want it any other way. Decision making would indeed be difficult in a society where the form of the argument was more important than its content. Thus, the language factors discussed here are not as important as the content of the argument or the predispositions of the audience. In some specialized segments of our culture, form is very important, however. One need only note the careful attention to language in fields like law and diplomacy to be aware of this reality. Indeed, it may well be that each field of argumentation has its own acceptable form of argumentative style, and failure to imploy it when arguing in that field will tend to be destructive. Although perhaps not as important as we have frequently been led to believe and surely not in the prescriptive way many have used the "rules" of grammar and usage, language is a vital part of argument. When we look for a modern understanding of the language of argumentation, we will do so by examining language through its traditional divisions of word choice, sentence structure, figures of speech and special strategies.

---

[2] John Waite Bowers, "A Response to John W. Black's 'Communication Behaviors: Acquisition and Effects,'" *Conceptual Frontiers in Speech Communication*, Robert J. Kibler and Larry Barker, eds., (New York: Speech Association of America, 1969), pp. 105–106.

WORD CHOICE

No one would deny that the words one chooses affect the adherence of receivers to arguments. Choices that make war into defensive action, death into eternal sleep, bombing into protective reaction, and garbage collector into sanitary engineer cannot be overlooked and such *euphemisms*, as they are called, are important. But why shouldn't a person be called a sanitary engineer instead of a garbage collector? Not too long ago committees had chairmen; now in many segments of society, they have chairpersons and the argument of many activists of all kinds that changing the language is an important part of changing the thought has validity. Thus, "Black" is a designation of awakened pride. It says something quite different when a man calls himself a Black than when he calls himself a Negro.

Such concerns with language serve to show that word choice is an active factor in argumentation. Like other elements of argumentation, it is a function of the relationship of speaker to receiver. Thus, one person's accurate term is another's euphemism. If a woman sees herself as a woman and not a girl, broad, chick, sweetie pie, or bitch, deviation from her choice should be made in full realization of the consequences.

Thus, the words we use give cues to others about our attitudes. There is evidence to show, in addition, that vocal cues in speech give receivers a rather good basis for judging the social status of speakers.[3] Of course, these cues are provided by more than word choice but such choice is important. What we can note is that there are ways of using language that reflect various roles in the society and one should be aware of the role projected by the language used.

In addition to role, we give signs in messages of our state of mind. Charles Osgood's study shows that suicide notes have significant differences on a number of language phenomena, such as repetition of words and phrases or allness references, which reveal the distressed condition of the writer: "Wherever there are competing motives operating in the encoder, evidence of compromise and conflict should appear in the message produced," says Osgood.[4] Obviously, we are interested in a different level of argumentative communication than suicide notes but such extremes should tell us something about other situations. Studies of non-

[3] James D. Moe, "Listener Judgments of Status Cues in Speech: A Replication and Extension," *Speech Monographs, 39* (June 1972), pp. 144–147.

[4] Charles Osgood, "Some Effects of Motivation on Style of Encoding," *Style in Language*, Thomas A. Sebook, ed., (Cambridge, MIT Press, 1960), pp. 300–301.

immediacy tend to confirm the point that language variations communicate to receivers about "the relationship between the speaker and the object he communicates about, the addressee of his communication, or the communication itself."[5]

Nonimmediacy is a complicated statistical analysis that measures the extent to which the speaker separates himself from the object under discussion or the receiver of the communication. A simple example used by Morton Wiener and Albert Mehrabian will indicate the nature of such study. A speaker describing a party might take quite different positions by change in pronoun: " 'I think I enjoyed myself,' 'I think we enjoyed ourselves,' 'I think they enjoyed themselves,' 'I think you enjoyed yourself.' These instances show variations in which the communicator included or excluded himself from the referent group."[6] The study of nonimmediacy is now only beginning to draw more explicit conclusions but we should be able to accept the position that the selection of words that tend to remove the speaker from the direct connection with the event or receiver makes the communication less personal. Thus, once again, word choice influences the meaning.

THE ABSTRACTION LADDER

Language can be identified on a variety of levels of nonimmediacy. Certain cases of special argumentation, like the judge in a law court, is expected to utilize the most noninvolved language possible. For much of general argumentation, however, we expect our disputants to be involved. We expect them to show that they are personally concerned about finding a workable decision or we find it difficult to give them our adherence. There has long been a counter view, which held that all language, to be clear, must be the product of less personal involvement. This "general semantics" point of view holds that language must be as closely related to the thing under discussion as possible. From this general point of view comes the conviction that concrete language is better than "abstract" language. S. I. Hayakawa, a major exponent of that point of view, has defined an abstraction ladder (see Figure 2). The lowest rungs of the ladder use words that refer to clearly referential material that the receiver would be expected to know. Words like bike, chair, table and door;

[5] Morton Wiener and Albert Mehrabian, *Language Within Language: Immediacy, A Channel in Verbal Communication* (New York: Appleton-Century-Crofts, Inc., 1968), p. 3.
[6] Wiener and Mehrabian, p. 29.

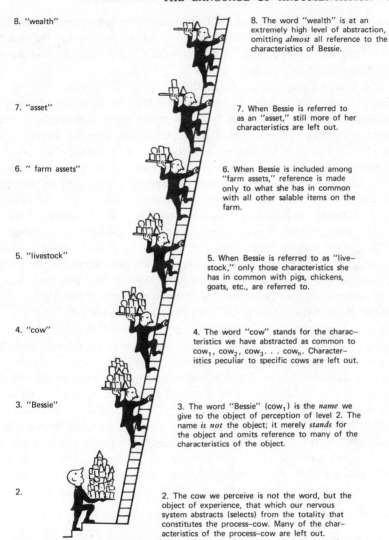

8. "wealth"

8. The word "wealth" is at an extremely high level of abstraction, omitting *almost* all reference to the characteristics of Bessie.

7. "asset"

7. When Bessie is referred to as an "asset," still more of her characteristics are left out.

6. " farm assets"

6. When Bessie is included among "farm assets," reference is made only to what she has in common with all other salable items on the farm.

5. "livestock"

5. When Bessie is referred to as "live-stock," only those characteristics she has in common with pigs, chickens, goats, etc., are referred to.

4. "cow"

4. The word "cow" stands for the characteristics we have abstracted as common to cow_1, cow_2, cow_3. . . cow_n. Characteristics peculiar to specific cows are left out.

3. "Bessie"

3. The word "Bessie" (cow_1) is the *name* we give to the object of perception of level 2. The name *is not* the object; it merely *stands* for the object and omits reference to many of the characteristics of the object.

2.

2. The cow we perceive is not the word, but the object of experience, that which our nervous system abstracts (selects) from the totality that constitutes the process–cow. Many of the characteristics of the process–cow are left out.

1. The cow known to science ultimately consists of atoms, electrons, etc., according to present–day scientific inference. Characteristics (represented by circles) are infinite at this level and everchanging. This is the *process level*.

Figure 2. "The Abstraction Ladder." Start reading from the bottom up. (FROM LANGUAGE IN THOUGHT AND ACTION, *by S. I. Hayakawa. Third Edition, Copyright, 1941, 1949 © 1963, 1964, 1972 by Harcourt Brace Jovanovich, Inc. and reproduced with their permission*).

physical objects fit in this class. At the top of the ladder are words like democracy, communism, truth, and God. At each step up the ladder words move away from physical referents and move toward those words that can be defined only by other words.[7]

There is an assumption here that the words on the lower rungs of the ladder, the concrete words, are to be preferred to those on the upper rungs. But such an assumption does not make sense. Democracy, communism, truth and God are important to people and they will argue about them (perhaps more often than they will argue about bikes, chairs, tables and doors). The competent arguer will not rely on one level of language but become versatile on all levels and sensitive to which level of language is appropriate for a particular situation. In some argumentation situations, such as scholarly argument, a special vocabulary is necessary. Even in general argumentation among educated people, specialized language is necessary. One cannot argue about communism merely by talking about physical conditions in the Soviet Union, the People's Republic of China or Albania. Such an argument will require the abstract language necessary to understand that philosophical system: capitalism, proletariate, dictatorship of the masses, bourgoise, even dialectial materialism.

Thus, the advantage to "concrete" language over "abstract" language is conditional on the use to which the language is to be put and the audience to which it is addressed. Whenever possible, arguments should be put in "concrete" terms—terms that refer to real things, which can be seen, heard or felt, but when one is forced to deal in more abstract subjects, more abstract language is necessary. In general argumentation we probably could stand by the convention that the more abstract the claim one argues, and the more abstract the terminology necessary, the more the arguer should take care to provide examples, analogies, definitions and synonyms that help make the argument more "concrete."

PRECISENESS

Certainly one means of making language clearer even on an abstract topic is the constant attention to precision in choosing words. What are the best words that will match the subject to the audience's perceptions? At the simplest levels, greater precision provides a sense of greater specificity and increases the credibility of the speaker:

A southern city—Atlanta, Georgia

A fine eastern apple—The Cortland Apple

[7] S. I. Hayakawa, *Language in Thought and Action* (New York: Harcourt Brace and Co., 1972), p. 153.

A National League baseball team—The Los Angeles Dodgers

A lot of people died in the fire—257 people died in the fire

On more complex levels, precise words can avoid misunderstanding. Democracy is an imprecise word (as is communism, fascism, and a host of others), that is, people may not be clear on its meaning. It is also *ambiguous.* That is, it clearly has several popular meanings. When you speak of the democracy of China, (or South Viet Nam, or Chile, or England) the word is ambiguous because these are quite different kinds of democracy. A "western democracy" is quite another thing from a "people's democracy." Such ambiguity should be avoided and the most precise terms should be used and supported by definitions, analogy and example. There is experimental evidence that points to the conclusion that when you increase the content of an argument or its specificity you decrease the number of alternative words or ideas a person can conceive of as filling out your meaning.[8] Thus, you achieve greater preciseness for the receiver.

One word of caution. When we talk about preciseness in language we should remember that there is no right way to use a word. Dictionaries help to identify word meanings, but a dictionary only tells what the current usage was at the time of publication and the evidence shows that individuals are bound by their own understanding of meaning, not by dictionaries.[9] Meaning in language, and preciseness in language, is determined by social conventions and individual preferences, not by arbitrary definitions.

SPECIAL VOCABULARIES

Books on style usually suggest that *cliches, slang* and *jargon* be avoided.[10] With cliches this is, of course, true. A cliche is by definition a piece of tired and worn out language that will receive a negative reaction because the receiver perceives it as tired and worn out. Jane Blankenship presents a representative group of expressions that will be generally recognized as cliches:

---

[8] I. Kaplan, T. Curvellas, and W. Metlay, "Effects of Content on Verbal Recall," *Journal of Verbal Learning and Verbal Behavior, 10* (April 1971), p. 207.

[9] Erwin P. Bettinghaus, "Cognitive Balance and the Development of Meaning," *Journal of Communication, 13* (June 1963), p. 103.

[10] Jane Blankenship, *A Sense of Style* (Belmont, California: Dickenson Publishing Co., Inc., 1968), p. 62; Mary G. McEdwards, *Introduction to Style* (Belmont, California: Dickenson Publishing Co., Inc., 1968), p. 31.

goes without saying	all in all
after all was said and done	blissfully ignorant
none the worse for wear	busy as a bee
easier said than done	drastic action
last but not least	breathless silence
method in his madness	ardent admirers
more than meets the eye	festive occasion
ignorance is bliss	vale of tears
few and far between	ripe old age
equal to the occasion	reigns supreme
beat a hasty retreat	sweat of his brow
tired but happy	worked like a horse
wee small hours	clear as crystal

Cliches may be used as new and interesting statements with slight but meaningful changes: "It is as clear as night from night," or "my speech to that group was a case of casting false pearls before real swine," or "he left no stone turned." Some years ago we recall an intercollegiate debate where one of the debaters enthusiastically reached for a cliche and came up accidentally with a memorable line: "If the plan of the affirmative is put into effect, we will lose our liberties in one swell foop."

Although cliches should be avoided, slang and jargon are quite another matter. Each are a question of audience and the slang expressions of ghetto Black English are perfectly communicative to that audience. Slang changes quickly, of course, and one needs to think seriously of the audience. The slang of this generation of college students may not be intelligible to their parents and the slang of one region or cultural sub-group may not be intelligible to another but within the group the slang provides a colorful means of communication.

Jargon is similar; it is the technical slang of a specialized group. One does not expect historians and plumbers to speak alike. Each profession requires a specialized vocabulary. What can be expected is that one who speaks or writes for others outside the profession will not use his specialized jargon to confuse receivers. Mike Royko, *Chicago Daily News Service*, syndicated columnist, gives this humorous example of the way jargon works.

WORD LISTS MAKE IT EASY TO TALK LIKE EDUCATORS

BY MIKE ROYKO, CHICAGO DAILY NEWS SERVICE

Until now, only professional educators knew how to speak educatorese, that mysterious language with which they befuddle the rest of us.

But now, for the first time, anyone can learn to speak it.

All you need is the new guide: "How to speak like an educator without being educated."

And as a public service, the guide is being printed in its entirety below.

In a moment, I'll provide instructions on its use. But first, a word of credit to its creators.

SIMPLE TO USE

The guide is the work of two rhetoric and speech teachers at Danville (Ill.) Junior College, Barbara Stover and Ilva Walker. They compiled it after years of wading through administrative circulars.

They did it for fun, but some of their students have found that the phrases are useful in preparing papers for sociology classes.

SIMPLE TO USE

The guide is simple to use.

Take one word from each of the five columns. It doesn't matter which word. Take them in any order, or in no order.

For instance, if you take the second word of column "A," the fourth word from column "B," the sixth word from column "C," and the eighth and tenth words from the last two columns, you will have:

Flexible ontological productivity implement control group and experimental group.

That doesn't make sense, does it? But now add a few connecting words, and we have:

Flexible and ontological productivity will implement the control group and experimental group.

That still doesn't make any sense. But it sounds like it does. Which means it is perfect educatorese.

You can do it with any combination of the words. As an example, use the first five digits of my office phone:

This works out to:

Adaptable reciprocal nucleii terminate total modular exchange.

Add a few little words and you have a splendid sentence, worthy of at least an assistant superintendent:

"Adaptable and reciprocal nucleii will terminate in total modular exchange." And you can quote me on that.

START WORKING

Go to it, with this guide you say things like:

"The interdisciplinary or supportive input will encapsulate vertical team structure."

Or "optimal ethnic accountability should facilitate post-secondary education enrichment."

Try it yourself. Once you get the hang of it—who knows?—You might wind up with Supt. Redmond's job.

—A—

Comprehensive
Flexible
Adaptable
Culturally
Perceptual
Evaluative
Innovative
Interdisciplinary
Conceptual
Ideological
Optimal
Minimal
Categorically
Unequivocally
Intrapersonal
Interpersonal

—B—

Cognitive
Reciprocal
Stylistic
Ontological
Prime
Supportive
Workable
Resultant
Behavioral
Judgmental
Ethnic
Attitudinal
Multicultural
Encounter
Counterproductive
Generative
Cognate

—C—

Nucleii
Interaction

Focus
Balance
Chain of Command
Productivity
Conference
Panacea
Rationale
Input
Throughput
Accountability
Feedback
Objective
Resources
Perspective
Curricula
Priorities
Diversity
Environment
Overview
Strategies
Posture
Methodologies
Introvision
Posits
Concept
Gestalt

—D—

Indicates
Terminate
Geared
Compile
Articulate
Verbalize
Facilitate
Implement
Incur
Sensitize
Synthesize
Integrate

Fragment
Minimize
Maximize
Energize
Individualize
Encapsulate
Orientate

—E—

Total modular exchange
In-depth discussion
Multipurpose framework and goals
Serial communication
Serial transmission of applicable
cable tools and instrumentation

Post-secondary education enrich-
ment
Changing needs of society
Motivational serial communications
High potential for assessing failure
Control group and experimental
group
Student-faculty relationships
Identifiable decision-making process
Sophisticated resource systems anal-
yses
Vertical team structure
Translation in depth
Classroom context
Individual horizons[11]

MEANINGFULNESS OF VALUE WORDS

In Chapter 6 we examined the role of values in argument and we observed that these values and value systems are revealed through certain words. It is worth mentioning here that since some words carry high value implications for the receivers of the message, they must be carefully selected. Their meaningfulness, it has been shown, is related directly to the strength of the personal values of the receiver.[12]

INTENSITY OF LANGUAGE

In recent years there has been considerable research on the relative effectiveness of intense language.[13] Language intensity is defined by John

[11] Mike Royko, "Word Lists Make It Easy To Talk Like Educators," reprinted with permission from the *Chicago Daily News*.

[12] W. A. Bousfield and Gloria Samborski, "The Relationship Between Strength of Values and the Meaningfulness of Value Words," *Journal of Personality, 23* (June 1955), pp. 375–380.

[13] John Basehart, "Message Opinionation and Approval—Dependence as Determinants of Receiver Attitude Change and Recall, *Speech Monographs, 38* (November 1971), pp. 302–310; John W. Bowers, "Some Correlates of Language Intensity," *Quarterly Journal of Speech, 50* (December 1964), pp. 415–420; Michael Burgoon and Lawrence J. Chase, "The Effects of Differential Linguistic Patterns in Messages Attempting to Induce Resistance to Persuasion," *Speech Monographs, 40* (March 1973), pp. 1–7; Carl W. Carmichael and Gary Lynn Cronkhite, "Frustration and

W. Bowers as "the quality of language which indicates the degree to which the speaker's attitude toward a concept deviates from neutrality." He further notes that "apparently, a culture enforces on its members enough common experiences with connotative dimension of language so that with some training and under controlled circumstances two groups within a culture can agree almost perfectly on direction and strength of language intensity."[14] Obviously, under less controlled situations there would not be such perfect agreement but most within a culture would agree to a significant extent on which terms were the strongest labels of good or bad on a person, thing or concept.

Some of the research in this field is contradictory but a number of interesting and worthwhile points for the student of argumentation can be made. More intense language is most appropriate when the audience shares the point of view of the speaker. When high intensity language is used on an audience that is in disagreement it produces a boomerang effect and damages the effectiveness.[15] High intensity language is also more effective in gaining adherence when it comes from a high credibility source, is not effective when the source has low credibility and is better accepted by receivers with a higher need for social approval from a credible source.[16] In another study, a higher intensity message was judged as clearer, more "logical" and its source more dynamic. But this was a case where the message topics in the experiment were not particularly ego-involving to the receivers and 13 of 55 subjects didn't perceive the high intensity of the language.[17] This could mean that with topics on which people have little personal involvement, intensity is perceived as dynamism and clarity and that the problem of boomerang applies only to cases where intense language is used on opposed and ego-involved persons.

Language Intensity," *Speech Monographs*, *32* (June 1965), pp. 107–111; William J. McEwen and Bradley S. Greenberg, "The Effect of Message Intensity on Receiver Evaluations of Source, Message and Topic," *Journal of Communication*, *20* (December 1970), pp. 340–350; R. Samuel Mehrley and James C. McCroskey, "Opinionated Statements and Attitude Intensity as Predictors of Attitude Change and Source Credibility," *Speech Monographs*, *37* (March 1970), pp. 47–52; Gerald R. Miller and John Basehart, "Source Trustworthiness, Opinionated Statements and Response to Persuasive Communication," *Speech Monographs*, *36* (March 1969), pp. 1–7; Gerald R. Miller and J. Lobe, "Opinionated Language, Open- and Closed-Mindedness and Response to Persuasive Communication," *Journal of Communication*, *17* (December 1967), pp. 333–341.

[14] Bowers, p. 416.

[15] Carmichael and Cronkhite, p. 111; Mehrley and McCroskey, pp. 51–52.

[16] Basehart; Miller and Basehart, p. 7; Miller and Lobe, p. 339.

[17] McEwen and Greenberg.

An interesting study by Michael Burgoon and Lawrence Chase reveals that when one wishes to create support for an argument in advance of its being made, the pretreatment argument should utilize intense language. Where one wished to induce resistance to the argument, however, the greatest change occurs when the language intensity is in conflict with the expectations of the audience.[18] Thus, if the speaker was perceived as a mild-mannered person, then intense language would produce the greatest change, but if that speaker was perceived as an intense person, less intense language would be most effective. This is a principle that many arguers would do well to consider. It is a technique used by many so-called radicals of the past decade to disarm audiences. Persons like Stokely Carmichael and Saul Aulinsky blunted later refutation of their positions by appearing not as wild men but as rather mild-mannered speakers. Too many arguers assume that greater intensity is always stronger. Not so, says this evidence, when you are perceived as being intense to begin with.

SENTENCE STRUCTURE

Common sense tells us, and some research evidence supports the conclusion, that an individual's own style developed as a personal response to language is more important than the choices deliberately made according to audience directed purpose.[19] Nonetheless, people can make some choices and the potentials of choice ought to be realized. The arguer who uses the same sentence structure without regard to audience or claim argued loses opportunity for variety that may strengthen the impact of the argument. What are the main sentence forms available in contemporary usage?

THE SIMPLE SENTENCE

The basic English unit is called a simple sentence. For instance:

He is a male chauvinist pig.

The environment is in danger.

War must be ended.

---

[18] Burgoon and Chase.

[19] Jane Blankenship, "A Linguistic Analysis of Oral and Written Style," *Quarterly Journal of Speech, 49* (December 1962), p. 422.

The essential ingredients of a simple sentence are: subject (he, the environment, war) connected to a verb and its related adjectives, adverbs and prepositional phrases. In its shortest form (He is, The environment is) of subject and verb it may still be a simple sentence but this is also true if the statement is much longer but contains only these elements. Note:

He is a male chauvinist pig, a jerk and a fool.

The environment and all of us in it is in danger.

War, famine and disease must be ended forever.

This movement from subject to verb represents the normal word order and any change from it puts one on alert to expect something different. That something different may also be less clear, particularly in spoken argument. Following the normal word order is the best practice where one is unsure of the audience and/or the subject.

THE COMPOUND SENTENCE

When one combines two simple sentences with a coordinating conjunction (and, or, but), a compound sentence is created. Each could stand alone, but we join them together because they are related. For instance, the previous sentence or the following:

A man is innocent until proven guilty, and that is fundamental to all law.

The Arabs and Israelis have declared a truce, but I don't believe it will last.

The Mets may win the game, or they may choke in the end.

In writing, a compound sentence may be formed without a conjunction by the use of a semicolon:

China is now a major power in the world; she must be reckoned with.

Since semicolons do not exist in speech, such a sentence for the speaker really becomes two sentences. For oral language, the conjunction is important. Why join two sentences with a conjunction? Because it provides an indication of the relationship that the speaker sees between the two statements. It is a different kind of argument. Note that in this sense the "and" conjunction is another form of the semicolon. It is a way of saying "and another thing." It adds little new information to the argument. If used too much it sets up an annoying pattern that implies that each statement is of the same weight and relation to every other. "But" and "or," on the other hand, give more information about the relationship. "But" indicates that a contradiction is about to be heard:

The Arabs and Israelis have declared a truce, but [watch out for a contradiction] I don't believe it will last.

"or" tells you another alternative is present:

The Mets may win the game, or [watch out for an alternative possibility] they may choke in the end.

THE COMPLEX SENTENCE

When one combines units that are not complete sentences, or weaker units that are technically sentences, with a complete sentence they are called complex sentences. The conjunctions joining them together also provide some information about relations (when, who, that, which, while, what, although, after, if, because). For instance:

Abortion laws should remain as they are although I object to some provisions in them.

A President can do a lot for the country when he cares to.

A return to the free enterprise system is necessary now while there is still time.

Note that in the first and third examples the last clause could stand alone but not with the same meaning. They are clearly dependent for meaning on the first clause, unlike the second clause in the complex sentence.

THE COMPOUND-COMPLEX SENTENCE

When we combine independent and dependent clauses we get a combination of the compound and complex sentence.

A man is innocent until proven guilty, and that is fundamental to all law though it is sometimes ignored in the courts.

The Arabs and Israelis have declared a truce, but I don't believe it will last because of the deep animosity between the two.

CHANGES FROM THE NORMAL SENTENCE ORDER

We have observed that the normal word order proceeds from a subject to a verb and its associates. One study has identified twenty-one different variations from that order. We shall not go into those changes but it may be worth looking at the five basic characteristics of the adaptation of sentences from the normal word order. They are, repetition, omission, suspension, inversion and antithesis.[20] We will discuss antithesis in the next section as a figure of speech. Let us look now at some examples of what happens when each of the other four principles is used.

Repetition

"Government, of the people, by the people, for the people, . . ."

A man is innocent until proven guilty, and that is fundamental to all law, fundamental to all religious truths and fundamental to all common sense.

Omission

"Sighted sub; sank same."

Plant a tree, protect the future.

Suspension

When he cares to, a President can do a lot for the country.

While there is still time, a return to the free enterprise system is necessary.

Inversion

To be reckoned with is China, now a major power.

A male chauvinist pig is he.

The last two factors, suspension and inversion, are probably the most important in general argumentation because they reverse the normal order and may be more often constructed by the average speaker or writer than the other two. It is generally considered that they provide interest and, therefore, increase the clarity of the message to listeners and readers. One study tends to confirm the value of unusual word orders in making the message more comprehensible. Lawrence R. Wheeless and James C. McCroskey found that while use of these syntactical changes from the usual word order had no impact on attitude, credibility or behavior, the results suggested an effect on comprehension. Difference in syntax did affect a receiver's perception of the message. It may also be that there would be impact on attitudes, credibility and behavior had Wheeless and McCroskey used more significant topics.[21]

[20] Ronald H. Carpenter, "The Essential Schemes of Syntax: An Analysis of Rhetorical Theory's Recommendations For Uncommon Word Orders," *Quarterly Journal of Speech, 55* (April 1969), p. 161.

[21] Lawrence R. Wheeless and James C. McCroskey, "The Effects of Selected Syntactical Choices on Source Credibility, Attitude, Behavior, and Perception of Message," *Southern Speech Communication Journal, 38* (Spring 1973), pp. 213–222. See also on repetition, Ray Ehrensberger, "An Experimental Study of the Relative Effectiveness of Certain Forms of Emphasis in Public Speaking," *Speech Monographs, 12* (1945), pp. 94–111.

There appears to be no reason to deny long standing notions that normal word order provides the generally most easily understood form of the sentence but that some changes to unusual word orders can add comprehension by catching the attention of receivers and holding it.

FIGURES OF SPEECH

In a sense, all variations in sentence structure are figures of speech. They establish an unusual pattern and, therefore, provide a basis for response irrespective of content. At this point, however, it is useful to describe a few of the most striking and popular figures of speech that one might use in enlivening argument. There are long lists of discrete figures, but we choose here to discuss a few of the most useful distinctions: metaphor, simile, personification, antithesis, irony, anaphora and oxymoron.

METAPHOR

The most important figure of speech is surely the metaphor. It is well that we spend some time on it. I.A. Richards has argued that metaphor is not an ornament to language but "the omnipresent principle of all its free actions."[22] Such a conclusion makes a good deal of sense as metaphor involves, in Aristotle's words, "an eye for resemblances" and much of argument is a matter of seeing how one idea resembles another. If metaphor is not fundamental to all language use, it surely is fundamental to argumentation.

Metaphors abound in our language. Simply identified, a metaphor implies an identity between two things which would not usually be seen there. The speaker or writer sees a resemblance that clarifies and argues.

"A house divided against itself cannot stand. I believe this government cannot endure, permanently half slave and half free." Abraham Lincoln.

"The infidels to the gospel of liberty raved, but the flag swept on." Albert J. Beveridge.

"I have a dream that one day every valley shall be exalted, every hill and mountain made low, and rough places will be made plane and crooked

[22] I. A. Richards, *The Philosophy of Rhetoric* (New York: Oxford University Press, 1965), p. 90.

places will be made straight, and the glory of the Lord shall be revealed, and all flesh shall see it together." Martin Luther King, Jr.

These examples point up the wide variety of ways in which metaphor develops. Abraham Lincoln provided clues by saying things like "I believe." His metaphor leaves less to the imagination than does Albert Beveridge's. Martin Luther King's statement is not only a metaphor but a whole series of metaphors and it is not only a metaphor linking the words of his dream with racial justice but it calls on biblical allusion to give it even more power.

Since the metaphor tries to establish adherence through relating one subject to a seemingly unrelated but analogous subject, the most important part of this phenomenon are the "forces which formulate lines of association." Michael M. Osborn and Douglas Ehninger call these the "qualifiers" and they are of four kinds: contextual, communal, archetypal, and private.[23]

Contextual Qualifiers. Indications of the limits of the metaphor that are provided within the text are contextual qualifiers. For example, consider this metaphor:

She was a real tigress about equal rights for women.

The phrase "about equal rights for women" puts the focus on the specific area where she is to be seen as having the characteristics usually ascribed to a tigress and eliminating all other factors.

Communal Qualifiers. When the qualifiers come not out of specific words used in the metaphor but out of the general understanding of the society, they are called communal. Thus, in the example given above we would know that the metaphor did not mean that she walked on all fours, had a striped skin, a long tail and cat-like whiskers coming out of the sides of her face.

Archetypal Qualifiers. Those qualifiers that have persisted over a period of time and are, therefore, more firmly established we call archetypal. They are common to many nations and times. One can debate the question of whether or not they are fundamental to man's nature. We choose to believe that they are not, because no archetypal qualifier is always treated the same. For instance: there is a problem with the black-white metaphor. In many societies and times to say something is black is to say it is bad and to say it is white is to say it is good. But this is not always true. Note how rich black coffee and white wash indicate that there are

[23] Michael M. Osborn and Douglas Ehninger, "The Metaphor in Public Address," *Speech Monographs*, 29 (August 1962), pp. 228–230.

times when the pattern is reversed so the relationship cannot be fundamental to human nature. But such an archetypal qualifier surely is prevalent. Note how the conscience of Afro-Americans was raised by attacking the black-white archetype with notions of black nationalism, black is beautiful, etc. Archetypal qualifiers would be best viewed as high level and persistent communal qualifiers. Typical archetypal qualifiers are black-white, up-down, light-dark, day-night, land-sea.

Private qualifiers. Some qualifiers are supplied by the receiver on the basis of private associations. Thus, the private joke, where only the speaker and the listener understand the meaning even though there are others who hear. Another example of private qualifiers is when persons speak metaphorically in a specialized discipline. Others may not understand the metaphors of law or physics or theology because they are private to a select group.

SIMILE

Still metaphorical but in a weaker form is the simile. The simile explicitly expresses a comparison between two things. It uses such terms as "like" and "as" to show such relationships.

He is as big as a house.

He was talking like a machine gun.

We say that the simile is weaker, not because there is evidence that it is less effective, but because it takes less of a chance than a metaphor and so loses some of the chance for a surprise to the reader or listener. Suppose Abraham Lincoln, instead of the famous metaphor, had said, "Our nation is like a house (a house understood as a family) and a house divided against itself cannot stand.

PERSONIFICATION

Personification is closely related to metaphor and simile. It too establishes a relationship between two things, in this case, between something human and something nonhuman. We personify nonhuman things; we make them persons. Another form of personification (referred to by the technical term metonymy) is when we give human characteristics to something nonhuman by associating it with parts of the body.

Justice is blindfolded.

The tree reaches its arms to the sky.

The nation with weeping eyes views the scene.

ANAPHORA

Anaphora is the name given to the figure of speech in which one repeats the same word or group of words at the beginning of successive clauses.

"Slavery, unless I will open my mouth in its defense, asks me to give the lie to my professions, to degrade my manhood, and to stain my soul. I will not be a liar, a poltroon, or a hypocrite, to accommodate any party, to gratify any sect, to escape any odium or peril, to save any interest, to preserve any institution, or to promote any object."
William Lloyd Garrison.

OXYMORON

When one joins two seemingly contradictory statements together it is called oxymoron (pronounced ox-im-er-on). Thus, saying that the speaker was met with a thunderous silence or that the young man was ruggedly weak or telling the terrible truth is oxymoron.

ANTITHESIS

The most well known example of antithesis is John F. Kennedy's statement:

"Ask not what your country can do for you. Ask what you can do for your country."

Thus, contrasting ideas are put one after another by Kennedy so that he can better point up the answer one is expected to make.

These are but a few of the identifiable figures of speech. These constitute, we believe, the major ones that will be found in general argumentation. The metaphor is, by far, the most important figure of speech and the only available research has been done on it. That research shows that metaphorical conclusions brought about more change in audiences than more literal but intense conclusions. This research also showed that trite metaphors boomerang.[24] There is no reason to believe that such a con-

---

[24] John Waite Bowers and Michael Osborn, "Attitudinal Effects of Selected Types of Concluding Metaphors in Persuasive Speech," *Speech Monographs, 33* (June 1966), pp. 147–155.

clusion would not apply to all figures of speech. Thus, we might note that figures of speech can clarify and produce some audience change if well done. But if not well done, or if overdone so as to call attention to themselves, they will produce a negative reaction.

SPECIAL STRATEGIES OF LANGUAGE

Thus far we have discussed the nature of word choice, sentence structure and figures of speech, and how they can aid in creating adherence to arguments. The following special strategies are special only in that they do not fit neatly into any other package, but they do represent specific linguistic techniques that have been found to have some usefulness.

LABELING

A number of studies reveal that at least in spoken argument there is some advantage, to directly labeling what one is doing. One study showed that the most effective way to get retention of content is to use what the experimenter called a "proactive" statement. Such phrases as "now get this" or "this is something you should remember" are helpful in increasing retention over no such statement. Another study of opinionated language mentioned earlier in this chapter indicates that if one gives explicit cues to what the receiver is expected to believe, it will strengthen the adherence to the argument. Carl Hovland and Wallace Mandell found that there is greater opinion change when the conclusion is clearly drawn than when left to the audience to draw. Another study shows that belief is increased just by the process of labeling a statement as a fact. Negative labeling, another study shows, establishes an "initial direction of thinking." It does not change a well structured belief but because it sets a matrix it has an effect on the direction the thought must initially go.[25]

There are reservations expressed by the experimenters about virtually all of these studies but taken together they provide rather impressive evidence of the value of labeling as a means of reinforcing points of view of the communication, and there is no evidence to the contrary. The most

[25] Ehrensberger, p. 111; Miller and Lobe, p. 341; Carl I. Hovland and Wallace Medell, "An Experimental Comparison of Conclusion-Drawing By the Communicator and By The Audience," *Journal of Abnormal and Social Psychology*, 47 (July 1952), pp. 581–588; George Horsley Smith, "Beliefs in Statements Labeled Fact and Rumor," *Journal of Abnormal and Social Psychology*, 42 (January 1947), pp. 80–90; Herbert G. Birch, "The Effect of Socially Disapproved Labeling Upon a Well-Structured Attitude," *Journal of Abnormal and Social Psychology*, 40 (July 1945), p. 310.

sophisticated kinds of literary writing, where aesthetic criteria are foremost, probably call for avoiding obvious labeling, but in the overwhelming majority of the cases, argumentation calls for it.

PSEUDOLOGICAL ARGUMENTS

We have already noted elsewhere that no argument in general argumentation is logical in the technical sense of that term. One does not argue from syllogism as a matter of general practice, for instance. But such a technique may, like labeling (it is a kind of labeling), strengthen the argument for the receiver. It is no more "logical" than the more informal form but it will, for some audiences, give the impression of greater logicality and clarify the argument. It will be seen most often in refutation when a speaker wishes to analyze another's informal argument and question the premise. He says, "let us see what you are arguing. In order to arrive at your conclusion you have to claim a major premise of X and a minor premise of Y. Now let's test those premises." There is a certain added advantage gained by the seeming greater logicality of the language.

CONCLUSIONS

Language is fundamental to all argument, but the sense in which we have used it here is narrowed to style and those items that are open to choice. Specifically, in our use here we have confined it to word choice, sentence structure, figures of speech and certain special language strategies of argumentation. The conventions, that govern such stylistic uses of language should be the product of the social standards of general argumentation, not the aesthetic standards of literary excellence. Any judgments we make about language are not as important as content and audience attitude in determining adherence but they are important.

The speaker or writer can aid his efforts to gain the adherence of his associates by paying attention to a number of factors related to *word choice*. The words that we select give cues to others about our social status and how we feel about a particular issue or the person to whom we address the argumentation. Words have varying levels of abstraction but "concrete" terms are not automatically better than abstract words. That decision depends on the particular needs of the argumentation. If abstract language is necessary, it should be given the utmost clarity through as much use of examples, analogy and definition as possible. Special vocabularies should be limited to those audiences that understand and appreciate them.

The arguer would do well to consider the uses of language intensity. More intense language is not automatically more effective than less intense language. Intense language can boomerang on the speaker. The decision on the value of intense language must be based on the predisposition of the listener.

Sentence structure can add variety and interest to one's language although the clearest kind of communication comes from the normal order of subject-verb. To the simple sentence, one can add compound, complex and compound-complex sentence compositions and changes in sentence order based on repetition, omission, suspension and inversion. Although people tend to develop a natural style, conscious use of some of these techniques can add variety to style.

Likewise, the conscious attempt to use such figures of speech as metaphor, simile, personification, anaphora, oxymoron, and antithesis add interest to an argument and there is evidence that, in the case of metaphor, at least, figures of speech produce more change in audiences than literal statements.

Labeling a statement so that the intention of the speaker cannot be misunderstood through such pointing words as "this is important" can strengthen the adherence to an argument as can the deliberate use of formal logical arguments, such as the syllogism.

PROJECTS

1. Examine a current speech or essay, provided by your instructor, for the word choice of the speaker or writer. Where would you put the language on the abstraction ladder? To what extent does the speaker or writer use jargon; precise language?

2. Develop several arguments for presentation in class where the essential content is the same (as much as possible) but the intensity level of the language changes. Discuss with your classmates which versions would be most effective and why.

3. Write a short, no more than two page, argumentative essay using simple sentences. Then rewrite the essay using more complex and compound sentence forms. Compare the writing for clarity and effect.

4. Examine some highly figurative piece of argumentation (such as Martin Luther King, Jr.'s, "I have a dream") and note the kinds of figures of speech used. Do the figures of speech help the argument? Would it be the same argument without the figures of speech?

11

Argumentation in Law

During the Classical period of Greece and Rome, and well into the Medieval period, the study of rhetoric and preparation for the practice of law were the same. Even into modern times students of law investigated theories of rhetoric alongside their work as legal apprentices. With the emergence of the formal study of law in such places as the Inns of Court in Great Britain and law schools in the United States, the two became separated, although much that now is taught in law reveals clear traces of rhetorical heritage.[1] Today it can be said that the study of argumentation is to the practice of law as political science is to politics or as biological science is to medicine.

Professors of law as well as practitioners readily agree that law is a communicating profession. Walter Probert, a professor of law writing in 1972, asserted that "the heart of the common-law-process-in-courts is not rules but rhetoric!"[2] He goes on to say, "and law is so much involved with words: What are laws, constitutions, statutes, regulations, rules, and principles made of, after all? And what do lawyers work with, in court,

[1] For a full discussion of this subject see Richard D. Rieke, *Rhetorical Theory in American Legal Practice*, Unpub. Ph.D., The Ohio State University, 1964.

[2] Walter Probert, *Law, Language, and Communication* (Springfield, Illinois: Charles C. Thomas, Publisher, 1972), p. 21.

in negotiating, drafting, interpreting, counseling, and all the rest?"[3] In a 1968 conference entitled "Law in a Changing America," practicing attorney Richard W. Nahstoll said what many other practitioners have said about the relationship of law and communication:

"In common with others, the lawyer functions in various ways and situations as a "peacemaker"—negotiating, arbitrating, seasoning his client's demands with a sprig of objectivity or structuring a situation to allow people, essentially desirous of working their way out of a situation that they find distasteful, to "save face" and reestablish communication.

"Fundamental to the broad spectrum of the lawyer's work is the art of communication—communication both sending and receiving, communication in the relatively informal setting of ex parte' *interviewing of clients, witness or associates, communication in the relative formality of the courtroom, communication in the negotiation process, communication (perhaps to an unidentified audience) through the written word, whether the document be a letter to be understood on receipt of tomorrow's mail, or a lease or a contract to be understood 10 years hence. Nor, as we have more recently been made aware, can the subtleties of "nonverbal communication" be ignored."[4]*

Of course, the particular theory of argument advanced by various legal scholars and practitioners is not always the same. In fact, the conflicting theories discussed in Chapter 1 are particularly noticeable in the study of law and legal argument. Later in this chapter, during the discussion of appellate argument, we will see that the major conflict is one between those who would subscribe to an essentially Platonic theory of argument and those who could best be described as Aristotelian. The rise in power of American law schools has led to another conflict relevant to the study of argument. Law scholars have suggested that knowledge of statutes, legal decisions, precedent in the common law, and legal philosophy are sufficient to become proficient in argument. Those who practice law, on the other hand, claim that while such knowledge is surely important, it is far from sufficient. They claim that experience in practice, working in the law office, counseling clients, interviewing others, negotiating with opponents, and appearing in the court are indispensable to the development of expertise in legal argument. Reflecting this, their concept of the constitutents of argument includes many more factors than men-

[3] Probert, p. 55.

[4] *Law in a Changing America*, Prepared by The American Assembly, Columbia University (Englewood Cliffs: Prentice-Hall, Inc., 1968), p. 128.

tioned by most scholars—understanding the elements of persuasion is most often mentioned.[5]

As a result of the legal scholar's disdain for the practicalities of legal practice, much of the following discussion will refer to the writing of practicing attorneys rather than representatives of law schools. This merely reflects the burden of published materials. The organization of the chapter is in terms of arenas of legal argument, and *in toto*, the chapter will describe the variety of legal practices as well as theories of legal argument.

LEGAL INTERVIEWS

In a discussion of legal argument many would envision only the courtroom. In fact, however, the greatest portion of time spent by attorneys is in what could be broadly described as legal interviews. In such person-to-person communication as lawyer to client, lawyer to witness, and lawyer to lawyer, the bulk of the work is done in preparing and settling cases. Because the interview serves the dual function of providing the source of evidence for more formal legal argument alongside the equally important task of negotiating settlements of cases prior to entering the courtroom, it may be the single most important element in legal argument. The ancient Roman rhetorician Quintilian placed much stress on this aspect of the law: "Very important are interviews between lawyer and litigants, for in such interviews the orator will discover the real issues."[6] This process of interviewing and counseling has been called "one of the most grievously undertaught skills in legal education."[7]

In the ordinary course of legal practice, lawyers must listen to clients's problems and make an assessment of their merits if ever required to constitute arguments before a judge. Many people fail to understand this and believe instead that a lawyer simply informs a client as to what the law "is." Of course, lawyers frequently express themselves so as to give this impression. In the final analysis, however, the lawyer's decision is an expression of what he believes a court would decide if ever asked to do so. It is one thing to read statutes and precedents and interpret them, but only the appropriate court can make an interpretation of the official law

---

[5] A more thorough discussion of conflicting theories of legal argument can be found in Richard D. Rieke, "The Rhetoric of Law, A Bibliographical Essay," *Today's Speech*, *18* (Fall 1971), pp. 48–57.

[6] Charles Edgar Little, trans. and ed., *Quintilian the School Master—The Institutio Oratoria of Marcus Fabius Quintilianus* (2 vols.), (Nashville: For George Peabody College for Teachers, 1951), p. 322.

[7] Probert, p. 211.

as it applies to any case. Therefore, in the legal interview, the first requirement is to learn as much as possible about the potential case. Those
experienced in the process say that no guiding or leading should be
employed. Instead, the attorney should instruct the client at the first as to
what procedures to follow, then the client should be left free to tell the
story without interruption. After all has been freely said, it is acceptable to
ask specific questions in order to search out even more facts. The client
will be simply telling of a problem—an accident, a conflict with someone,
a possible crime, or merely a plan proposed that may or may not be legal.
The lawyer will be listening with the view of someone who might need to
prove as fact what the client is telling. The lawyer will be assessing the
story as potential evidence in an argument. As the Board of Student
Advisers of the Harvard Law School tells students:

*"Much of a lawyer's work is concerned with ensuring that his client's acts
will not give rise to a lawsuit. Even where a dispute seems likely, the lawyer
often guides his client's acts and correspondence so as to settle short of the
courtroom, or to strengthen the client's chances of winning if the case does
go to trial. This phase of law-work is commonly called counselling and
occupies the time of many lawyers. One aspect of such counselling may be
to assay the client's chances of winning before a judge or jury."*[8]

Of course, in preparation of either a written memorandum or a case for
trial, it is common for lawyers to interview many other individuals in order
to obtain as much potential evidence as possible. The client may be the
chief source of evidence, but certainly not the only one.

Most likely the first opportunity to employ information gained through
interviews in a formal argumentative form is a legal memorandum. The
memo is "intended to inform the reader of all the possible legal issues
and legal and policy arguments from both the plaintiff's and the defendant's points of view, and from probable outcome of any given case."[9]
The memorandum shows the client what the lawyer believes would be
the outcome should the questions be put to the court. It constitutes a professional opinion, one in which the lawyer authorizes the client to put
considerable stock, and is therefore a formal argument as well as an
assessment of probable arguments. The attorney wants the client to place
adherence in the arguments advanced in the memo, and this is often a

[8] The Board of Student Advisers, *Introduction to Advocacy*, 7th ed., (Cambridge,
Massachusetts: Harvard Law School, 1962), p. 14.
[9] John S. Searles, *Advocacy in the Moot Court Program*, 3rd ed., (Cincinnati: The
W. H. Anderson Co., 1971), p. 1.

difficult problem in argumentation. A survey of practitioners revealed many sources of difficulty in communication between lawyer and client. The clients often are highly ego involved in their case, have developed misconceptions about the legal merits related to their problem, and often fail to understand the lawyer's role or his particular terminology. Thus, it is often quite a task for a lawyer to write a memorandum to which the client will subscribe.[10]

An equally important form of legal interview is the negotiation process between lawyers representing opponents in any conflict. For a wide variety of reasons it is more desirable to agree on a settlement in a case than take it to court. But this is predicated on the assumption that an agreement can be found such that neither side feels it would be better served by letting a judge or jury decide. This is negotiation as described in Chapter 2. "Working out a settlement frequently turns on your ability to persuade your adversary."[11] To engage in this form of argument the lawyer must be thoroughly prepared to argue his case in court. If he has looked toward settlement from the start and thus has not fully prepared, he may well find his negotiating position weakened. Further, negotiation requires a brutally realistic assessment of the merits of one's case. This is no time for Quixotic determination to win or die trying—it is the client who dies. If the offer made by an opponent is better than what can reasonably be expected from a court's evaluation of the lawyer's arguments, it may be wise to accept it. "In many instances, effecting a settlement involves the highest degree of advocacy by the trial lawyer.[12]

PLEADINGS

Even though the great majority of problems can be settled short of full use of the judicial system, settlement and success in courts depends on full and effective preparation. A significant factor in preparation is setting out the claim to be examined legally and the issues of which it consists. In law this portion of the argumentation is called the pleadings: "that branch of legal science that deals with the principles governing the formal written statements made to the court by the parties to a suit of their respective

[10] Wayne N. Thompson and S. John Insalata, "Communication from Attorney to Client," *The Journal of Communication, 14* (March 1964), pp. 22–23.

[11] John C. Elam, "Settlement: The Real Target of any Trial," in Grace W. Holmes, ed., *Excellence in Advocacy* (Ann Arbor, Michigan: The Institute of Continuing Legal Education, 1971), p. 7.

[12] Elam, p. 4.

claims and defenses as to the suit."[13] In any argumentative situation, success of one position is enhanced if that side can determine what issues will be argued and how they will be phrased. In pleadings, opposing attorneys write out their view of the case, their concept of the issues, and propose interrogatories that they hope will extract useful admissions from the other side. In this sense, pleadings resemble cross-examination in academic debate in that each side hopes to obtain admissions that will ultimately be useful.

By design, the pleadings serve to clarify the controversy so as to make the ultimate decision a product of only relevant and important issues. In practice, opposing lawyers employ the pleadings to delay coming to trial, use them to maneuver for position, and employ the process to obtain information about the opponent's case and evidence while revealing as little of their own as possible. Also, in the pleadings, each side will seek to set up claims that they believe their evidence and argument will justify— this will not be a time for over-statement of prospects for fear the actual argument will suffer, if too great a promise has been originally advanced.[14] Effective preparation of this paper-work will advance the legal argument in two ways. First, unless this is done according to prescribed patterns, success in trial may be blocked on technicalities, and second, without effective pleadings it may be impossible to succeed in the negotiations for settlement because opponents will not believe that you are serious about going to trial.

EVIDENCE IN LAW

Evidence in legal argument is the subject of massive books and legal decisions and will not be described in detail here. Furthermore, what will be accepted as evidence will vary from jurisdiction to jurisdiction and generalizations may be misleading. However, it is possible to discuss the overall characteristics of evidence in law and compare them to that in general argumentation.

Aristotle distinguished between evidence in deliberative (or legislative) rhetoric and that in the forensic (or legal) situation. In the former, people are deciding matters of community interest of which they are a part. Their self-interest is involved in the outcome, and they will judge

[13] Charles E. Clark, *Handbook of the Law of Code Pleading*, (St. Paul, Minnesota: West Publishing Co., 1947), p. 1.

[14] Alexander H. Robbins, *A Treatise on American Advocacy* (St. Louis: Central Law Journal Co., 1913), p. 44.

evidence accordingly. In a legal argument, however, the judge or jury is deciding matters in which they have no involvement—they are selected precisely because they have no stake in the case. "Here the judges made award regarding interests that are not their own; if they view these in the light of their own feelings, and yield to the gratification of their ears, they lend themselves to the more plausible speaker, and so decide the case. They do not *judge* it."[15] The goal is to make a judgment on the case, not merely to pick a winner. To assure this, even in ancient times limitations were placed on the evidence that could be submitted in a court of law. Efforts were begun then, and continue today, to define the kind of evidence that would more nearly yield decisions based on sound judgment. The law of evidence stands between the advocate and the judge or jury as a kind of filter, letting through only that evidence that meets requirements of probity, that is, meeting minimum requirements of honesty, relevancy, factuality, etc. The "probative value" of evidence is the test of its ability to meet such standards. Of course, such a concept as probative value raises philosophical questions about the nature of evidence or support in argument. The theory advanced in Chapters 5, 6, and 7 of this book would generally be in conflict with a notion that evidence serves to reveal the "truth" of the matter. Instead we have suggested that support is a process of finding starting points between what the audience will perceive as factual or already within their value system, and what the advocate wants to claim. This conflict exists among philosophers and practitioners of law.

The more traditional (and more common) perception of evidence in law would be predicated on the belief that the events that become the subject of legal argument "actually happened" in a distinct form, and in the courtroom lawyers use evidence to recreate the events in the minds of jurors. For example, if a contract were signed three years ago and two people were present and participated in the signing, a trial over a difference in interpreting the intent of that agreement today would seek to bring that event back to life in front of the jury. The contract itself would be presented and read. The two individuals would be brought forward and asked about their understanding of the agreement. Perhaps documents arising out of the agreement would be presented to show what was intended—plans, orders, budgets, memoranda, etc. Ideally, at the end of the trial, the jury would be as clear about the event as they would have been had they actually been present during the signing. They can then decide what were the "facts" of the situation.

---

[15] Lane Cooper, *The Rhetoric of Aristotle*, © 1932, Renewed 1960. By permission of *Prentice-Hall, Inc.*, Englewood Cliffs, New Jersey, p. 4.

A conflicting view of the function of legal evidence would be to describe the trial at law as a creative process rather than a re-creative one. That is, instead of bringing back from the past what "actually" happened, legal evidence serves to construct a conception of the "event" which will best serve the ends of justice today. Felix Cohen argued that it is unacceptable to suggest that one "event" happened. Instead, he would suggest that each signer of the contract had a perception of the event, as did lawyers who drew up the document, and those later affected by the agreement. Similarly, those in the courtroom today would have had their own view had they actually been present. Cohen would suggest that it might be more useful to speak of the "events" related to the signing, and then the function of evidence would be to construct an event that most satisfies today's needs. He uses as an example the concept of the cause of an accident. In deciding personal injury cases, evidence is presented to show who caused the accident. But cause is not a clear-cut concept. If two drivers collide, the "cause" might be described as the path of one car, the engineering of the road, the parents of the drivers (if they had not been born, there would have been no accident), or the employers of the drivers who sent them out on an errand. In most jurisdictions, it is possible to sue the employer of the driver under specified circumstances. Cohen would say this is not discovering that the employer was indeed "the cause" of the accident; it merely is a conception of the situation the courts find consistent with today's needs for justice.[16]

Walter Probert, writing more recently, would take a similar point of view. He would suggest that the concept "fact" is actually a convention in language to describe certain kinds of claims, and not a slice of reality. He says, "If we allow the power of the word 'facts' to take our eyes off the statements that are thus being labeled, *to fail to see them as words*, we inevitably fall prey to one of the most powerful forms of rhetoric yet evolved."[17] Regardless of the point of view held, it is the object of the trial at law to secure the adherence of judge or jury to a set of claims to the extent they will be labeled "facts." Both sides will assert what they believe to be factual descriptions of an event in the past over which there is now controversy. They will present evidence in the form of testimony of individuals who had access to some direct experience with the "event" or a related one, and physical evidence in the form of documents and objects (including photographs) that are a part of the events under examination. The judge or jury will listen to all this and then announce what version of

---

[16] Felix S. Cohen, "Field Theory and Judicial Logic," *The Yale Law Journal*, 59 (January 1950), pp. 238–272.

[17] Probert, pp. 96, 177.

the story will obtain the official label as facts. It is important to note that there is virtually no appeal from this judgment. Although a judge may direct a verdict because of the clear preponderance of the evidence, in his judgment, toward one side, and a court of appeals may rarely determine the jury strayed too far from acceptable procedures in determining the facts, for the most part, once this judgment is made, it is considered finished and final in the eyes of the law.

Once again, the focus of legal evidence is on bringing to the attention of the jury those people and objects associated with the source of controversy. Different from other rhetorical situations that typically involve forming judgments about what might happen in the future if certain actions are taken, law cases seek to make a judgment about that which has already occurred. The stress, therefore, is not on authoritative judgments as is the case in policy debate, but is instead on reports of witnesses or participants in the past activity, and objects that are a part of it and, therefore, contribute to forming an image of the activity. The primary measure of evidence is its probative value or its ability to reveal as nearly as possible an acceptable image of the event. A category such as "direct" evidence exists to describe that which of itself establishes a fact. For example, if the question is whether or not a will existed, the presentation of the will directly shows an answer. Testimony by those who were present, if believed, constitutes direct evidence of an occurrence. Another category, "circumstantial" evidence describes testimony and objects that establish a basis for an inference in answering a question. For example, finding your fingerprints on a table provides the basis for an inference that you were present at the place the prints were found.

The filtering process, described earlier, of rules of evidence is illustrated by these policies suggested by the Advisory Committee on Evidence Rules of the Judicial Conference of the United States. (1) Evidence must be relevant to the questions at hand to be considered. (2) Those claims generally known within the territorial jurisdiction of the court or which are capable of accurate determination by reference to a source whose accuracy cannot reasonably be questioned may be accepted without evidence through "judicial notice." (3) If the probative value of evidence, even though it is relevant, is outweighed by the damage of unfair prejudice, misleading the jury, confusion of issues, or if it causes undue delay, it may be excluded from consideration. (4) Opinion evidence is admissible even from a lay person when it is rationally based on his perception and is helpful to a clear understanding of the testimony. (5) Hearsay evidence, that which reports what a witness said to a second or third party, is inadmissible except when the witness himself is not available or even when he is available when the nature of the statement and the special circumstances under which it is made offer assurances of accuracy not likely to be enhanced by calling the witness himself.[18] These examples show how the rules of evidence are based on rhetorical or argumentative considerations. The rule makers have in mind the *kind* of decision they want made, although they leave entirely to the judge or jury the specific decision. To help ensure the right kind of decision, rules are made to filter out all but selected evidence. The choice is made on the basis of an expectation of the kind of impact a type of evidence will have on decision makers. Although the rules are phrased to coincide with a traditional notion of truth-discovery, they function to affect human response to arguments.

For example, the greatest proportion of legal evidence consists of testimony by witnesses, and a great deal has been done to ensure that witnesses report what they believe to be the truth so as to take the emphasis off the question of whether the jury believes what is said. Threats ranging from fines and imprisonment on the present scene to cutting off hands or execution in the past have been used to this end. Yet, witnesses continue to report that which they do not believe to be true, as in the Watergate scandal where apparently several fine lawyers committed perjury. And, people continue to draw different meaning from the same experience and report different testimony as truthfully as they can.

Thus, in the final analysis, the test of the evidence is whether or not the jury believes it. In contrasting physical evidence with testimony, one lawyer said,

"There are other kinds of evidence, however. They are usually a minor part, and often an important part of trials of any kind. A document, a thing, a photograph—something that is a persuader—carries its own image or its own inference. A human being is a mass of criteria. A beautiful young lady who might after the trial meet you for a drink is much easier to believe than a crotchety, old, unwashed man. These are the things that interfere with testimonial evidence; but a document, a good clean document whose signature is not denied, may well be uncontested. . . . the object is to persuade."[19]

[18] The Advisory Committee on Evidence Rules of the Judicial Conference of the United States, Appointed by the Chief Justice of the United States, Report issued March, 1969, cited in Charles W. Joiner, "Rules of Evidence: Do They Help or Hinder Persuasion?" in Grace W. Holmes, ed., *Persuasion: Key to Damages* (Ann Arbor, Michigan: The Institute of Continuing Legal Education, 1969), pp. 182–187.

[19] F. Lee Bailey, "How to Persuade with Nontestimonial Evidence," in Grace W. Holmes, ed., *Excellence in Advocacy*, pp. 43–44.

Another practitioner reported saying the following to expert witnesses that he planned to use:

"Doctor, you are an expert in medicine, . . . but I have been in court every day for years and I know what approach will interest jurors. Understand that I am not attempting to influence your opinion in this case. We both know that I wouldn't do that, and you wouldn't allow it. I am saying only that the way you express yourself—the image you project to the jury—is vital to our case."[20]

Because judges and jurors determine "facts" by listening to witnesses, and making a judgment as to their credibility is mostly judged by the observable, nonverbal elements of the testimony, witnesses are carefully coached by lawyers as to their manner of presentation. Thus, finding the witnesses and physical evidence is only the first step in legal argument. The manner of communicating it is tremendously important, and that is discussed in the following sections.

CASE BUILDING

Legal argument is more analogous to a persuasive campaign than to a single speech because the lawyer must orchestrate a variety of elements to yield a final product of a favorable decision. From the selection of jurors to presentation of witnesses and cross-examination of opposing witnesses, the lawyer must keep in mind the image being formed by the jury. In theory, a trial functions to set forth all the evidence—witnesses as well as other forms—before the jury begins to form an opinion. Then the attorneys make what is called the closing "argument" where the evidence that has been advanced is discussed in argumentative form with a view toward leading the jury to a decision. In the legal sense, all that has happened prior to these closing statements is not argumentative. However, in operation this image is not apparent. On the contrary, all that happens in the courtroom, including jury selection and opening statements, is observed by the jurors and becomes a part of their ultimate decision. At any point during the trial the judge or jury may reach a decision and then begin seeking support or reinforcement for it rather than listening objectively.

[20] John C. Shepherd, "Relations with the Expert Witness," in Grace W. Holmes, ed., *Experts in Litigation* (Ann Arbor, Michigan: Institute of Continuing Legal Education, 1973), p. 22.

To develop a case, then, the attorney must consider what aspect of his total campaign will most likely produce the desired effect—where should emphasis come? Lawyers speak of developing a theory of the case—a strategy or rationale that will be persuasive. Perhaps the theory will be the client himself—his story and his apparent high character. Perhaps the focus will be on refutation of the opposition arguments. Sometimes the theory is to defend as well as possible, seeking errors that might permit success at the appellate level. For the most part, however, only the legally trained person can effectively develop such case theories, and they cannot be explained here. A practicing lawyer describes his manner of case construction in this way:

"My first step in preparing a case is to get together all the facts I can find. . . . Once I have the facts assembled, everything goes backwards. I ask myself, "What will the judge charge the jury?" The charge is the final argument, and it is the one to which the jurors listen most attentively. . . . Therefore, my final argument must be directed to arguing the principles that I anticipate will be in the charge. If that is the final argument, what evidence do I need to justify it? And what evidence do I have? That is what I put in the opening statement."[21]

Developing such an integrated case includes consideration of the order in which witnesses are to be heard. Some rely on the drama involved in a trial and put the key witness, such as the plaintiff, on the stand first. They believe in the law of primacy—that which is heard first will be the most meaningful and lasting. Others suggest this is a dangerous tactic because the impact of cross-examination of this witness also would come immediately. They would suggest, instead, starting with an unimpeachable witness such as a police officer and establishing a strong, although minor point first. Because of the latitude given lawyers as to the order of witnesses, this is a major point of decision in case building.[22]

Many legal terms have become common to many argumentative situations, but probably the most common are "burden of proof" and "prima facie" case. In law, as in most uses of the term, burden of proof suggests an artificial presumption of the decision to be made in the absence of a clear preponderance of evidence for either side. A prima facie case is

[21] Craig Spangenberg, "What I Try to Accomplish in an Opening Statement." Reprinted with permission from Holmes (ed.), *Excellence in Advocacy*, © 1971 by The Institute of Continuing Legal Education, pp. 22–23.

[22] William H. Erickson, "Cross-Examination of the Expert," in Grace W. Holmes, ed., *Experts in Litigation*, pp. 52–53.

one that meets the demands of the burden of proof by offering evidence in support of each of the essential elements of the question at hand. Essential elements are typically a function of the legal question being considered and will be set during the pleadings and finally defined by the judge in his charge or instructions to the jury. Books in law have been written outlining the requirements of *prima facie* cases in various legal situations. But, as in all other argumentative contexts, in the final analysis the success or failure of a case depends on the willingness of decision makers to grant their adherence. In fact, one lawyer has said, "There is no burden of proof. If we required a man to carry the burden of proof, it would be a state of absolutism and everybody carrying that burden would lose, with rare exception. The burden of proof, be it civil or criminal, . . . is in fact the risk of nonpersuasion."[23]

Although these statements on case building emphasize the importance of structuring a legal case, evidence suggests that it is not a common practice in the United States for trial attorneys to prepare formal trial briefs. This is contrasted with the custom in the United Kingdom in which a solicitor generally prepares a complete brief so that the barrister who eventually must argue the case in court can be informed as well as possible.[24] Those practicing lawyers who write on this subject, however, tend to encourage the practice of brief writing. The purpose of the brief is to organize all the materials to be used in presenting the case to the court in the most effective manner possible. The attorney aims at setting out the facts clearly and relating them to the issues established in the pleadings. It is in the brief that the order of presenting witnesses is established.[25] To illustrate, a brief for a civil action should include (according to the American Law Institute) first, a statement of the action, or such procedural data as the type of suit and the time of its origination. Next, a statement of facts should be included. Presumably, this section should contain information—what one side believes to be fact—and should not be overtly argumentative. However, "the order in which the facts are to be presented is a matter of strategy to be decided differently in different cases."[26] The facts can be arranged chronologically, or in the order in which the case is to be presented, or in some other way. The statement of facts should

[23] F. Lee Bailey, p. 41.

[24] Henry Hardwicke, *The Art of Winning Cases or Modern Advocacy*, 2nd ed., (Albany: Banks & Co., 1920), p. 12.

[25] John C. Reed, *Conduct of Lawsuits*, (Boston: Little, Brown and Co., 1912), p. 215.

[26] Wilford R. Lorry, *A Civil Action—The Trial*, American Law Institute and the American Bar Association (Philadelphia: American Law Institute, 1959), pp. 16–17.

include a clear indication of what is desired from the court. Following the statement of facts should be a clear indication of the issues arising under the litigation and then a section with the attorney's argument of the issues. The final step in the trial brief is a conclusion that points out the presence of all the necessary and important elements of the case and the justification for the decision requested. With this, the lawyer is ready for trial.

THE OPENING STATEMENT

Actually, the first step in a jury trial is the *voir dire* or selection of the jurors. At one time lawyers were permitted to question prospective jurors rather freely and could thereby begin the argumentative process at that stage. Now it is increasingly common for the judge to question jurors and the opportunity for structuring the decision making panel and getting started with surreptitious argument is slight. Thus, that stage will not be discussed here as a critical element in legal argument.

For major purposes of argument, the first stage of the trial is the opening statement. Of course, those who are specialists in law will shrink from calling this step argumentative for here it is only expected that each lawyer will inform the judge or jury of the facts they *intend* to prove when evidence is presented. But "argument" in the legal sense is more restrictive than the term has been used elsewhere in this book. Notice the distinctions a lawyer makes: "One is persuading, not arguing. Lawyers are under ethical requirements in the opening statement not to argue the case. But there are many ways that one may persuade without arguing."[27] The jury is instructed not to perceive what a lawyer says as evidence, but most lawyers believe they do so anyway. The jury is instructed to listen to the opening statement as merely alerting them to what the case is about and what to look for when evidence is actually presented, but instead they respond, often, to the opening statement as if it were evidence. In fact, the University of Chicago Jury Study found that before the end of the trial, a majority of jurors make a firm decision in the case.[28] For these reasons, the opening statement must, indeed, be looked on as an argumentative element in the trial.

[27] John C. Elam, "Persuasion in the Opening Statement: The Defendant's Approach," in Grace W. Holmes, ed., *Persuasion: Key to Damages*, p. 97.

[28] Harry Kalven and Hans Zeisel, *The American Jury* (Boston: Little, Brown and Co., 1966), pp. 476–491.

Unfortunately, many lawyers, accepting the assertion that the opening statement is not part of the argumentative process, fail to prepare fully for the speech, and sometimes they waive the opportunity altogether. Often, the opening is only a perfunctory description of the case in general terms. Yet at this time the lawyer's role, *vis-a-vis* the jury, is being permanently set. If they perceive him as uninterested, unprepared, uncommitted to his position, it will color their reaction to him throughout the trial. Although the jury is repeatedly told that what a lawyer says is not evidence, there is strong reason to believe that jurors accept such statements as evidence, often failing to recall that they were actually said by an attorney.[29] Theorists of persuasion are uncertain whether or not primacy or recency (what is heard first or closest to decision) outweigh one another in ability to influence. But in some situations what is heard first makes the lasting impression. There is a chance this is so in the trial at law, and, therefore, the opening statement becomes even more crucial to the argumentative situation.[30] One writer on the subject said it is reasonable that at times the first speaker is so effective as to "channelize" the thinking of some jurors from that point on "so that all evidence thereafter received is not heard with the same objectivity as would be the case were such an opening statement not to be made."[31]

Typically, the opening statement is in chronological order, describing a series of events that will become the object of contention in the trial. The attorney avoids objection for trying to "argue" by avoiding language that will be perceived as emotional and by resisting the lure to elaborate and draw implications from the events being described. Although trying to describe the events in a way that is most helpful to his case, the lawyer will at the same time tell of evidence that will come out as unfavorable to the client. In this way an image of fairness may be generated and an avoidance of apparent surprise when the evidence is actually presented is accomplished. The way in which information is to be combined with persuasion is to make the facts as presented sufficiently dramatic that they make their own conclusions. "Very few persons," states an early commentator, "comprehend the force that there is in a clear, succinct, orderly narrative of facts." He continues, "There is a logical power about such a narrative that exceeds often the mere force of ingenious reasoning. It is the natural logic of the facts."[32]

[29] Spangenberg, p. 19.

[30] Spangenberg.

[31] Lorry, p. 49.

[32] Joseph W. Donovan, *Modern Jury Trials* (New York: G. A. Jennings Co., Inc., 1927), p. 240.

PRESENTATION OF EVIDENCE

For the most part, trial evidence is presented through the testimony of witnesses under the direct examination of the counsel who called them and as modified by the cross-examination of opposing counsel. In most argumentative situations, the advocate is in total control of the supporting materials because they are given in the form of quotations. The lawyer, however, must present evidence through a dialogue with a witness. The advocate speaks to judge or jury through the words of the witness. "Often he is trying to do more than one thing at once, and he is communicating on several levels . . . talking to the witness and the several jurors simultaneously, to the trial judge, and potentially to the . . . appellate court via the record of the case."[33]

Court rules and practitioner experience suggest that the dialogue should be structured as much as possible so as to let the witness tell the story with minimum interference from counsel. Witnesses should use their own words in response to open-ended questions. Leading questions (those that either directly suggest the answer desired or that embody a material fact and may be answered "yes" or "no") are usually not allowed in direct examination.

Much more than a recitation of perceived facts is going on in the dialogue of direct examination. Unless the decision makers agree that what is said should be believed, it goes for nothing. For in any argumentation, support is supporting only if it is part of the decision maker's value system. Testimony produced from witnesses is argumentative support only if the witnesses are believed. To this end, lawyers spend considerable time in advance of the trial coaching witnesses. Although some might think this is sophistry and should be avoided, it is defended by noting that honest witnesses, if they testify poorly, may be disbelieved. Prospective witnesses are told how to dress (conservatively for the most part), how to speak (confidently but not arrogantly, usually), how to respond to questions (don't delay too long or people will think you are trying to remember a made-up story), and how to respond to cross-examination (never become belligerent). Because witnesses are almost always unfamiliar with the trial environment, they may be frightened, they may completely change their manner, they may even tell a story widely unlike that told the lawyer earlier in his office. Because of this, direct examination is unpredictable and a difficult form of communication. Yet, the lawyer must

[33] Probert, p. 67.

keep in the background and permit full attention to the witness. Counsel must not comment on answers, seek to draw argumentative conclusions from them at this point, or otherwise get into the center of attention. At this stage in the trial, it is the testimony that counts. If one's witnesses are believed, most of the argumentative task is accomplished. In a study of legal decision making, subjects were asked to describe witnesses in a trial using forty selected adjectives. A factor analysis of their responses and an analysis of variance of these ratings in relation to the decisions suggests two predominant perceptions of witnesses that lead to favorable decisions. First, the witness should be perceived as rational and reasonable. Second, the witness should be thought of as a human, nice person.[34] If counsel can communicate these concepts to the jury alongside the specifics of the testimony, the direct examination should be successful, at least to the extent permitted by the overall strength of the case.

CROSS-EXAMINATION

Cross-examination is a form of refutation aimed at denying or weakening support used by an opponent, or turning opposing support to one's own advantage. It is performed, again in dialogue form, although here counsel uses almost totally leading questions: those that can be answered "yes" or "no" by the witness. By doing this, the lawyer retains control of the dialogue by placing the substance in the question rather than leaving it to the answer. For example, a leading question might ask, "Was it raining at the time of the accident?" rather than merely inquiring "What was the weather like?" The cross-examiner does not merely probe what has been said on direct examination. An argumentative goal must be set, such as damaging the credibility or ethos of the witness, obtaining factual admissions that weaken the effect of the testimony, obtaining factual admissions beneficial to one's own case, obtaining materials for closing argument, or showing such contradiction among opposing witnesses as to destroy the total effect. Again and again experienced trial lawyers say the best cross-examination is no questions at all. They mean that often nothing has been said by a witness that damages the lawyer's case, and so no cross-examination is called for. Or, the witness has been so poor in testifying for the other side that he has done all the damage that could be done to himself. Or the testimony has been so devastating that it could

[34] Richard D. Rieke, "The Role of Argument in the Trial at Law," paper presented at the Speech Communication Association Convention, San Francisco, California, December 1971.

not be shaken and the only possible effect of cross-examination would be to strengthen the damage done. "Do not examine at all if no purpose can be achieved or if you are uncertain of your ability to control the responses."[35] Above all, the cross-examiner should never ask questions when he does not know the answer. Cross-examination is not an investigatory process, it is a refutative one. The questions come from the attorney's knowledge of other information that, when put in the form of questions, will refute the testimony. The goal is simply to force the witness to say what must be said (if perjury is to be avoided) to weaken the impact of direct testimony.

It is possible to view cross-examination as a game situation that begins by an identification of roles—the witness at least is identified in favor of his own testimony and frequently identifies himself with the side that called him; the cross-examining attorney is the opponent. To the extent one gives in, the other gains. This relationship is clearly more true in the case of a perjured witness, but usually occurs with any witness. Before the game can begin, the attorney opposing the testimony must decide whether to gamble on playing—does the chance of gain offset the chance of loss? To what extent has his position been damaged by the testimony? If there has been little damage, no questions may be the best bet. Also, if the cross-examiner to be is not fully prepared to go ahead, it may again be best to pass. Preparation means gathering every detail and document together for ready reference during cross-examination. Pretrial discovery of opposition evidence, and depositions from prospective witnesses are vital. Cross-references of all the advance information must be available for checking against actual trial testimony, for the typical approach to cross-examination is to expose contradictions, omissions, distortions, and other variations between pretrial documents and depositions and what is said in court. The goal is to diminish confidence in the evidence as support for arguments ultimately to be made, and to diminish confidence in the witness as a reliable source.

If the decision is made to cross-examine, a variety of methods are employed. One may proceed to question in the same order as was used on direct examination. Or, to gain advantage of what is freshest in the mind of the jury, one may begin at the end of the testimony. Sometimes, it is recommended to select a series of untruths that may individually be trivial but in rapid combination their exposure may destroy the credibility of a witness quickly. At times, the best approach is to "go for the jugular."

---

[35] William H. Erickson, "Cross-Examination of the Expert," in Grace W. Holmes, ed., *Experts in Litigation*, p. 58.

That is, select the essence of the testimony, the biggest point against you, and drive immediately at its destruction.

If "no questions" is often the best form of cross-examination, then knowing when to stop questioning is the second most important restraint necessary to the lawyer. The questioner must know to stop when he has all that can be obtained from the witness through cross-examination. There is a point of climax that is reached in cross-examination when the greatest amount of value has been obtained by a given line of questions. To proceed further on that line might permit the witness to explain away any harm that has been done him or at least to distract the attention of the jury from the particular conclusion the cross-examiner has obtained. The jury is not trained in the evaluation of testimony. They tend to make fairly gross distinctions—a witness has told the truth or not; the fact is as the witness said or not, and so forth. Sometimes a truly significant accomplishment of cross-examination such as the exposure of a major misstatement by the witness may be lost in extended questioning around the point and in the final analysis count very little toward the decision. Observers sometimes feel the cross-examiner is unfair in preventing elaboration, but if it is called for it may be done through redirect examination. It is not the obligation of the cross-examiner. Interestingly, for many, many years practicing lawyers have objected to the image portrayed by Perry Mason, the fictional trial attorney. He cross-examines witnesses until they confess, and real lawyers suggest this simply never happens. On the contrary, only the most naive cross-examiner, after securing a series of factual admissions, goes on to ask the last question, "Then we really shouldn't believe what you said?" The witness will simply not grant an affirmative answer, and will instead present an argument in defense of his now challenged testimony that may destroy the cross-examination.

Finally, it is important to adjust the tone of cross-examination to fit the witness. Although dramas of the courtroom often depict the cross-examiner as a harsh, intimidating challenger, it is probably more often valuable to be courteous and gentle. Some witnesses, such as clergymen, children, old people, or those who are ill cannot be cross-examined at all for fear the effort will be perceived as improper and more will be lost than gained. The ordinary witness has just finished telling a story under the careful coaching and direction of a skilled lawyer, and the jury has probably granted credence. The cross-examiner is, therefore, challenging a new-found friend of the jury, and must proceed cautiously for fear of alienating the jury. Unlike Perry Mason, the cross-examiner will probably not win or lose on the challenge of any one witness and he should not try to gain more from this element of legal argument than can reasonably be expected.

CLOSING ARGUMENT

It is in the closing argument or summation that the lawyer is able to relate evidence with claim and ask the decision makers to conclude with one side or the other. In essence, here the attorney makes an argumentative speech quite similar to any other with the exception that in this case the audience has just spent considerable time observing the development and testing of the sources of support that will be used. Also, the audience is a captive one—the law requires that they remain until the end. Wide debate exists over the effectiveness of this aspect of legal argument. Some say this: "Within the last decade, I have arrived at the view that final argument is the most important single feature of any lawsuit. . . . I now believe that a case is won or lost in final argument;"[36] or this: "In the final argument you pour your whole personality out to the jury. You win or lose right there."[37] On the other hand, others say, "The final argument is not where the advocate wins the lawsuit. . . . Jurors decide which side they believe by the end of the opening statements."[38] In a study of jury decision making, it was found that jurors tend to decide who, if anyone, was at fault in a civil suit (liability) before the final argument, but they were still withholding decision as to the amount of damages, if any, that should be awarded.[39] Most trial counsel take the argument seriously because it *may* make a difference.

An equally vigorous debate arises over the role of so-called emotional appeals in the summation. It is popular to denounce emotionalism when speaking on the subject because our society does not approve of such an approach to argumentation. However, an examination of the transcript of selected final arguments leads quickly to the conclusion first, those arguments that probably would be labeled emotional by most observers abound, and second, what observers are actually saying is the common observation, "My arguments are made of sound logic while my opponent is using pure emotion." It would seem that the best advice is to use arguments that the jury or judge will not *label* as undue emotionalism.

Most of the rules of persuasion apply to the closing argument. However, some specific observations can be made. The jury must be analyzed

[36] Murray Sams, Jr., "Closing Argument: New Answers to Some Old Problems," in Grace W. Holmes, ed., *Excellence in Advocacy*, p. 73.

[37] John C. Shepherd, "Closing Argument: The Defendant's Last Chance," in Grace W. Holmes, ed., *Excellence in Advocacy*, p. 86.

[38] Bill Colson, "Arguing Expert Testimony in the Summation," in Grace W. Holmes, ed., *Experts in Litigation*, p. 83.

[39] Rieke, "The Role of Argument in the Trial at Law."

as to their reaction to the trial—what testimony has been impressive to them, what has been their reaction to litigants and counsel, toward which side are they tending, which points should be reiterated in closing argument for greatest effect, what opposing points have done the most damage and require careful rebuttal? The entire trial record, including the judge's instructions, should be studied prior to making the argument. In evaluating conflicting testimony, the lawyer will try to show that probability favors his interpretation. Attorneys put a great deal of emphasis on the jury's judgment of what seems to make sense—the side that demonstrates that its evidence makes more sense is likely to win.

In the closing speech the advocate will be wise to use the record of evidence to support his position. There seems to be general agreement that the closing speech is best when it sticks to the evidence and does not move off into appeals not directly supported by testimony. One practitioner has a table set in front of the jury and places on it copies of the record, pretrial depositions, and other documents that he uses for references or simply as props to increase the credibility of his speech. Moreover, the jury will have access to some, if not all, of these materials during their deliberations. It may be that if arguments are tied to them, they will have more lasting effect.

As in most argumentation, the goal is not to stampede an audience to immediate action. Instead, the final argument must advance claims in such a way that they will survive the impact of opposing arguments and what will be hours or even days of deliberation. In the closing argument, as noted earlier in this chapter, the court's instructions to the jury must be anticipated and dealt with. The issues must be restated in the light of the evidence, and finally an overall concept of the case, permitting a decision in your behalf, should be claimed. There is wide variation in the length of such speeches from a few minutes to many hours. There is little evidence relating to a preferred length. Instead, concentration on effectiveness in speaking is paramount, and if that takes a long time, let it. Regardless of one's philosophy, if there is a place for eloquence in the trial, it is in the closing argument.

APPELLATE ADVOCACY

The advocate, on appeal, has two channels of communication to the court: the brief and the oral argument. When most effectively used, one will complement the other. In English appellate courts, the emphasis is placed on oral argument. In the United States, much greater stress is placed on the brief without suggesting that oral argument is not critical.

The value of the brief varies with the practice of the court. If briefs are read only after oral argument, and if the court has been persuaded to decide the case one way, the brief becomes the peg on which it can hang its decision. If briefs are read in advance of argument, then the brief acts as a first step in persuasion. Finally, in a very close case where legal materials must be studied carefully, "the brief becomes the factor on which the entire case will be won or lost."[40] In the brief the attorney puts down the facts of the case selected from the record of the lower court's proceedings, indicates the body of law—precedent cases and other authority— which he feels support his interpretation, and works all of them into issues raised on the appeal accompanied by his claim. The brief provides an opportunity for detail and elaboration, or order of argument not possible in oral argument.

The function of the oral argument is to emphasize and clarify the written argument in the brief. The oral argument should not seek to review the long series of decisions on which the appeal is based. Rather, it should select one or two most convincing cases and discuss them. Rather than read from the lower court record or from the decisions of previous cases, the attorney during oral argument should speak with the court on the question of whether his interpretation of the law is to be accepted over that of his opponent. At this stage of legal argument, it is reasonable to assume that both sides have compelling cases and the court could justify going either way. It is in oral argument, primarily, that the advocate convinces the court that law and good sense, alongside justice, indicate a decision in his behalf. For the lawyers who choose to waive their right of oral argument, many judges suggest that cases are won or lost at this point. One put the point this way: some cases cannot be won (or lost) because they are one-sided, but in at least half, oral argument is critical. In fifty to eighty percent of the cases coming before Federal appellate courts, the opinion judges hold after hearing oral argument is the same as their final decision, suggesting the power of that element.[41]

Prominent attention is given by practitioners to the rhetorical effectiveness of the structure of brief and oral argument. There is agreement that structure makes a difference in effectiveness. The arrangement of the brief is essentially standardized into the following major divisions: (1) resume of the opinions of lower courts; (2) questions presented in the appeal; (3) statement of facts; (4) summary of arguments; (5) argument; and (6) a brief conclusion. The arrangement of the oral argument is sub-

[40] Frederick B. Wiener, "Oral Advocacy," *Harvard Law Review*, 62 (November 1948), p. 37.

[41] Frederick B. Wiener, *Briefing and Arguing Federal Appeals*, (Washington, D.C.: B.N.A. Incorporated, 1961), pp. 31–32.

ject to greater variance of opinion. In the first place, most appellate courts reserve the right to interrupt the speaker at any point to pose questions that may not be relevant to the particular point being discussed, and may cause wide deviation in the planned arrangement. Because of this, the advocate must be thoroughly informed about the case and must be prepared to respond to questions, some of which are clearly antagonistic, quickly and intelligently. Moreover, the questions often reveal that the division of opinion among a three or nine member court that the advocate must discern if responses are to be phrased in such a way as to give most strength to those tending in the advocate's direction. Persuasion among judges during their conference may be enhanced if the advocate provides good ammunition in the form of arguments to his proponents.

Usually the oral argument will deal first with the relevant facts from the trial in lower court that will be important to the appeal. Then, the advocate will address issues and present argument. If a full brief has been presented to the court, it is not necessary to cover every point in oral argument. Usually it is best to select the strongest points and drive them home. Because of the stability of membership on courts of appeal, it is possible for the advocate to have much knowledge of the tendencies of each judge prior to argument. Some prediction can be made as to the likely attitude toward the case, and oral argument can be specifically adjusted to change the opinions of those likely to oppose the position advanced, and to strengthen the attitude of those favorable judges. There is no excuse, here, for failing to derive arguments from the values and opinions of the audience.

Because many appellate courts present written opinions that include reasons for the decision, judicial decision making provides both an insight into the kinds of arguments those judges respond to, and an example of legal argument worthy of study *per se*. Although many judges would argue that they are merely stating how their decision was reached, scholars as well as practitioners are increasingly inclined to perceive the judicial decision as a species of legal argument.[42] Instead of combining the "law" with the facts of a particular case and drawing the decision as a conclusion in formal logic, judges now often describe their work as making a decision and then generating arguments that will justify it in the eyes of the litigants, other judges, the legal community, and others who may be interested. One scholar said this:

"Lawyers should certainly re-explore the "rhetorics" of the ancient world, and [their] elaboration in the "new rhetorics," as a conduit of more orderly

---

[42] Richard D. Rieke, "The Rhetoric of Law, A Bibliographical Essay."

transmission of ideas of justice and of the facts of social life into the mobile and shifting body of legal propositions of which the common law consists. Though this is certainly not a simple task, even a first glance suggests that some features of appellate judicial process that resist rationalization in terms of deduction from preexisting legal propositions, fall more easily into place in terms of the notions with which rhetorics work."[43]

In other words, this scholar perceives judicial decisions as a form of rhetoric for the purposes of some analyses at least.

CONCLUSIONS

Argumentation in the specialized field of law has been examined in terms of the various argumentative tasks regularly performed by lawyers. Worthy of note is the fact that much legal argument does not occur in the courtroom. Instead, in the interview context where lawyers communicate with clients, potential witnesses, other lawyers, etc., seeking to work out an understanding on a question of law or to settle a difference, most legal argument takes place. Even though an attorney rarely goes to court, he will still write memoranda, negotiate settlements, and generally interact with others argumentatively. When the courts do become involved, a sequence of argumentative processes takes place, starting with pleadings, moving to the gathering of evidence and the preparation of a case, and finally heading into the courtroom itself with opening statements, direct examination of favorable witnesses and cross-examination of opposing witnesses. The closing argument, typically thought of as the prime instance of legal argument, merely completes a long and complicated process that may have begun months before. If the decision of a lower court is appealed, appellate argument takes place through the preparation of formal briefs and the making of an oral argument. Because appellate courts consist of several (typically three or nine) members who sit together for years at a time, argument at this level offers an unusually good opportunity for analysis of the audience and the relating of advocacy to it. Moreover, because many appellate courts write opinions explaining their decisions, it is possible to observe the influence of lawyers' arguments on judicial thinking, and to observe how appellate courts argue in defense of their own decisions.

[43] Julius Stone, *Legal System and Lawyers' Reasonings* (Stanford: Stanford University Press, 1964), p. 333.

PROJECTS

1. Spend some time sitting in a local court listening to legal argument. Report to your class the special characteristics you see in it. Which might you use in other situations and which seem to you to be bound by the legal circumstances?

2. Interview an attorney to learn about interviewing and the writing of memoranda.

3. Read one of the following First Amendment decisions of the Supreme Court of the United States. Engage in a discussion with some of your classmates on which evidence and argument seemed most believable to the court. Can you reconstruct the two cases from reading the decision?

> New York Times Company v. L. B. Sullivan, 376 US 254 (March 1964)
>
> Red Lion Broadcasting Company v. Federal Communications Commission 395 US 367 (June 1969)
>
> Robert Watts v. United States, 394 US 705 (April 1969)
>
> Irving Feiner v. People of the State of New York, 340 US 315 (January 1951)

4. Participate in a trial in class by preparing a fictionalized situation and assigning roles. For ideas on this, see the yearly books published by the Institute of Continuing Legal Education, Ann Arbor, Michigan cited in the footnotes of this chapter. You might also want to use a case from Harry Kerr, *Opinion and Evidence* (New York: Harcourt Brace & Co., Inc., 1962).

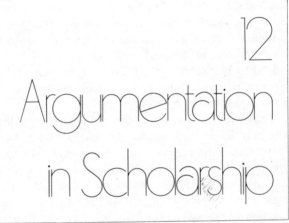

12
Argumentation
in Scholarship

For most of this book we have looked at general argumentation—the way in which we make arguments and test those of others in our every day activities of business, politics and social actions. But people also engage in special kinds of argument where special conditions and vocabularies are taken into account and special rules apply.

In Chapter 11 we discussed one of these: legal argument. In Chapter 13 we will look at the special form of argumentation found in intercollegiate and interscholastic debate. In this chapter we will look at the special argumentation of the scholar.

In this, we are primarily interested in the kind of scholarship usually carried out in the social sciences and the humanities though, as we shall see, there are relationships to the natural sciences and mathematics on the one hand and the fine arts on the other.

TWO CONFLICTING VIEWS OF SCHOLARSHIP

From the most ancient of times to the present it has been popular to suggest at least two distinct objectives of scholarship. The first with which we have concerned ourselves in this book is argumentative. That is, it is concerned with testing ideas in the light of an audience's needs and responses. Such a relativistic point of view has been in direct conflict with the objective of other scholars who engage in inquiry perportedly to demonstrate certainty independent of audiences. This point of view has been in recent years most often associated with the natural sciences, mathematics and symbolic logic. It has been popular to assume that arguments capable of demonstration (that is to say, arguments that show truth regardless of the acceptability of them to any audience) constitute the highest order of scholarship. Furthermore, it has been assumed by adherents of this point of view, that all other arguments emulate, or seek to emulate, these demonstrations. Thus, in this system of scholarship some questions can be decided with certainty and others can at best only be judged to be probably so. Probability is characterized as approaching but not reaching certainty, and it is achieved by use of logical forms suitable in the higher order of investigation.

Thus, science, mathematics and symbolic logic become the ideal scholarly forms and history, sociology, psychology and literary scholarship become (if they are any use at all) inferior reproductions of these using the same forms and tests but not achieving certainty.

Important also is the presumption that the means of testing all of these argumentative forms inheres in the arguments themselves and is not a function of the critical evaluation of people to whom they are addressed. A review of the theories of Plato discussed in Chapter 1 may be helpful in recalling this notion. Essentially, Plato believed that a universal and permanent Truth exists and it remains for men to search until they find it. A "True" argument, therefore, is true whether human beings agree with it or not. Those who fail to believe when confronted with a true argument are merely fools to be dealt with as such. Descartes was a highly influential spokesman of such a notion. He felt that arguments must begin with "self-evident" truths, those which cannot possibly be doubted, and then build from that foundation systematically by means of mathematical regularity. Mathematics was, in Descartes' eyes, the model of certainty, and all argument should seek to emulate it—as argumentation approaches the order and certainty of mathematics, it approaches Truth. For him, therefore, "The proper order in philosophy is to start from the most simple and clear truths, containing only the most simple notions, and to advance step by step towards more complex truths, making sure that each step of the argument is indisputable."[1]

Descartes, of course, began his philosophy by seeking to rid his mind of

---

[1] Stuart Hampshire, ed., *The Age of Reason* (New York: Mentor Books, 1956), p. 60.

all but self-evident truths, and finally reached the claim that, "I think, therefore, I am," and felt this was undeniable. From this he went on to build a systematic philosophy that included a proof of the existence of God.

In recent years, the popular notion has followed Descartes. Such statements as "science says . . ." "science has found . . ." "science tells us . . ." illustrate this view. Many philosophers of science, however, reject this Cartesian view of the scientific method as naive.

Karl R. Popper, in this book, *The Logic of Scientific Discovery*, observes that new ideas are put forward tentatively as a hypothesis. From this, conclusions are drawn by deduction. These conclusions are compared with one another and with other relevant statements so as to see relationships. Important to our discussion here is that the key to the survival of a scientific theory is its testing. From such testing, positive results can only temporarily support the theory and negative results *at any time* can overthrow it.[2]

Such an understanding of scientific method makes natural science not that much different from history. Louis Gottschalk is using essentially the same point of view in establishing and maintaining historical truth.

"There can be no doubt, for example, that on a day conveniently labeled "October 12, 1492," a group of sailors captained by a man known in English as "Christopher Columbus" landed on an island which was apparently the one now called "Watlin Island." The truth of that event is proved by a series of documents so carefully tested for authenticity and credibility that, until more authentic and more credible documents are discovered which would call it in question, the historian considers it a fact, or more accurately a series of facts, and the layman doubts it no more than he does the multiplication table."[3]

It was on exactly the same basis that Newtonian physics survived as truth until surplanted by quantum physics, although some applications of Newtonian physics still survive where its conclusions continue to provide a basis for understanding as in much of civil and mechanical engineering.

To summarize, two approaches to scholarship have been briefly described. One approach, the more traditional, views scholarship as

[2] Karl R. Popper, *The Logic of Scientific Discovery*, (New York: Harper Torchbooks, Harper & Row, 1969), pp. 32–33.

[3] Louis Gottschalk, *Understanding History*, (New York: Alfred A. Knopf, 1969), p. 8.

"truth centered" and scholarly arguments are assessed in terms of intrinsic characteristics and without regard for the human beings to whom they are addressed. The other approach suggests a more audience centered view of scholarship in which arguments are assessed as rigorously as ever, but the rules of assessment are seen to be a function of the people who use the scholarship. In the latter perspective, all approaches to scholarship have equal merit in their potential to serve mankind. This is the perspective that we shall take in discussing scholarship as argument.

SCHOLARSHIP AS ARGUMENT

Our goal, therefore, is to examine the process of scholarship from the perspective of an audience centered theory of argumentation. The basis of an arguementation centered theory of scholarship is that there is no "correct" method for the discovery of truth. What matters is the method to which the appropriate decision makers subscribe. This does *not* suggest that scholarly research under this perspective is subject to whimsical and arbitrary acceptance or rejection. On the contrary, it is evaluated by highly specialized audiences who apply rigorous standards of criticism to all scholarly claims. But in the final analysis, willingness to grant adherence to such a claim is a function of audience judgment in relation to the scholarly argument, and not merely a function of the discovery of the inherent "truth" of the claim. Such an argumentative perspective allows one to subscribe to any one of a number of theories of knowledge, or a combination of them. It does call your attention back to Chapter 2 in the diagram of the decision making process. There, you will recall, highly specialized techniques may be employed early in the decision making pattern, but before the recommendations of such specialized procedures can become action they must be expressed in the language of a system of argumentation.

Popper suggests an argumentative approach to science when he says that knowledge progresses by "unjustified (and unjustifiable) anticipations, by guesses, by tentative solutions to our problems, by *conjectures.* These conjectures are controlled by criticism, that is, by attempted *refutations*, which include severely critical tests." He continues,

"They may survive these tests; but they can never be positively justified: they can neither be established as certainly true nor even as "probable" (in the sense of the probability calculus). Criticism of our conjectures is of

decisive importance: by bringing out our mistakes it makes us understand the difficulties of the problem."[4]

A conjecture, in Popper's vocabulary, can be used in place of claim in the vocabulary of this book for purposes of this chapter. For Popper, proof consists of surviving refutation—conjectures are not demonstrated as "true" so much as they are not shown to be false. His argumentative perspective is clearly revealed in the following assertion:

"Those among our theories which turn out to be highly resistant to criticism, and which appear to us at a certain moment of time to be better approximations to truth than other known theories, may be described, together with the reports of their tests, as the "science" of that time. Since none of them can be positively justified, it is essentially their critical and progressive character—the fact that we can argue about their claim to solve our problems better than their competitors—which constitutes the rationality of science."[5]

Thomas Kuhn's position is similarly argumentative in nature. For him, the key word is "paradigm," which describes a broad scholarly rationale toward some problem, such as Newton's in physics or Lavoisier's in chemistry, which was "sufficiently unprecedented to attract an enduring group of adherents away from competing modes of scientific activity" and which was "sufficiently open-ended to leave all sorts of problems for the redefined group of practitioners to resolve."[6] Paradigms, then, are concepts shared by practitioners of a scientific specialty, and who, therefore, constitute a scholarly community.[7] For Kuhn, the individual scholarly studies within a paradigm may be evaluated by standards and instrumentation specified by the paradigm, and are, therefore, relatively stable. But the movement by scholars from one paradigm to another within a specialty is much more clearly argumentative.

"To discover how scientific revolutions are effected, we shall . . . have to examine not only the impact of nature and of logic, but also the techniques of persuasive argumentation effective within the quite special groups that constitute the community of scientists."[8]

[4] Karl R. Popper, *Conjectures and Refutations, The Growth of Scientific Knowledge* (New York: Basic Books, Publishers, 1962), p. vii.

[5] Popper, *Conjectures and Refutations.*

[6] Thomas S. Kuhn, *The Structure of Scientific Revolutions*, 2nd ed., Enlarged (Chicago: University of Chicago Press, 1970), p. 10.

[7] Kuhn, p. 177.

[8] Kuhn, p. 94.

Such an idea, as we shall see in more detail later, does not indicate that scientific inquiry is whimsical and arbitrary. Each paradigm, and the individual studies that emerge from it, will be subjected to rigorous criticism and selected only after it is decided that they serve the scholarly function better than alternatives. But ultimately, the viability of a paradigm must be explained in terms of argumentation rather than some intrinsic and permanent measure of correctness.

Carl L. Becker offers an argumentative view of historical scholarship when he claims that, "In the history of history a myth is a once valid but now discarded version of the human story, as our now valid versions will in due course be relegated to the category of discarded myths."[9] The "validity" of an historical claim is a function of the needs and perspectives of those to whom it is addressed. Historians do not find the whole truth or even a part of it; they do not let the facts speak for themselves, says Becker:, "Left to themselves, the facts do not speak; left to themselves they do not exist, not really, since for all practical purposes there is no fact until some one affirms it."[10] Thus, historical claims are advanced for the critical evaluation of an audience, and their acceptance or rejection cannot be separated from that audience;

"It must be obvious that living history . . . cannot be precisely the same for all at any given time, or the same for one generation as for another. History in this sense cannot be reduced to a verifiable set of statistics or formulated in terms of universally valid mathematical formulas."[11]

To consider scholarship from an argumentative perspective, however, requires a new exploration of familiar territory. From the point of view of argumentation, what are the theories of knowledge that set the basis for the paradigm and control the selection of methods and materials of research and justification? How do paradigms function for communities of scholars? What are the dominant aims of scholarship? These are the questions that will direct the remainder of this chapter. It will not be possible to exhaust the discussion of each by any means, but enough will be said to lay a framework for the reader's continued analysis.

[9] Carl L. Becker, "What is Evidence: The Relativist View—'Everyman His Own Historian,'" in Robin W. Winks, ed., *The Historian as Detective*, (New York: Harper & Row, Publishers, 1969), p. 16.

[10] Becker, p. 19.

[11] Becker, p. 13.

THEORIES OF KNOWLEDGE

It is common when looking for different approaches to scholarship to talk about different disciplines. History, literary scholarship, psychology, artistic criticism and political science are disciplines we say. All too frequently we go so far as to delineate differences by looking at academic departments in a University and assuming we are looking at disciplines. But literary history is more like history, poetic creation more like painting and linguistic analysis more like mathematics. Yet all can be found in an English Department. Some sociology is highly mathematical, some is not. More important to understanding different methods of scholarship are the broad theories of knowledge that separate scholarly communities, not along discipline lines, but along lines of their theories of knowledge. Clearly individuals from quite different disciplines will adhere to the same theory of knowledge and individuals will find themselves at odds with persons from their own discipline. There are six relatively distinct theories of knowledge that we shall differentiate here. Each of these will tend to prescribe for its adherents the particular standards of evidence, credibility, values and argument form that they must use if their arguments are to survive the refutations.

RATIONALISM

You will recall from Chapter 1 that Aristotle believed that Truth and Justice are by nature stronger than their opposites, and if given full opportunity to compete in the market place of ideas, will always emerge. In his *Areopagitica*, the famous defense of free speech, Milton said about the same thing, although more eloquently: "Let her and falsehood grapple; who ever knew truth put to the worse, in a free and open encounter?" For Milton, as well as Aristotle, if a bad decision is made it merely means that the advocates did not do their job and Truth was not effectively advanced. Thus, there are means by which reasonable men can find the truth and explain that truth to others. Those means are systematic and social in their basic approaches.

Other than this most popular, essentially *rationalistic* theory of Truth, over the years a variety of rationales have been employed to describe some notion of "knowledge."[12]

---

[12] The structure for this review is taken from Morris R. Cohen, *Reason and Nature —An Essay on the Meaning of Scientific Method* (Glencoe, Illinois: The Free Press, Publishers, 1953), pp. 8–75.

PSYCHOLOGISM

Not to be confused with the study of psychology in general, psychologism posits "that human institutions are matters of growth rather than creation, and that the great achievements of life are the result of unconscious spirit rather than conscious deliberation."[13] In the chapter on values we discuss the value system of transcendentalism that is substantially based on the way of knowing of psychologism because its cornerstone is the superiority of intuition over reason.

A modern version of a similar idea comes from B. F. Skinner's extension of conditioning. His view is far from that of the transcendentalist in his interest in social control but his emphasis on nonconscious, nonrational (if you wish) decision making makes his views similar to the believer in psychologism as a theory of knowledge. "Behavior is shaped and maintained by its consequences . . . the environment not only prods or lashes, it selects. Its role is similar to that in natural selection."[14] He goes on later to say,

"The fundamental mistake made by all those who choose weak methods of control is to assume that the balance of control is left to the individual, when in fact it is left to other conditions. The other conditions are often hard to see, but to continue to neglect them and to attribute their effects to autonomous man is to court disaster."[15]

Skinner believes knowledge is merely an unconscious response to aversive and rewarding stimuli in the environment, and not the product of deliberation.

HISTORICISM

Historicism is a theory that reduces everything to the facts of history. Such pithy expressions as this, "There is nothing so powerful as an idea whose time has come," illustrate the belief that reality is a function of cycles and movements in history. To understand the detailed nature of human institutions such as government and religion, according to this

[13] Cohen, p. 8.

[14] B. F. Skinner, *Beyond Freedom and Dignity* (New York: Alfred A. Knopf, 1971), p. 18.

[15] Skinner, p. 99.

point of view, one need only examine the actual history of them. Such historians as subscribe to this theory would argue that the facts should be allowed to speak for themselves, and the scholar should avoid abstractions. Note also that in this theory as in psychologism people are controlled by forces that they are incapable of adjusting by rational means.

EMPIRICISM

Empiricism offers observation in the place of human reason. Knowledge exists in nature and must be observed and carefully reported if human beings are to make use of it. The pure empiricist would seek to rid himself of all human involvement in the knowledge process. He would use his perceptions as vehicles in gathering data and his ability to communicate merely to report what his senses told him, but beyond this he would seek to avoid his own thoughts, feelings, proclivities, desires, etc. Peirce, quoted in Chapter 2 called for some means of satisfying doubt without resort to human judgment. He looked, instead, for some "external permanency" over which thinking has no effect. He proposed the adoption of the empiricism of the natural sciences by those in all fields of scholarship. Listen to his words characterizing his method: "There are Real things, whose characters are entirely independent of our opinions about them; those Reals affect our sense according to regular laws, and . . . by taking advantage of the laws of perception, we can ascertain by reasoning how things really and truly are. . . ."[16]

KINETICISM

Kineticism argues that only change is real and that nature contains no constant elements.[17] Darwin's theory of the evolution of the species illustrates such a theory by describing current flora and fauna including human beings as a phase in a long process of natural selection. Survival becomes a key word in kineticism, because "reality" consists of constant change, with some elements disappearing while others survive into the next period, and so on. Morris R. Cohen regards kineticism as essentially romantic "because it makes explicit the romantic impatience with the fixed, clear, and orderly routine of reason."[18]

[16] Charles S. Peirce, "The Fixation of Belief," in Justus Buckler, ed., *Philosophical Writings of Peirce* (New York: Dover Publications, Inc., 1955), p. 18.
[17] Cohen, p. 18.
[18] Cohen, p. 20.

Kuhn subscribes to an essentially kinetic theory in his book, *The Structure of Scientific Revolutions*:

"What is built into the neural process that transforms stimuli to sensations [knowledge] has the following characteristics: it has been transmitted through education; it has, by trial, been found more effective than its historical competitors in a group's current environment; and, finally, it is subject to change both through further education and through the discovery of misfits with the environment. Those are characteristics of knowledge."[19]

Kuhn, of course, rejects the suggestion that his point of view is romantic and in opposition to orderly routine. It merely posits a different character to the particular order currently in vogue.

PURE BELIEF

Faith or mysticism or intuition are words frequently used to describe an approach to knowledge based on individual experience or insight and not subject to the verification of others. *A priorism* is another name for essentially the same theory. Those who adhere to this kind of an idea would argue that knowledge comes to individuals in the form of inspiration, revelation, or some other contact with an unseen, and perhaps unknowable source of knowledge. Sometimes this source is called "God;" sometimes other characterizations such as "fate," "the spirits," "the stars," "Karma," "the Devil," are used to identify the source of knowledge. Often, no source at all is announced. One simply "knows," because he knows. Often distinguished from it, but clearly related, are such sources of knowing as "commonsense," "instinct," and "creative imagination," although they may also be, and often are, related to a concept of intelligence or innate capacity. Again, they are highly personal sources of knowledge and, perhaps most important, they cannot be tested by anyone other than the person who first uses them.

PARADIGMS AND SCHOLARLY ARGUMENT

Scholars tend to form communities focusing on a particular specialty such as clinical psychology, nuclear physics, medieval history, group communication, constitutional law, and so forth. Such communities of scholars share common educations, perceptions of themselves, and read

---

[19] Kuhn, p. 196.

the same literature. Communication among members of such communities is frequent and occurs in language that may be quite esoteric. Some communities find it necessary to communicate frequently to nonspecialists in order to explain and justify their work; others rarely must do so. We noted earlier Kuhn's use of the word "paradigm" to signify what is shared by communities of scholars. He suggests several shared components: (1) "symbolic generalization," which are starting points for argument, the maxims and topoi or commonly accepted premises; (2) "shared commitments to . . . beliefs," which are similar to the first but constitute more broad generalizations about the specialty under investigation such as models of the phenomenon; (3) "values" such as the commitment to prediction, internal consistency, authenticity of sources; and (4) "exemplars," or examples of successful problem-solutions that have become classics within the specialty and are widely read during one's studies. These exemplars may deal with substantive experiments or research reports, or highly regarded commentaries on methodology or reconstructed logic.[20] We should add, of course, that fundamentally a community of scholars shares a theory of knowledge for if they did not all four of the shared items mentioned above would be impossible.

Adherence to a paradigm controls what a scholar will perceive as a legitimate problem for study, what "facts" will be observed in the study, the kinds of measuring instruments suitable for study, the methodology or reconstructed logic to be employed, the language to be used in preparing the research report, and so forth. Paradigms can be compared to theories, but paradigm designates shared characteristics more broad than those now typically meant by the use of "theory." As suggested earlier, paradigms can be illustrated by mentioning Newton's work in physics, Lavoisier in chemistry, Darwin in biology, Watson in psychology, Keynes in economics, Aristotle in rhetoric, and so on. Because of their greater need to communicate with those outside the scholarly community, members of such disciplines as the humanities, social sciences, and arts, more frequently operate from less clearly defined paradigms as those in some of the natural sciences, but communities and paradigms tend to form in all scholarly activities. In communication, for example, rhetorical criticism for years was responsive to Aristotle's work in rhetoric, and that of other writers who developed and elaborated on his ideas. It has been characterized by Edwin Black as neo-Aristotelian criticism.[21] Those who shared this paradigm were guided into studies of speakers along relatively

[20] Kuhn, pp. 177–189.
[21] Edwin Black, *Rhetorical Criticism: A Study in Method* (New York: The Macmillan Co., 1965).

prescribed lines. They noted intrinsic elements in selected speeches, such as enthymemes, and employed such Aristotelian terminology as ethos, pathos, and logos. In more recent times, the community of rhetorical critics has moved away from this single paradigm toward a more pluralistic approach. Others in communication have left the community of critics altogether to orient themselves around a more empirical paradigm that they feel will better give them knowledge. They do not even consider the observations of critics to be data. Instead, they examine other phenomena, perceive different "facts," employ different measuring instruments, different design and methodology, and speak in quite a different language. Still others operate in several paradigms depending on the problem and the material.

Such scholarly communities and the paradigms they share have major implications to the study of scholarly argumentation. First, the paradigm to which one subscribes will dictate the manner of assessing scholarly arguments. Second, argument designed for one paradigm will be unlikely to win adherence from those committed to another paradigm, even when both are located within essentially the same discipline. Third, when a new paradigm is proposed to replace another, extremely intense and difficult argumentation will take place. Each of these observations requires some added discussion.

The paradigm to which one subscribes will dictate the manner of assessing scholarly arguments. As Toulmin observes, field dependent characteristics of argument play a vital role in their assessment.[22] It is from the paradigm that the field dependent elements of scholarly argument come. In another place, Toulmin states clearly his concept of assessing scholarly arguments:

". . . in studying the development of scientific ideas, we must always look out for the ideals and paradigms men rely on to make Nature intelligible. Science progresses, not by recognizing the truth of new observations alone, but by making sense of them. To this task of interpretation we bring principles of regularity, conceptions of natural order, paradigms, ideals, or what-you-will: intellectual patterns which define the range of things we can accept . . . as "sufficiently absolute and pleasing to the mind." An explanation, to be acceptable, must demonstrate that the happenings under investigation are special cases or complex combinations of our fundamental intelligible types."[23]

[22] See Stephen Toulmin, The Uses of Argument (Cambridge: At the University Press, 1958); also reexamine Chapter 4 for a discussion of this topic.

[23] Stephen Toulmin, Foresight and Understanding, An Enquiry into the Aims of Science (New York: Harper & Row, Publishers, 1961), p. 81.

Kuhn notes that "paradigms provide scientists not only with a map but also with some of the directions essential for map-making. In learning a paradigm the scientist acquires theory, methods, and standards together, usually in an inextricable mixture.[24] Therefore, an argumentative case prepared in the form of a scholarly book or paper may be judged to be of high quality by those sharing the paradigm while being rejected by those subscribing to another paradigm, even within the same field. The scholar is wise to know his paradigm and his audience before advancing an argument.

An argument addressed to those outside the paradigm might be judged negatively not only in terms of conclusions drawn, but the very research problem itself might be considered negligible. As Toulmin says, "Men who accept different ideals and paradigms have really no common theoretical terms in which to discuss their problems fruitfully. They will not even *have* the same problem: events which are 'phenomena' in one man's eyes will be passed over by the other as 'perfectly natural.' "[25] It is equally fruitless for present day scholars to look back on work of past years with scorn—the earlier work was not necessarily wrong, it merely came from another paradigm. If, therefore, a scholar must address an argument across paradigms, it will be necessary to search them both for common assumptions, values, language, etc. If they exist to any extent, it may be possible to prepare an argument for both. But this is unlikely. Most probably, it will be necessary to avoid such argumentative situations, or seek to move outside the language of scholarly argumentation and cast the material in popular form.

Finally, when a new paradigm is proposed to replace another, extremely intense and difficult argumentation will take place. Of course, this does not occur often. First, because paradigms by definition are sufficiently broad in scope to facilitate considerable research they should last for some time. Second, when scholars have been educated and experienced in working within a paradigm, it is painful and expensive to shift. The more experienced scholars will find it difficult to perceive the discipline in terms of a new paradigm. To change, they would be required to develop facility in a totally new set of instruments and procedures, in addition to changing many of their values. They will, in other words, find it much easier simply to reject the arguments being advanced under the new paradigm. Because older scholars tend to be in positions of importance and prestige, it usually falls to younger, less prestigious individuals to advance a new paradigm, and because of this, winning adherence to

[24] Kuhn, p. 109.
[25] Toulmin, *Foresight and Understanding*, p. 57.

their arguments is slow. The pattern of decision emergence discussed in Chapter 2 gives a good general description of this process. Old paradigms are not rejected simply because they increasingly fail to account for phenomena being observed or ideas being nurtured. Only when an alternative to take the place of the old system is effectively proposed will a former paradigm be rejected, and then only after a painful interchange. Listen to Kuhn on this subject:

". . . the choice [between paradigms] is not and cannot be determined merely by the evaluative procedures characteristic of normal science, for these depend in part upon a particular paradigm, and that paradigm is at issue. When paradigms enter, as they must, into a debate about paradigm choice, their role is necessarily circular. Each group uses its own paradigm to argue in that paradigm's defense.
"The resulting circularity does not, of course, make the arguments wrong or even ineffectual. The man who premises a paradigm when arguing in its defense can nonetheless provide a clear exhibit of what scientific practice will be like for those who adopt the new view of nature. That exhibit can be immensely persuasive, often compellingly so. Yet, whatever its force, the status of the circular argument is only that of persuasion. It cannot be made logically or even probabilistically compelling for those who refuse to step into the circle . . . . As in political revolutions, so in paradigm choice— there is no standard higher than the assent of the relevant community."[26]

Paradigm debates, as in the decision making model in Chapter 2, work on a form of natural selection or emergence. The most viable, in the judgment of those deciding, is selected from among the competitors. The decision is not necessarily the "correct" or "true" one, but the one judged best among alternatives.

Kuhn outlines some of the potential arguments that can be advanced in favor of a new paradigm. First, one can argue that the proposed model will solve problems that have troubled the old one. Second, the new paradigm may be strengthened if it can predict phenomena that have gone totally unsuspected in the former procedure. Third, one can argue that the new pattern is more suitable, more simple, neater, than the old. John Waite Bowers uses the term "elegant" here, meaning the new paradigm "makes a great number of predictions from a small number of statements."[27] In the final analysis, however, selection of a new paradigm

[26] Kuhn, p. 94.
[27] John Waite Bowers, *Designing the Communication Experiment* (New York: Random House, 1970), p. 18.

must be done without the certainty that has long been claimed for the process. In fact, Kuhn says such a choice can be made only on the faith that the new plan will work better in the long run.[28] Thus, all the elements of argumentation discussed in this book apply to scholarly argumentation as well.

CENTRAL AIMS OF SCHOLARSHIP AS ARGUMENTATION

Thus far, we have observed that the special argumentation of the scholar still maintains its orientation to audience as does general argumentation but that it is a special audience which is addressed. This audience consists of a particular community of scholars who share a particular paradigm. This paradigm will be based on a particular theory of knowledge and, consequently, on certain assumptions, beliefs, values and exemplars that limit the kinds of arguments which can be made within that paradigm.

There is no space here for us to detail the various paradigms of modern scholarship or even one of them, but we can look at several central aims of scholarship that will give some indication of the outcomes that are sought by various paradigms.

KNOWLEDGE

Frequently, scholarship is described as the search for truth. Often, the work of scholars is looked on as cumulative in nature—they are putting a puzzle together by adding bits and pieces of knowledge to form that larger picture that is the truth. Some scholars even perceive their own activities in that way by suggesting they must hurry on with their research for there is so much yet to be learned before we can rest. Of course, historians can never rest for while they describe history, more of it is being made. But medical science has had a strong influence on this kind of thinking by suggesting that there are certain diseases that we are learning to conquer one by one. Curiously, there always seem to be plenty to work on even after hundreds of years of conquest. Perhaps, like history, while some are managed, others are being made. Yet, the traditional image of scholars, after thousands of years of formal and recorded scholarship, is one of working toward that time when most knowledge is recorded and our picture of truth is virtually complete. Some approaches

[28] Kuhn, pp. 153–159.

to information science seem to be based on this image by calling for the establishment of data banks containing all that has ever been written on a given subject. Then, presumably, the time will come when any scholar can punch the proper request into the computer and receive print-outs of all one would ever need to know.

Such a view embodies the aim of a scholarship that claims to determine truth independent of audiences. But the same position may be held by an exponent of the argumentation view of scholarship. Truth in this case means the accepted truths of the paradigm that can be built one on the other toward some higher level of understanding. Thus, for many scholars, the primary objective of their work is knowledge regardless of its form or usefulness. In such an argumentative theory of scholarship the central aim is one of human decision making and the intelligent understanding required for that purpose. Intelligent understanding must always be a combination of whatever knowledge exists apart from human beings' thinking and human thought. Thus, no matter what external permanency there may be, it must always be understood in human terms if it is to become useful in decision making. For this reason, a cumulative view of scholarship cannot be totally saitsfactory at any given time because each generation will bring new biases and understandings to its problems and will, accordingly, require new scholarship expressed in these terms. As Toulmin puts this claim,

"The central aims of science . . . lie in the field of intellectual creation: other activities—diagnostic, classificatory, industrial, or predictive—are properly called 'scientific' from their connection with the explanatory ideas and ideals which are the heart of natural science . . . .
"The central aims of science . . . are concerned with a search for understanding—a desire to make the course of Nature not just predictable but intelligible—and this has meant looking for rational patterns of connections in terms of which we can make sense of the flux of events."[29]

PREDICTION

The medium by which a variety of theories of knowledge have gained prominence is prediction. That is to say, human beings seem universally to be impressed with forecasting abilities. When someone announces an event to occur in the future, and it does occur, that person is generally judged to have access to a powerful source of knowledge. Those who

[29] Stephen Toulmin, *Foresight and Understanding*, pp. 38, 99.

employ this mechanism tend to rely on the acceptance of the idea that all reality is orderly and governed by some form of law: the law of god, of nature, of the spirit, the stars, etc. If such is indeed the case, then all that is to happen in the future can be predicted on the knowledge of what is knowable today. Astrologers, by studying the movement of the planets, and combining that with the belief that all that happens is foreordained, suggest they can predict the future. Scientists, by studying the physical world with the belief that all that happens is a function of causes also existing in the physical world, predict future events within that world. Mystics, by studying their own visions or revelations, combining that with the belief that the future is a function of some supernatural power, predict a variety of events. Devines, by studying Scripture alongside their own revelations, combining that with the belief that God is omniscient and omnipotent, frequently make predictions. Prophecy is a powerful tool in many systems of knowledge.

LOGICALITY

For a long time, as was suggested in Chapter 1, the role of formal systems of logic in argumentation has been a troublesome subject. Essentially, it has been held that logic sets the norm that should guide our thinking process, and the extent to which we conform to logic governs the validity of our thoughts. Efforts have been made to set up rules of logic that are universal and permanent to guide all thought. Although an audience centered theory of argumentation does not subscribe to such a notion, it may utilize logicality as an aim of scholarship.

Kaplan distinguishes between what he calls "logic-in-use," which describes the actual patterns of thinking used by scholars, and "reconstructed logic", which describes the idealized patterns of discourse through which scholars justify their conclusions. In the process of discovery, says Kaplan, imagination, inspiration, and intuition play an enormous role, but the discoveries are not without a logic-in-use as well. Methodologists and logicians are concerned with the logic of discovery as well as the reconstructed logic of justification of conclusions. It is in the process of reconstructed logic, that process by which conclusions are justified or proved, that argumentation is involved.

Viewed argumentatively, that which most people refer to with the name "logic" designates an idealization of the process of discovery. It is a pattern or reconstruction developed to permit scholars to talk about their thoughts in such a way that others may understand and grant or deny adherence. There are many reconstructed logics that have been employed to prove or justify various conclusions—contrary to popular belief, Aristotle did not begin and end the subject, says Kaplan. He claims that the function of reconstructed logic, as in the case of the hypothetico-deductive pattern currently employed in science, is to "throw light on the sound operations actually being used" by scientists.[30] When it no longer is useful to report discoveries in this format, a new reconstruction will be needed. For Kaplan, and many other methodologists, the function of logic (or reconstructed logic) is to illuminate the logic-in-use. To the student of argumentation, reconstructed logic has in addition to illumination, the burden of communicating the claims of scholars so that they win the adherence of those to whom they are addressed.

Says Kaplan,

"What a scientist does in a particular case may be more or less reasonable, sensible, intelligent. What makes it such is not something in his psychology nor in ours who are appraising what he does, but something in his problem and in the appropriateness to it of the operations of his understanding. This latter something is the subject-matter of what I am calling logic."[31]

Logic, therefore, does not perform the normative, absolute function of leading us to truth, says Kaplan, but it does help us call attention to the characteristics of a problem that are important to what we seek in our scholarship. It should facilitate the making of the kinds of decision we desire. But, the student of argumentation must add, logic will be successful only so long as it serves the needs of the relevant audience. When a scholarly argument cast in a particular reconstructed logic no longer is recognized by the scholarly community, it will be necessary to rebuild the argument using a logic that is recognized. When scholars allow themselves to be controlled by their own reconstructions rather than *vice versa*, says Kaplan, "the autonomy of science is subtly subverted."[32]

The most widely known reconstructed logics now in use include, as discussed briefly in Chapter 4, the verbal adaptations of what is essentially Aristotelian logic. Mathematical systems and models are also widespread in scholarship and with the assistance of computers, becoming more so. As Kaplan observed above, the experimental design involving hypothesis testing under laboratory conditions in which selected variables can be observed alone while others are controlled or eliminated constitutes the

[30] Abraham Kaplan, *The Conduct of Inquiry* (San Francisco: Chandler Publishing Co., 1964), pp. 8–18.

[31] Kaplan, p. 18.

[32] Kaplan, p. 11.

backbone of science both natural and social. The scholar advances conclusions framed in this hypothetico-deductive format so that his statistical analysis can eliminate chance as an explanation for his observations, and his research design focuses attention on the action of his hypothesis. The primary argumentative element in such a logic will frequently be prediction—if the hypothesis *does* predict the observations, it is more likely to win the adherence of others. In recent times, however, prediction alone has come to be less compelling, and new logics are already being employed.[33] In fact, currently there is considerable dynamism among scholars to modify logics and build new ones.

APPLICATION

Frequently, the results of scholarship are judged by usefulness. The layman asks of the geneticist how his findings will be useful and the geneticist answers, "Well, it may have something to do with cancer." That satisfies the layman. The findings of research are useful.

It is not uncommon for scholars themselves to accept the ability to apply as a standard of judging scholarship. Among historians there is a common theory that the study of the past tells us about how we should live in the present. "Those who do not remember the past," said Santayana, "are condemned to relive it." Such a view is a modified form of historicism and should be recognized as a prevalent view by every reader of this book.

AN INTERACTION OF DATA AND RESEARCHER

Ordinarily, scholars claim that bias does not enter into their work, but an argumentative analysis would counter that this is not only impossible but undesirable. For scholarship to serve its purpose, under this analysis, it is critical that research reports be communicated in such a way that they can be meaningful to the contemporary audience whether they be scholars or others. Neil McK. Agnew and Sandra W. Pyke, in their introduction to research in the behavioral sciences, define science as the process of "construction or creation rather than discovery,"

". . . *bringing biased sensing devices—sense organs, brains, points of view, instruments—in contact with nature, and then fitting the constructed pieces*

[33] David H. Smith, "Communication Research and the Idea of Process," *Speech Monographs, 39* (August 1972), pp. 174–182.

together as best we can with the system of biases operating at the time and with the resources at our disposal. Science becomes the game and art of describing a pattern within a system of sensing and conceptual biases or limits."[34]

These authors relate science to other forms of human discourse such as politics and religion where the critical role of bias is more recognized and accepted. In politics, for example, disagreement among informed and reasonable people creates no alarm—it is expected. The function of human perspective in political decision making is widely accepted. The same, say Agnew and Pyke, should be accorded science.

"These disagreements suggest that man is not a simple detector, recorder, and reporter of nature's pieces. Alternatively, seeing science as creation or invention helps to account for disagreements between observers of the same event, or between researchers sampling from a great data stream. The invention model proposes that man and nature combine to make patterns—man processes experience—he spins his own truths."[35]

Abraham Kaplan, also writing on research methodology for the behavioral sciences, advances the notion that the scholarly work should advance claims which "can enter into the making of a decision, and its meaning is analyzable in terms of the difference it makes to the decision taken." He goes on to say that, "To believe a proposition [claim] is not to lay hold of an abstract entity called 'truth' with a correspondingly abstract 'mind'; it is to make a choice among alternative sets of strategies of action."[36]

THE ABILITY TO STAND UP TO CRITICISM

Although all of the aims of scholarship we have previously mentioned are a part of an argumentative theory of scholarship, the ability to stand up to criticism is centrally argumentative. In addition, all of the other aims frequently contain phases of this one. We are tempted to say that this is the dominant aim of scholarship.

For Marc Bloch, the archaeologist who finds an urn filled with the bones

---

[34] Neil McK. Agnew and Sandra W. Pyke, *The Science Game* (Englewood Cliffs: Prentice-Hall, Inc., 1969), pp. 173–174.

[35] Agnew and Pyke, p. 174.

[36] Kaplan, p. 43.

of children to be a case of human sacrifice, uses the "simple reasoning" of "eliminating all other possible explanations."[37] We have previously mentioned Gottschalk's illustration of the "facts" of Columbus' landing and Popper' explanation of the testing of scientific theories. There is no question that the ability to stand up to criticism is an aim of scholars in fields as widely divergent as history and physics.

CONCLUSIONS

The traditional hierarchy among arguments, with the ones coming from systems of scholarship that claim certainty (particularly those with scientific, mathematical and logical claims) having the highest order, is questioned by this discussion. In its place, an audience centered theory of scholarship is advanced. In viewing scholarship as argumentation we acknowledge that arguments are addressed to highly specialized audiences but they are always subject to testing. They do not yield certainty.

Basic to each community of scholars who test arguments is an acceptance of one or more theories of knowledge. Six such theories are here identified as the basis of a possible paradigm of scholarship (rationalism, psychologism, historicism, empiricism, kineticism, and pure belief.)

Paradigms of scholarship are important to identify. They control the data to be observed, the measurement instrument, the methodology and the language of explanation. Each paradigm is representative of a community of scholars and based on a way of knowing. Arguments between paradigms are particularly difficult because the participants do not share the same basis of knowledge. They virtually cannot talk to one another. Such a dispute requires that the participants look for shared "facts," presumptions and values.

Each paradigm will acknowledge an objective or aim of its scholarship. Some of the most popular are knowledge, prediction, logicality, interaction of data and researcher, application and the ability to stand up to criticism. The purpose of a community of scholars is to define its aim so that by following a given theory of knowledge through established methodology, adherence may be found to a series of ideas by the members of the community.

---

37 Marc Bloch, *The Historians Craft* (New York: Alfred A. Knopf, 1961), p. 52.

PROJECTS

1. Make a list of all the things you know for certain and then test them on your classmates. Are some, while not certain, acceptable to most of you because you agree to a theory of knowing? Would this change if you believed in some other theory?

2. Select a field of study most familiar and interesting to you (such as history, psychology, or sociology), and interview several professors from that field to see if you can identify the major paradigms that currently are most important to it. Remember, none of these fields have just one paradigm.

3. Which aim of scholarship do you consider most important? Be prepared to defend it in class against others who prefer another aim.

13
Argumentation in
Educational Debate

Possibly the oldest formal element of advanced education known in the Western Culture is education for argument. Accordingly, one of the oldest specialized fields of argumentation is that designed to prepare students for lifetime experiences through participation in classroom, intercollegiate and interscholastic debate. In this chapter we will show some of the historical background for the current educational practices and note the special characteristics of argumentation as it is practiced in the educational setting.

EDUCATIONAL DEBATE

Recently, specialists in pedagogy have announced what they believe to be exciting new approaches to education—simulation and gaming. They find that education that simulates those life experiences being taught tends to be more meaningful and appealing to the students. Furthermore, they suggest that if the simulation can be put in some kind of game format, the excitement of competition will motivate students to greater involvement in the educational process. Those knowledgeable in educational debate can only smile at such announcements, for simulation and gaming have been characteristics in their field for over 2000 years!

About 2400 years ago, Protagoras, a Greek teacher, invented themes for his students to argue.[1] The practice persisted and was developed into a highly regarded pedagogical device in Rome, still more than 2000 years ago. The Romans called the practice declamation or *declamatio*, and it was divided into debates over policy claims, called a *suasoria*, and arguments arising from legal claims, called a *controversia*. The procedure was for the teacher to propose a theme for discussion, then the student prepared a speech on the subject and delivered it to the class, and finally, the teacher spoke in criticism of the speech.[2] The practice of setting a theme, discussing alternative claims in reply to it, and then selecting a solution (even though the solution was typically the teacher's announcement of the "correct" answer) gave students opportunity to argue in situations approximating the forum and courts they would soon enter as adults.

A similar practice became common during the Medieval and Renaissance periods; its subjects were primarily theological and it was called a disputation or *disputatio*. "It may well have been one of the most important influences in European higher education between about 1140 and 1600."[3] This argumentative form, expressed in Latin even in schools and colleges in America during the Colonial period, put most attention on Aristotelian logic with emphasis on the syllogism and topics. The students were given a claim to which one replied and then there were objections to the first position taken, and then a decision, which again was a statement of "truth" by the teacher. Typically, one person spoke in defense of the claim, and there were four opponents. A moderator was chosen from among the students to keep order. Disputation constituted a regular part of the curriculum for hundreds of years, and was used as a form of display to show off students' talents.[4]

Such syllogistic disputations were carried from Europe to America and for a time continued relatively unchanged. Then, as political activity grew around the question of the colonial status of those in America, education became less a training ground for theologians than for politicians and lawyers. Students objected to the irrelevancy of speaking in Latin, and debating such abstract claims as the relative beauty of prose

---

[1] Lester Thonssen and A. Craig Baird, *Speech Criticism* (New York: The Ronald Press Co., 1948), p. 37; for a more detailed discussion of debate training in Ancient Greece, see George Kennedy, *The Art of Persuasion in Greece* (Princeton: Princeton University Press, 1963).

[2] James J. Murphy, "Two Medieval Textbooks in Debate," *Journal of the American Forensic Association, 1* (January 1964), p. 1.

[3] Murphy, p. 3.

[4] Angelo M. Pelligrini, "Renaissance and Medieval Antecedents of Debate," *Quarterly Journal of Speech, 28* (February 1942), pp. 15–17.

and poetry. So they formed their own debating societies to speak, in English, on urgent questions of the day.[5] The practice of submitting questions that were of interest to students, not faculty members, soon led to pro and con arguments on matters of practical concern.

A reasonable outgrowth of debating societies was the challenge of the society at one school by another. When students grew impatient with the competition of collegues, they wanted to test their skills against the best from another school. School pride was also a part of it. Before the beginning of the twentieth century, intercollegiate debate had become established.[6] The debates then were quite unlike those seen on campuses today. Typically, there were three men on a team, they dressed in formal attire, had an auditorium filled with people, and spoke for two or more hours with musical interludes. Sometimes there were school cheers before the debate, between speeches, and while the judge's decision was awaited. Commonly, each speaker came with a prepared address of about twenty minutes, and the one or more of them were permitted about five or ten minutes for rebuttal. Speeches did little to react specifically to what opponents had said, even the rebuttals were prepared in advance.[7] Later, some use of blocking, as described in Chapter 9, emerged so that the speech of reply could be generally adjusted to conform to the basic pattern of the constructive speeches to which they applied.

A characteristic of early debating was the small number of students who could participate, and the relative infrequency of participation. On a campus, the debating society would meet regularly, but not many members could participate in the formal presentations of each debate. For intercollegiate debates, try-outs were often held, and only the top students were allowed to represent the school. Even these students might engage in only one or two debates a year. Clearly, little opportunity for debate, criticism, and improvement existed. Even though students gradually began to ask faculty members to help them prepare for debates, there were still few chances for practice and participation.

In 1923, Southwestern College of Winfield, Kansas launched what has come to be the intercollegiate debate tournament. The first tournaments were like the modern variety in that a host school invited a select group of other colleges to come together at the same time, each with an affirma-

---

[5] David Potter, *Debating in the Colonial Chartered Colleges*, (New York: Bureau of Publications, Teachers College, Columbia University, 1944), pp. 25–31.

[6] Egbert Ray Nichols, "A Historical Sketch of Intercollegiate Debating, II," *Quarterly Journal of Speech*, 22 (April 1936), p. 213.

[7] L. Leroy Cowperthwaite and A. Craig Baird, "Intercollegiate Debating," in Karl Wallace, ed., *History of Speech Education in America* (New York: Appleton-Century-Crofts, Inc., 1954), pp. 262–267.

tive and a negative team, to debate each other, and each school was to provide a judge as well. At a tournament, each team would debate at least three times. In a single weekend, a debater could get as much experience as he previously had had in a whole year of home and home debates.

At that early time, however, the debates held to the three-man team and longer time limits than now used.[8] Before long, time limits were reduced to ten minute constructive and five minute rebuttals so that more debates could take place during a tournament. Team size was reduced to two persons, some say to allow for more debates per day, others have said that the three-man team went out with the horse and buggy—the automobile could conveniently accomodate four students and a judge, but not six students. For whatever reason, the modern style of tournament debate came to be two teams, consisting of two persons each, and representing two schools, who would argue for one hour before a critic judge, who gave a decision.

CONTEMPORARY EDUCATIONAL DEBATE

With the establishment of two-man teams and interest in the tournament as the main forum for student experience, the essential pattern for educational debate that persists to the present was set. Of course, over the years there have been changes, but they will not be discussed in detail here for they do not impinge significantly on the basic format. For example, a major change was the move from debating one side of a claim to both sides. For many years, a school attending a tournament brought two teams, an affirmative and a negative. In competition, they would meet their opposite numbers from other schools, thus, always defending the same side. The theory was that no student should be asked to defend a policy that did not reflect his own point of view. Gradually, this has changed for a number of reasons. First, modern educational debate takes as its model, forensic debate such as occurs in the courts. There, the adversary system is manifest in the person of professional advocates who are assigned to defend one side or the other on the notion that all points of view deserve a fair defense. The advocates are not expected to lie or misrepresent. They are simply charged to say all that could reasonably and fairly be said in behalf of their side. They need not personally subscribe to the conclusions in order to advance the available arguments. Second, it is characteristic of the claims (always referred to as proposi-

---

[8] Cowperthwaite and Baird, p. 274.

tions) selected for debate in college that they are concerned with broad policy questions such that a variety of arguments could be advanced pro and con, and regardless of the particular ideology of the debater, it is likely that a case can be built on either side that is consistent with personal beliefs. Finally, many have observed that high school and college students often have no firmly developed ideology on the proposition at hand, and they are not offended by being asked to argue both sides. Even those who begin the year with bias often discover their opinions change as they investigate the various perspectives on the resolution. In any event, it is now most common for teams to alternate from affirmative to negative over the course of the tournament.

Another major change has been the predominance of debate as the activity of choice in forensic programs. Speech or forensic activities in high school and college have traditionally featured various events such as delivering original or unoriginal orations, extemporaneous speaking, reading, drama, after dinner speaking, and so forth. Although there is still considerable support and practice in such events, debate has become the predominant activity, particularly in college.[9] In colleges and universities, the greatest proportion of forensic programs are concerned either with debate alone, or with debate as the major feature with some attention to other events.

Another major change in educational debate during the past few years has been the role of women. Even in the 1960's it was not uncommon for tournaments to feature men's and women's divisons. Teams featuring a man and a woman were described as "mixed," were relatively rare, and debated in the men's division. Some faculty members directing debate still argued that women could not deal intellectually with the same level of argumentation of which men were capable. Women were thus protected, as in athletics, from the alleged superiority of men. Even in open competition, some coaches refused to enter women debaters in major tournaments on the theory they could not win. In 1962, when the first woman participated in winning the National Debate Tournament, that theory lost some force. By the 1970's most such overt discrimination against women had disappeared.

Typically, contemporary educational debate is pursued through a debate program that is heavily oriented toward intercollegiate competition. Most programs serve between 16 and 25 students per year, and students are expected to work for the full year. Usually, a full-time faculty member is assigned to direct the forensic program, although forensics will not usually

[9] Richard D. Rieke, "College Forensics in the United States—1973, *Journal of the American Forensic Association, 10* (Winter 1974), pp. 127–133.

constitute a full load—they sometimes teach a full load as well. Coaching methods are varied, but usually they include close teacher-student consultation, practice sessions, small group conferences, advanced students helping younger ones, and occasionally lectures on theory.

At most institutions of higher education, any student interested in educational debate is welcomed on the debate team, and many programs actively seek to interest students in participating. Faculty members report that their educational objectives for such work are primarily improved decision making ability, and more effective analysis of issues and arguments.

Support for travel to tournaments is provided by various combinations of academic funds and student activity fees, with some help coming from alumni. A typical four year college spends from $3000 to $5000 per year for forensic travel. In doing so, they attend from 11 to 26 tournaments per year. Half of the colleges and universities sponsor one or more high school and college tournaments per year. Throughout the United States, there are more than 400 tournaments held each year.[10]

Although there is a continual process of adding new forensic programs and ending them elsewhere, at the present time, almost half of all colleges and universities in the United States have active programs in debate and other speech activities. Virtually all the four year institutions have such programs, and many junior and community colleges have them as well.[11]

FIELD DEPENDENT CHARACTERISTICS

Even though educational debate is not an end in itself, but is intended instead to prepare students for general argumentation in later life or advanced study in specialized fields such as law and education, the use of simulation and gaming necessarily generates some characteristics of educational argument that are unique to that process. Some controversy has come from this fact. Many teachers would modify the educational process so as to reduce or eliminate field dependent characteristics. They would do so by increasing the accuracy of the simulation until it virtually recreates the process being studied. For example, in preparation for general argumentation in policy making, students would engage in legislative sessions such as mock congresses and United Nations patterned after their actual counterparts. To learn about conference decision making,

[10] Estimated from Rieke survey.
[11] Rieke.

students would engage in model discussion sessions. These techniques have been tried, and continue to be discussed. In prelaw situations, particularly in law schools themselves, moot courts are operated along the exact lines of a trial in a particular jurisdiction.

However, for the undergraduate, educational debate is most often done in the forensic debate, which is a specialized argumentative form created from a combination of legislative and legal decision making and used almost exclusively within the schools.

The format is forensic (legal) in the sense that it functions with advocates assigned to defend a particular position before a judge who is empowered to make the decision. It is legislative in the use of propositions (claims) of public policy, and the cases and arguments employ evidence produced by the advocates themselves rather than through the use of witnesses and various forms of physical evidence. The system is unique in the consideration of a single public policy question at a time, in isolation from competing policy proposals and not in relation to an overall budget and revenue source. It is also unique in that a designated approach to policy goals is prescribed by the proposition, and the affirmative must defend it to the end even when it would be obvious to most observers that a compromise would yield a single piece of legislation satisfactory to all concerned.

To illustrate the unique character of educational debate notice that in law, each case is unique—although there may be precedents quite similar to the one at hand, by definition, no other case deals with the same people, is concerned with the same problems, and considers the same arguments and evidence. Similarly, the decision of a judge or jury is unique. No presumption is made that all other judges or juries would decide the same. The only test on appeal is whether or not some error occurred that would make it unlikely that the decision emerged from a proper argumentative context. As was seen in Chapter 11, a court of appeal will not consider a case simply because it does not agree with the decision. Therefore, each case can, in terms of its particular facts, be considered in isolation.

In legislative policy making, on the other hand, no policy is considered in total isolation from others. Even the question of whether there is time to deal with an issue because of the pressure to consider other bills prevents single attention to one item. Furthermore, no legislature can ponder the merits of one policy without considering its cost in relation to what else might be done with the money. Finally, while idealistically each policy should be considered on merits alone, in most political situations the desires of constituents must be taken into account. Accordingly, legislators may be agreed on the high quality of a bill and still vote it down because they cannot as yet justify it to the public.

In educational debate, the combination of legislative and forensic models creates changes. Students are unable to call witnesses before the judge, so they report, through quotations, what witnesses might have said, thereby becoming witness and advocate at the same time. Because it is impractical for students to consider a complex of legislation together, and because they would find it difficult to create a simulated annual budget, they deal with proposed policies as unique questions for debate. Finally, students have no constituents and would be hard put to simulate them. Therefore, they consider what "ought" to be enacted, but do not take on the responsibility of showing that it "will" be. Thus, an educational debate topic is always on a policy claim, always has the word "should" in it, and the word should means ought to be enacted, but not necessarily will be. Accordingly, student debaters rarely deal seriously with the financial considerations of their proposals; they rarely consider the policies that will be denied by virtue of choosing theirs, and almost never discuss the political ramifications of their proposition.

Another characteristic feature of education for argument is the statement of a proposition by outside sources. In both high school and college, topics for debate are chosen by committees or popular vote of coaches or other faculty persons. Then, the students are told what they will debate. This process resembles the legal context in which the attorneys are given a case, but is totally foreign to legislators who, when a topic comes up, are free to write many bills, weigh them, amend them, debate them, and only after all this interaction, do they vote on them. Even after voting, if a bicameral legislature is involved, a conference committee may be forced to write a somewhat different bill from that passed by either house in order to obtain a final consensus.

Being given a proposition, the affirmative debaters must devise their own specific interpretation of it and plan to effect it. They must come up with something that can be clearly distinguished from that complex of systems then in operation, and any reasonable extension of them. That is to say, if the affirmative does not offer a plan different from current systems, the negative may be able to show that a reasonable modification of present systems will yield the same result. Even when the negative and affirmative seem anxious to do about the same thing in almost the same way, a debate may continue on whether or not the affirmative proposal genuinely makes the change deemed necessary to fulfill their requirement set by the wording of the proposition. Sometimes it is a race to see whether the affirmative team can claim a policy under the proposition before the negative claims it as an extension of the *status quo*.

This competition, plus the general desire to come up with an analysis that will catch opponents off-guard, generates another characteristic unique to educational debate: the question of topicality. That is, what specific proposals may legitimately be considered under one generally worded topic. Consider, for example, one topic debated in 1972: Resolved: That greater controls should be imposed on the gathering and utilization of information about U.S. citizens by governmental agencies. During that year, a variety of interpretations emerged, including cases on legalization of marijuana, federal aid to education for law enforcement officers, abolition of grand juries, parolee rights, invalid eye-witness testimony, and many others. One writer suggested that common sense would not permit such a wide variety of interpretations on the same topic. The respondent replied that all had been challenged on "topicality" and "extratopicality" and had survived to win as often as they lost. Therefore, if the judges bought the case, it must be all right. Such an issue over whether or not the affirmative is arguing "within the topic" is unique to competitive debate.[12]

Also unique to educational debate is the value of surprise, and the immediate decision. The game character of the activity requires that a winning side be selected immediately on the completion of a one-hour debate so that the tournament may proceed in an orderly fashion. As described earlier, in virtually no other decision making environment is this the case. Even in law there is opportunity for delay, discovery of the opponents' evidence, and ultimately appeal. Because of this, educational debate may be more highly influenced by those in possession of more recent data, or less well known information. Those debaters who are most diligent in keeping themselves informed, and in engaging in continuing analysis in search for original approaches to the proposition may prove to be more successful. This also makes educational debate more susceptible to the use of distorted evidence. In one championship college debate, of 71 pieces of evidence, there were 23 misrepresentations and three outright fabrications.[13] In another sample of 18 debates it was discovered that 22.1% of the evidence used contained inaccuracies, and the rate of inaccuracy increased as the experience or competence level of the debaters increased. The type of inaccuracy discovered in this study was most often an inaccurate paraphrase, or taking evidence out of context, or

[12] David W. Shepard, "Burden of What?" and Kathy Corey, "The Spirit of '72: A Response to David Shepard," *Journal of the American Forensic Association*, 9 (Winter 1973), pp. 361, 365.

[13] Robert P. Newman and Keith Sanders, "A Study in the Integrity of Evidence," *Journal of the American Forensic Association*, 2 (January 1965), p. 8.

mistaking the source.[14] There are no data to relate the occurrence of such evidence and the decisions ultimately made, nor have there been any studies to relate the frequency of inaccurate evidence in educational debate with that in general argumentation, or in the various specialized fields of argumentation. However, it may be that because of the immediacy of decision, the judge's discretion in punishing what is perceived to be improper use of evidence is greater than elsewhere.

The immediacy of decision, when combined with the fact that this field deals exclusively with young (or learning) debaters, yields perhaps greater susceptibility to "trick" or what have been called "one-tournament" cases. These are cases that have a superficial reasonableness about them and an underlying fatal weakness. The theory is that by the time the opponents discover the weakness, the debate is over. Sometimes, such a case can win extensively over the course of two or three days, only to be exposed a week later when opponents have had time to study it. Presumably by that time the case is no longer being used. Again, there are no studies to suggest that such gamesmanship is more prevalent in college and high school debate than in other argumentative situations. However, the immediacy of decision may cause them to have more effect.

Judging of educational debates is unlike the judging process in other decision making situations. Already discussed above is the fact that the judge must decide immediately. In many tournament situations, judges are discouraged from even fifteen minutes of review and contemplation. Because most school debate occurs in a contest situation, considerable attention is given to obtaining clear statements of who won the debate, and rating points are desired as much for their tie-breaking quality as for their feedback. But the situation is an educational simulation, not actual decision making. Therefore, the judge is not deciding on the intrinsic merits of the question but on the qualities of the debaters. At least two schools of thought obtain on this question. For some, the duty of the judge in educational debate is to act as one with no preconceptions about the topic and evaluate the issues raised in each debate and decide in terms of the relative merits of the arguments and issues. Another school of thought would have the judge examine the overall qualities and preparation of each team and decide in terms of which team demonstrates the superior attainment. Debate ballots typically ask the judge to select the team which did the better debating, but they almost never define the concept. Under the former school of thought, it is possible for a judge to say that the over-

---

[14] James A. Benson, "The Use of Evidence in Intercollegiate Debate," *Journal of the American Forensic Association*, 7 (Spring 1971), p. 267.

all better debating was done by the affirmative, for example, but a key issue was won by the negative, which accordingly is given the decision.

Although many current judges do not agree with this distinction, probably more than half employ a primarily issue oriented, or "logical" approach rather than evaluating the overall qualities of the debaters.[15] Generalization about judging behavior, however, must take into account the fact that those who judge educational debate tend to be young. In one study of 223 judges, nearly half were under 27 years of age, and over 80% had not reached forty.[16] Differences in age and geographic location seem to be responsible for differences in judging behavior. Those living in different parts of the country seem to develop different philosophies of debate and they are reflected in their decisions.[17] Such data suggest the possibility that even though the debating is intended to be educational and to develop universal principles of good argument, those judging do so, as the theory in this book would suggest all judges do, in terms of values that may be personal, group-oriented, regional, etc. Debaters would be wise to adjust their arguments to each judge.

Debate ballots typically ask judges to withhold decision until the end of arguments, and to comment to the debaters by means of ratings, rankings, and discursive comments. Presumably these reactions are to instruct students so that they may do better in the future. A common set of criteria given on a debate ballot would include analysis, reasoning, evidence, refutation, and delivery.[18] The ballots often ask judges to rank the four debaters from best to worst. However, there is evidence to suggest that many find it difficult to retain the educator's role. Reasons for the decision are frequently omitted completely, and sometimes may consist only of brief comments.[19]

Furthermore, judges probably do not withhold judgment until the end of the debate. Instead, they operate like judges in most decision making situations, they seek relief from doubt, and as the debate goes on they often find enough information to warrant moving into a decision phase

15 Dennis P. Dunne, Herschel L. Mack, and Robert Pruett, "Empirical Evidence on the 'Logical'-'Proficiency' Dichotomy in Debate Judging," *Journal of the American Forensic Association*, 7 (Winter 1971), p. 204.

16 Dunne, Mack and Pruett.

17 Dunne, Mack and Pruett. See also William D. Brooks, "Judging Bias in Intercollegiate Debate," *Journal of the American Forensic Association*, 7 (Winter 1971), p. 199.

18 For examples of debate ballots commonly used, write to the Secretary of the American Forensic Association.

19 Carol A. Berthold, "A Descriptive Study of Selected Characteristics of Debate Judges' Ballots," *Journal of the American Forensic Association*, 7 (Winter 1970), pp. 30–35.

and begin to seek arguments in support of the decision toward which they are tending. The most common form of the debate involves four constructive speeches alternating affirmative, negative, affirmative, negative and four rebuttal speeches alternating negative, affirmative, negative, affirmative. Judges who, after hearing the first affirmative speech, are inclined more toward the affirmative than the negative, will give significantly more decisions to the affirmative than negative. And with each additional speech, the judge becomes significantly more able to say which side will win the round.[20] In terms of shifting judges' inclinations, the first affirmative constructive is critical, and the first negative constructive is equally important to that side. The fifteen minute block of negative speaking coming in a combination of the second negative constructive and first negative rebuttal is perhaps the second most important presentation in an educational debate. Then, the two affirmative rebuttals become important either to secure an already established victory, or to work to change an increasingly strong inclination by the judge to vote negative.[21]

Whether a judge is still "objectively" seeking information to help in determining a decision or is engaging in dissonance reduction—searching for arguments to support that position already selected—will influence the argumentative approach to be taken by the debaters. Of course, they have no certain feedback on this subject. But with experience, debaters develop their own ability to analyze the flow of arguments and make a judgment as to their status with the judge.

In the most common form of educational debate as explained earlier, in which there are four ten minute constructive speeches, with affirmative speaking first and negative last, followed by four five minute rebuttal speeches begun by the negative and with the affirmative giving the last speech, the responsibilities of the various speakers emerge from data on judging. The *first affirmative* must set forth clearly and persuasively the overall case to be defended throughout the debate. The interpretation of the proposition is most often given operationally by describing the specific plan to be proposed. Then the arguments calling for the plan are advanced. Recall that following this speech many judges become inclined toward one side or the other to such an extent that it may influence their final decision. The *first negative* constructive speech must describe the

[20] John F. Schunk, "A Quantitative Study of Decision-Making in Academic Debate," *Journal of the American Forensic Association*, 7 (Spring 1971), pp. 274–275. These data must be considered with the reservation that the research design asked subjects to state after each speech which side they were inclined toward. This very act of responding may have caused a commitment that would influence reaction to future arguments.

[21] Schunk, pp. 276–277.

overall position of the negative and establish a preliminary clash with the entire affirmative case, with special emphasis on the reasons given for the proposal, but including some attention to the merits of the plan itself. Here, the negative has the opportunity to convince the judge that there will indeed be a debate. If they fail to do so, he may begin at once the process of reducing dissonance that surrounds an affirmative decision. Of course, the negative may also convince the judge that there will be no debate—the negative will prevail. The *second constructive* speeches by both affirmative and negative serve to reinforce positions in response to attacks, provide secondary evidence to support points previously made, and generally strengthen positions made in the first two speeches. The second negative constructive speaker will typically develop a careful analysis of the practicality and desirability of the specific affirmative proposal, offering constructive arguments against its adoption. The *first negative rebuttal*, coming as it does immediately following the second negative constructive, has the opportunity to return to arguments advanced in favor of the proposition, secure the negative position regarding them, and put the affirmative so behind in the mind of the judge that it will be unlikely that they will recover.

For this reason, the *first affirmative rebuttal* is a particularly important speech. Because there can be no negative reply following the last affirmative speech, some judges tend to require at least a basic affirmative reply to *all* outstanding negative arguments by the first affirmative rebuttal. By indicating the basis of response, the judges believe, they will at least give the negative a chance to counteract it before the end of the debate. With only five minutes to cover fifteen minutes of negative argumentation, the first affirmative rebuttalist must work efficiently. Here, the value of blocks is most apparent. By preparing in advance, brief and clear answers to typical negative arguments, this speaker can cover considerable argumentative ground in the short time available. The remaining *negative rebuttal* should be devoted to a clear focusing of the negative positions made in the debate. He will call attention to those arguments that have been unanswered or poorly answered. The full extent of the burden still remaining to the affirmative will be specified. Some have said that the duty of the second negative rebuttal is to write the last affirmative speech, that is, specify what the affirmative must answer or the negative position will prevail. Unfortunately, by this point in many debates the speakers are so concerned with merely answering everything asserted by the opponents that they lose sight of this rhetorical burden on them.

The *final affirmative speech* may be the most important or least important speech in the debate depending on the state of mind of the judge. As suggested earlier, by this point, many judges are fairly well committed to their decision. The final affirmative speaker must make an estimate of whether or not this is so in the particular debate and then it must be decided whether the tendency of the judge is proaffirmative or pronegative. If proaffirmative, the speaker merely recapitulates the affirmative position *vis-vis* the negative in the most persuasive manner possible. The function is to provide justification for the decision the judge already is going to make. However, if the debater feels the judge is tending toward the negative, the duty is quite different. First, the judge must be made uncomfortable with a negative decision, and must be made to feel that additional information may shake confidence in the negative arguments. Only after returning the judge to a predecision position can the affirmative speaker proceed to give proaffirmative arguments with any hope that they will be received by the judge impartially. Debaters should keep in mind that if the judge has been inclined to vote for one side or the other since early constructive speeches, subsequent arguments may have been heard from one side only, or not heard at all. Rebuttalists may shake the confidence of judges late in the debate by asking, in effect, "Did you hear everything that was said in the last two speeches?" By thus creating doubt, the debater may succeed in winning the objective attention of the judge once more.

Again it must be recalled that a peculiarity of educational debate is the immediate, irrevocable decision. While in other situations time must pass, during which time, according to theories of persuasion, the effects of arguments may diminish or even reverse, in educational debate, short-term effects alone are sought. Because high schools and colleges typically use the same proposition for several months, the judge's reaction will be in part a function of all previous arguments heard on the topic. However, the reaction to any particular debate, whether the judge's point of view is to evaluate the overall proficiency of the debaters or the development of the specific issues, the arguments provided in the immediate debate probably constitute the primary basis of decision. The comments given on the ballot, whether they are perceived as educational suggestions, or justifications for the decision, should be noted carefully. It is common for debaters to speak contemptuously of judges' ballots—suggesting the judge did not understand, or was too ignorant of the topic or of the debate procedure to decide "properly." Instead, they should notice how, in fact, their arguments *were* received and thereby learn better how to predict the impact of their future arguments. If you recall, we said that judging values seem to vary from place to place and according to age and experience. Instead of insisting the judge conform to debaters' standards, debaters might seriously consider adapting their arguments to individual judges. They will have to do it for the rest of their lives.

SPECIAL PROCEDURES IN EDUCATIONAL DEBATE

Most of the processes in educational debate are essentially the same as those described in previous chapters and no further elaboration is required here. However, because this form of argumentation is that used to learn the rest, it may be of value to the reader to mention some special procedures worth knowing.

RESEARCH

In most instances of argument, individuals are operating in an area of their own professional competence such as politics, law, education, business, and so forth. School and college debaters are given new topics regularly, and they come from widely different fields. It is necessary, therefore, before engaging in the ordinary type of research and analysis to learn what are the standard sources of information and who are the respected authorities. Even though this contributes to the educational value of the activity, it puts an unusual burden on the student debater. Where can one go to discover the most fruitful sources of information and to become acquainted with the respected names? One study of the use of evidence found it useful to speak of seven categories:

1. *Newspapers.* Read newspapers regularly, both local editions and such national publications as *The New York Times, Christian Science Monitor*, and *The National Observer*.

2. *Newsmagazines.* Check regularly with such news magazines as *Time, Newsweek, U.S. News and World Report*, and *Business Week*.

3. *Popular magazines.* Keep track of special articles in such magazines as *Fortune, Commonweal, New Republic*, and *Harpers*.

4. *Government documents.* A vast amount of information is published regularly by the Federal, State and Local Governments. Pay particular attention to the *Monthly Catalog of U.S. Government Publications*, the index to the *Congressional Record*, and the published Hearings of Senate, House, and local legislative committees.

5. *Professional journals.* In virtually every field of endeavor there are specialized publications containing informative articles by noted authorities. These can be discovered best by consulting an authority in the field under investigation or by inquiring in any library.

6. *Pamphlets.* Again, specialized publications in pamphlet or monograph form are often useful sources of information. Check with the
librarian.

7. *Books.* Obviously, reference to the card catalogue in any iibrary
under the subject index will reveal books written on any subject.[22] A
study of 1231 instances of evidence used in college debate revealed
that 65.2% came from government documents, professional journals
and books, and championship debaters use references in this category
even more frequently.[23]

Any debater, no matter what the field, must develop some filing method
to permit ready reference to research materials. Educational debaters
have relied on various forms of card files or loose-leaf notebook systems.
It is a highly personal thing that each must develop. Whatever system is
used, it must permit debaters to find everything that they have found on
any issue quickly. In this age of inexpensive copying and close attention
to accuracy of evidence, many find it valuable to copy the original article
or page, use a highlighter to point up key ideas, and use some form of
index for quick references. With more familiarity in the subject matter
and experience in debate, the tendency to read verbatim will typically
give way to knowledgeable paraphrase. Championship debaters use direct
quotation only 35.5 percent of the time, presumably secure in the knowledge that if challenged, they have access to the document or a copy.[24]

ANALYSIS

Because of the broad topics used in educational debate, a major analytical requirement is to develop what is called in law a theory of the case;
that is to say, how shall the topic be approached? We have already seen
how many different "theories" were used in the debates on control of government information gathering. Not only must the debater discover
what seem to be the issues likely to emerge in an expert discussion of the
topic, it is necessary as well to find what debate judges will accept as a
reasonable interpretation. What, for example, will satisfy the affirmative
obligations in the debate—what scope of the problem must be covered
before the plan is considered to fulfill the obligations of the proposition?
This is usually found by systematic trial and error. Theories are developed
and tried before judges until acceptable ones are established.

[22] These categories were taken from Benson, p. 263.
[23] Benson.
[24] Benson.

CASE BUILDING

For years case building in educational debate followed the standardized pattern called "stock" issues: (1) Is there a need for a change? (2) Is the need inherent within the present system? (3) Is there a practicable plan to meet the need? (4) Can the plan be implemented with more advantages than disadvantages? This approach, relevant to the problem solution approach discussed in Chapter 8, seems best designed to deal with issues striking at the very substance of public policies. For example, debates questioning whether ownership of utilities or basic industries should be public or private; debates over whether it is the responsibility of the federal government or the state and local governments to provide education, debates over whether it is the public's responsibility to care for those unable to care for themselves, and debates over whether obscene communication falls within the protection of the First Amendment are topics susceptible to the stock issues approach. It is relevant to search for inherent evils—wrongs so much a part of a system that they can be remedied only by a complete change in the system. The great debate in the United States over whether war should be eliminated as an instrument of public policy is such a question. There was virtually no room for minor repairs to the system. Those who rejected war, rejected it totally.

Recently, however, debaters have discovered that the type of topics assigned to them and the state of mind of people in this country do not lend themselves to such analysis and case building. Even when the topic concerned the responsibility of the Federal Government to provide a guaranteed minimum annual income, the issues did not deal with socialism versus individualism. Instead, the question typically turned on the *best method* of assuring a minimum income. Negative teams objected to pay without work, but they tended to agree it was a public responsibility to provide the work. There was hardly a Social Darwinist in the country. The result of this is a change in the form of cases advanced.

The first major move was the use of comparative advantages cases. When students realized that the topics they were given did not call for sweeping changes, but instead for incremental additions to already established tendencies, they modified their cases accordingly. Even still, the obligations of argument did not differ significantly from those used under a stock issues approach. For example, the 1961 and 1973 college topics both concerned Federal provision of health care for all citizens. An examination of the final round of the National Debate Tournament for those years is revealing.[25] In 1961, Harvard University, on the affirmative, advanced a stock issues case with these elements:

I. We contend that the neglect of health is today causing needless death and suffering,
    A. Lives are needlessly lost each year,
        1. The Conference on General Welfare says ⅓ of a million lives are needlessly lost each year.
    B. Many suffer without the care they need,
        1. The U.S. Public Health Service says 49.9% of all acute disabling medical conditions receive no medical attention.
    C. Neglect of health endangers the health of all,
        1. Public Health Reports say contagious disease, if untreated, will spread to others.
II. The primary reason for the neglect is that people are led to make medical decisions on economic grounds,
    A. Many simply can't afford to pay,
        1. This is the testimony of Professor A. F. Weston of Washington U., Professor B. J. Stern of Columbia, and Professor Strauss of Columbia.
    B. Uncertainty as to what the ultimate cost will be leads them to postpone the care or forego it,
        1. This is the testimony of Professor of Sociology E. L. Kuhs.
    C. Even if we can pay, an economic deterrent remains,
        1. This is the testimony of Jerome Rothenberg in *The American Economic Review*.
III. This problem is inherent in the present system,
    A. No voluntary system can remove the need to make economic decisions in seeking medical care,
        1. This is the testimony of Professor Ernest Haverman.
        2. Public Health Reports agrees.

In 1973, Georgetown University was on the affirmative and argued the comparative advantages approach. Compare the two segments of the cases.

[25] The transcript of the 1973 NDT final debate can be found edited by Stanley G. Rives, *Journal of the American Forensic Association, 10* (Summer 1973), pp. 16–45. The transcript of the 1961 debate, which can be obtained from the A.F.A. can be found in Douglas Ehninger and Wayne Brockriede, *Decision by Debate* (New York: Dodd, Mead & Co., 1963), pp. 351–375.

I. The affirmative program better provides needed medical care to more U.S. citizens.
    A. Too often care is based on the ability to pay,
        1. This is the testimony of Senator Edward Kennedy.
    B. Cost leads to denial of care to millions,
        1. Task Force on Urban Coalition testifies to this: poor people have four times the chance of dying under 25 years of age, four times as much serious illness, twice the days of restricted activity, and a third longer hospitalization.
        2. This is also the testimony of Dr. Therman Evans and Senator Edward Kennedy.
    C. A thorough-going restructuring of our medical care delivery system is required,
        1. This is the testimony of Mayor John Lindsay of New York City.
II. The affirmative program will better guard against individual financial hardship,
    A. The costs of serious illness are both severe and extensive,
        1. Representative L. Hogan says the costs may be as much as $75,000.
        2. Senate Finance Committee says one million people annually are hit.
    B. For such people, costs can lead to tragic hardship,
        1. The Brookings Institution says ruin can come to middle class or wealthy individuals.
        2. This is agreed to by Representative L. Hogan.
        3. Hemophilia is an example of catastrophic illness.
            a. National Hemophilia Foundation says 100,000 people have the disease at a yearly cost of $22,000.
            b. Drs. Adams, Darilich, and McIntyre testify that there is no medical insurance for hemophiliacs.
            c. Dr. Jane Van Eyes, Dr. R. Matson, and Representative M. Griffiths agree.
III. The affirmative program will insure the highest quality of medical care,
    A. High quality in prescription drugs will be provided,
        1. *The Washington Post* reports Food and Drug Administration testimony that many physicians imperil health care of millions by massive overprescription and misprescription of drugs,
        2. Dr. H. Simmons of the FDA testifies that needless use of antibiotics causes 38,000 to 225,000 deaths yearly.

    B.   High quality of medical X-rays will be provided,

        1.   Dr. Karl Morgan of Oakridge Lab testifies that better training could reduce exposure levels of 90% thereby saving thousands of lives yearly, prevent physical and mental damage to unborn children, reduce many forms of cancer, and avoid genetic damage.

        2.   The National Academy of Sciences testifies that a continued rise in exposure levels may lead to 27,000 afflicted with serious genetic disease, and increased cancer deaths by as many as 6000 per year.

        3.   Dr. Karl Morgan testifies that most X-ray equipment is handled by nonradiologists.

In 1961, a stock issues case assumed the burden to prove that inability to pay for medical care caused much hardship and even death, and alleged this could only be corrected by a national health plan. In 1973, a comparative advantages case assumed the same burden. In both debates, the negative made its primary challenge in the area of denying a causal relation between income and health care and suggesting that already existing programs could easily take care of health needs. Presumably in 1973, the judge's demands on the affirmative were slightly modified by the use of a comparative advantages approach. In the latter case, the affirmative claimed only that their proposal would be comparatively advantageous over the present arrangement. They did not suggest, as did the stock issues approach, an inherent and, therefore, irrevocable weakness in the present combination of plans. It should be noted, however, that in 1961 medical care relied more on fee for service financing than was true in 1973 by which time public programs of medicare and medicaid had been well established.

With awareness of the changing character of policy questions being debated by students increasing, other case rationales are being tried. As suggested in Chapter 8, the criteria case is increasingly popular. Here, the focus is on a value or values discernible within our society that cannot be achieved through present policies, but which can be fulfilled by the affirmative proposal.[26] In the medical care question some debaters used a form of the criteria case by observing that no one should be denied adequate medical care because of inability to pay. This is a value shared by Americans but not met by present policies. Only a national medical plan, they argued, could fully do so. Some writers have argued that this

---

[26] For a discussion of this case format in the educational debate context see James W. Chesbro, "Beyond the Orthodox: The Criteria Case," *Journal of the American Forensic Association*, 7 (Winter 1971), pp. 208–215.

method should be called a "goal" case and that the criteria approach should seek to set up more desirable values for policies than are currently employed.[27] In this analysis, the criteria case would suggest, for example, that the current values in medicine favor highly expensive urban medical centers when the proper criterion of medical service is its availability to all the people wherever they are. They would then argue that a comprehensive national health plan would be the most advantageous way to accomplish this. Student debaters should be aware of these variations in affirmative case construction.

ANALYSIS WITHIN A DEBATE

Keeping track of every argument made by the opposition in relation to every point in one's case is probably more important in educational debate than in most other argumentative forms. Because decisions are made by a critic who is interested in how well the students have learned to debate, more attention will be paid to this aspect of argument. In earlier chapters, we've said keeping good notes is important. In educational debate, keeping a "flow" sheet is vital. Although there are variations in method, most contain some method of displaying arguments as originally advanced, as originally responded to, and as further developed in rebuttal. Notice this brief example from the 1973 debate mentioned earlier between Georgetown and Northwestern.

[27] John D. Lewinski, Bruce R. Metzler, and Peter L. Settle, "The Goal Case Affirmative: An Alternate Approach to Academic Debate," *Journal of the American Forensic Association, 9* (Spring 1973), pp. 458–463.

Affirmative	Negative	Affirmative
I. The affirmative program better provides needed medical care to more U.S. citizens,	I. Affirmative program no better than present plans,	I. Affirmative program better provides medical care to more citizens,
A. Too often care is based on ability to pay, 1. Sen. Kennedy	A. Signify and quantify the problems of middle class 1. Kennedy evidence only "blurb" assertion.	A. [No reply]

Affirmative	Negative	Affirmative
B. Cost leads to denial of care to millions, 1. Poor suffer 2. Millions suffer when they might have been helped.	B. We have a pluralistic system able to do the job, 1. Private insurance 2. Medicaid 3. Extended medicaid 4. Health centers 5. Free care	B. Negative must develop a counterplan to show their pluralistic system will work. 1. Will you prove extensions 2. Show where group practice now exists. 3. There are barriers to rapid expansion of group practice C. Negative must show how extension of present policies is comparatively more advantageous than either affirmative proposal or present system.

By glancing at this flow of argument that covers only three speeches, it is possible to see that the second negative speaker can claim no affirmative quantification or demonstration of significance of harm to middle class citizens as asked for by the first negative. Nor did the affirmative reply to several of the specific methods mentioned for providing medical care. On the other hand, the negative speaker can see the necessity of responding to the challenge to assume the burden of proof for the modifications proposed in the present system. A further glance at the flow sheet reveals no negative denial of the block of argument charging that cost leads to denial of care to millions. Here, the negative offered a defense of the present systems, but did not directly deny the evidence originally produced by the first affirmative. By using lines and arrows, the debater can keep track of what replies apply to what constructive arguments even though space on the paper will not allow putting them side-by-side. Without this ability to analyze during the debate, there will be no chance of selecting the arguments most likely to advance the debate. This will also allow debaters to "pull through" arguments. That is, they can readily remind the judge of arguments that have not been denied by the opposition. Merely arguing on without due regard to what has been said before is a common failing of inexperienced debaters.

COMMUNICATION STYLE

As in such specialized argument systems as law, educational debate has many unique protocols in communication. Probably the most noticeable to the outsider is rapidity of speech and the little time devoted to amenities. Those not familiar with academic debate sometimes find it impossible to comprehend what some debaters say. Even those who do not speak rapidly, speak in a code developed over months of arguing the same question. On the medical question they spoke of HIP, and OEO, and HMO, and OEO-CHC, NHI, without bothering to define them. It is important to notice, however, that the experienced critic-judge has little trouble following such speech. By careful note-taking and experience with the topic, these characteristics pose little barrier to comprehension. This is probably characteristic of any decision making situation where experts present arguments to other experts. Of course, when speaking to a general audience or an inexperienced judge (or an older one no longer willing to do the work of careful listening) it is imperative that debaters be able to change their style.

Probably the most important factor permitting debaters to speak so rapidly and still be understood is what might be called *verbal organization.* When academic debaters speak, they indicate main point, subordinate points, evidence, and transitions from point to point clearly by their selection of words, emphasis, and for key points, repetition. They will overtly announce that "This is my main contention." Then, they may repeat it immediately to be sure the judge was able to write it down. They will announce, "Please turn your attention to point II." Similar verbal organization permits constructive arguments to appear on the flow sheet of the judge and opposition in about the same structure as intended. Then, during the debate, attention can be directed to the point under discussion much more easily. Debaters develop a tendency to enumerate almost excessively. They will tick off point after point and identify them by number. This tells listeners when there is movement from one idea to another. Even in casual conversation, debaters tend to enumerate, "Let's go get some food, for three reasons, number one. . . ." It may seem excessive, but it is the only way to maintain comprehension while speaking so rapidly. Inexperienced debaters often learn to speak fast before they learn verbal organization, and this is disastrous.

Finally, a communicative pattern common to academic debaters is the frequent internal summary. Realizing that even careful note-takers may become lost during a debate, speakers will frequently bring them up to date and remind them of what has been said. These communication patterns, while mostly relevant in the school situation, may be transferred to other contexts. It must not, however, be assumed that academic debate generates a flexibility in communication patterns to serve all situations. Other educational experiences are necessary to accomplish that task.

CONCLUSIONS

Educational debate has been seen to be a venerable process, starting over 2400 years ago. Ancient Greek thinkers began the process, and Roman rhetoricians developed it thoroughly. During the medieval period, syllogistic disputations became a central part of education, and this remained so even into the Colonial period of America. It was student initiative that developed debates in English on topics of current urgency, and this led to intercollegiate debating and faculty coaches. The debate tournament was a natural culmination. Currently most major colleges and universities, and many community colleges and high schools have forensic programs. They stress competitive, intercollegiate debate.

Various hybrid characteristics of educational debate have been discussed. The combination of a forensic format with legislative questions is probably the key to such specialized development. The fact that people other than debaters select the proposition is also significant. Judges of academic debate have special responsibilities, but they tend to behave like most other decision makers, seeking relief from doubt as soon as possible.

Some discussion of the responsibilities of the various speakers in educational debate was given. Attention was given to the flow of argument in relation to the judge's need to reach immediate decision. Special procedures in educational debate were described. They included research, analysis, case building, analysis within a debate, and communication. Special attention was given to changing patterns of cases such as the move from a stock issues approach to the comparative advantages case.

PROJECTS

1. Listen to several educational debates and try to judge them using the format of a standard debate ballot. Compare your judgment with others who also acted as decision makers.

2. Prepare a case and debate it in class using a variation of the academic format.

3. Join the debate team.

Index

303